Law, Relationality and the Ethical Life

This first book-length study into the influence of Emmanuel Levinas on the thought and philosophy of Giorgio Agamben, *Law, Relationality and the Ethical Life*, demonstrates how Agamben's immanent thought can be read as presenting a compelling, albeit flawed, alternative to Levinas's ethics of the Other.

The publication of the English translation of *The Use of Bodies* in 2016 ended Giorgio Agamben's 20-year multi-volume *Homo Sacer* study. Over this time, Agamben's thought has greatly influenced scholarship in law, the wider humanities and social sciences. This book places Agamben's figure of form-of-life in relation to Levinasian understandings of alterity, relationality and the law. Considering how Agamben and Levinas craft their respective forms of embodied existence – that is, a fully-formed human that can live an ethical life – the book considers Agamben's attempt to move beyond Levinasian ethics through the liminal figures of the foetus and the patient in a persistent vegetative state. These figures, which Agamben uses as examples of bare life, call into question the limits of Agamben's non-relational use and form of existence. As such, it is argued, they reveal the limitations of Agamben's own ethics, whilst suggesting that his 'abandoned' project can and must be taken further.

This book will be of interest to scholars, researchers, graduate students and anyone with an interest in the thought of Giorgio Agamben and Emmanuel Levinas in the fields of law, philosophy, the humanities and the social sciences.

Tom Frost is based at the University of Leicester.

Law and Politics: Continental Perspectives

Series editors
Mariano Croce, *Sapienza University of Rome, Italy*
Marco Goldoni, *University of Glasgow, UK*

Law, Relationality and the Ethical Life
Agamben and Levinas
Tom Frost

Hermeneutics as a General Methodology of the Sciences of the Spirit
Emilio Betti

States of Exception
Law, History, Theory
Edited by Cosmin Cercel, Gian Giacomo Fusco and Simon Lavis

Foucault's Politics of Philosophy
Power, Law, and Subjectivity
Sandro Chignola

For information about the series and details of previous and forthcoming titles, see https://www.routledge.com/Law-and-Politics/book-series/LPCP

Law, Relationality and the Ethical Life

Agamben and Levinas

Tom Frost

Routledge
Taylor & Francis Group
a GlassHouse book

First published 2022
by Routledge
2 Park Square, Milton Park, Abingdon, Oxon OX14 4RN

and by Routledge
605 Third Avenue, New York, NY 10158

Routledge is an imprint of the Taylor & Francis Group, an informa business

a GlassHouse book

British Library Cataloguing-in-Publication Data
A catalogue record for this book is available from the British Library

Library of Congress Cataloging-in-Publication Data
A catalog record has been requested for this book

ISBN: 978-1-138-72630-7 (hbk)
ISBN: 978-1-032-05715-6 (pbk)
ISBN: 978-1-315-19144-7 (ebk)

DOI: 10.4324/9781315191447

Typeset in Bembo
by Taylor & Francis Books

Contents

Acknowledgements

No academic project is a solitary task. Certainly, that was the case here. The arguments I make in this book have their origins in my doctoral thesis. My first and biggest thanks go to Oren Ben-Dor, my lead doctoral supervisor, and Alex Conte and Ed Bates, my other doctoral supervisors. Specifically, without Oren's help, advice and support I would not be where I am today. Through many conversations over many cups of coffee at varying times of the day and night he helped me understand the detail and nuances of the thought of Giorgio Agamben, Emmanuel Levinas, Martin Heidegger and Michel Foucault. Panu Minkkinen as the external examiner to my thesis provided many thoughtful critiques which have helped my development as an academic. Chris Rodgers, Heather Keating, Donald McGillivray and Sally Kyd have been supportive Heads of Department at Newcastle, Sussex and Leicester.

Thanks are due to the series editors Mariano Croce and Marco Goldoni, both for their comments on the proposal and the draft of this monograph, as well as their agreement to host this work in the *Law and Politics: Continental Perspectives* book series. Thanks also to Colin Perrin, Commissioning Editor at Routledge, for helping to shape this project from its beginning. Without his help and support this book would not have been completed. Nicola Sharpe, Hannah Lovelock and Ajanta Bhattacharjee at Routledge and Taylor and Francis also assisted with the development and production of this work. Many conversations with many colleagues and friends over the years have assisted in both sharpening arguments and providing support and advice – thanks are due to Colin Murray, Aoife O'Donoghue, Patrick O'Callaghan, Kevin Brown, Ashley Wilton, Jo Bridgeman, Tarik Kochi, Kim Brayson, Amir Paz-Fuchs, Kenny Veitch, Verona Ni Drisceoil, and Tanya Palmer.

This monograph draws upon research which I have previously published in academic journals, including:

- Frost, T (2010) 'Agamben's Sovereign Legalization of Foucault', *Oxford Journal of Legal Studies*, 30, 545–77.
- Frost, T (2013) 'The Hyper-Hermeneutic Gesture of a Subtle Revolution', *Critical Horizons: A Journal of Philosophy and Social Theory*, 14, 70–92.
- Frost, T (2014) 'Thinking relationality in Agamben and Levinas', *Griffith Law Review*, 23, 210–31.

- Frost, T (2019) 'The *Dispositif* between Foucault and Agamben', *Law, Culture and the Humanities*, 15, 151–71.
- Frost, T (2020) 'Destituent Power and the Problem of the Lives to Come', *Etica & Politica / Ethics & Politics*, 22, 211–34.
- Frost, T (2021) 'Kierkegaard and the Figure of Form-of-Life' in *Agamben and the Existentialists*, Norris, M and Dickinson, C (eds), Edinburgh: Edinburgh University Press, 64–79.

All journals and publishers have given their permission for these articles to have their arguments developed in this book. I would like to thank all of the anonymous reviewers for these publications for their criticisms, suggestions and comments. This feedback has proven invaluable for the publications as well as this book's arguments. In Chapter Seven, I have drawn upon Giorgio Agamben's contributions in Italian to the *Quodlibet* publication. Any errors and mistakes in the translations are my own. Finally, thank you to my family for supporting me throughout my academic studies and early career, without which this book would not have been completed. Any mistakes or errors in the text are mine and mine alone.

Table of cases

(A) *A Hospital NHS Trust v CD* [2015] EWCOP 15 **217**
(B) *A Primary Care Trust v CW* [2010] EWHC 3448 (COP) **208**
(C) *Abertawe Bro Morgannwg University Local Health Board v RY* [2017] EWCOP 2 **206**
(D) *Airedale NHS Trust v Bland* [1993] AC 789 (HL) **202, 205, 208**
(E) *An NHS Trust and others v Y (by his litigation friend, the Official Solicitor) and another* [2018] UKSC 46, [2018] 3 WLR 751 **208**
(F) *Aintree University Hospitals Foundation Trust v James* [2013] UKSC 67, [2014] 1 All ER 573 **206**
(G) *B v D* [2017] EWCOP 15 **206**
(H) *Barber v Superior Court of State of California* (1983) 195 Cal. Rptr. 484 (Court of Appeal of California) **201**
(I) *Butts v Penny* (1677) 2 Levinz 201 **160**
(J) *Cruzan v Director, Missouri Department of Health* (1990) 110 S.Ct. 2841 (Supreme Court of the United States) **201**
(K) *Forbes v Cochrane & Cockburn* (1824) 2 Barn & Cres. 448, 107 ER 450 (KB) **161**
(L) *Gillick v West Norfolk and Wisbech Area Health Authority* [1986] AC 112 (HL) **174**
(M) *Gregson v Gilbert* (1783) 3 Doug 232, 99 ER 629 **159**
(N) *Heart of England NHS Foundation Trust v JB* [2014] EWHC 342 (COP) **205**
(O) *In re B (Consent to Treatment – Capacity)* [2002] 1 FLR 1090 (CA) **203**
(P) *In re F (Mental Patient: Sterilisation)* [1990] 2 AC 1 (HL) **205**
(Q) *M v Mrs N (By her litigation friend, the Official Solicitor)* [2015] EWCOP 76 **207**
(R) *Malette v Shulman* (1990) 72 O.R. (2d) 417 (Ontario Court of Appeal) **203**
(S) *Pearne v Lisle* (1749) Amb. 755, 27 ER 47 **160**
(T) *Planned Parenthood v Casey*, 505 U.S. 833 (1992) (Supreme Court of the United States) **174**
(U) *R (Pretty) v Director of Public Prosecutions* [2002] 1 AC 800 (HL) **205**
(V) *Re G (An Adult)* [2004] EWHC 2222 (Fam) **205**
(W) *Re SA (Vulnerable Adult with Capacity: Marriage)* [2006] 1 FLR 867; *Re SK* [2005] 2 FLR 230 **205**
(X) *Re T (Adult: Refusal of Treatment)* [1993] Fam 95 (CA) **203**

Table of statutes

Introduction
Continuing an abandoned project

The English translation of *The Use of Bodies* was published in 2016, and this brought to a close Giorgio Agamben's twenty-year multi volume *Homo Sacer* study, a study which Agamben, by his own admission, "cannot be concluded but only abandoned (and perhaps continued by others)".[1] As the *Homo Sacer* series of works draws to a close, we are able to reflect upon Agamben's optimistic,[2] comic[3] perspective on the coming politics.[4] This book is an attempt to continue Agamben's study, both in respect of his critique of Western politics and philosophy, and in considering the implications and viability of his coming politics.

Agamben's scholarship has had huge impact in the humanities and social sciences. A great deal of attention has been paid to the *Homo Sacer* study, and to Agamben's argument that *life* in Western political thought has been based on a division between a natural life (*zoè*) and a politically ordered life (*bios*) which inexorably produces a remainder, bare life, which is cast out from the *polis.* [5] As Adam Kotsko has explained, there are two aspects of life, and politics is concerned with articulating the difference between the two. We do not have access to the fact of natural life – it can only be experienced through its being taken up in the political system.[6] This bare life is left at the mercy of sovereign and governmental action and decisions and has as its exemplars the asylum seeker and the camp inmate, politically liminal figures who lack the rights and legal protections we take for granted. These examples may seem extreme, but as Agamben writes "it is only in the burning house that the fundamental architectural problem becomes visible for the first time".[7]

Before I outline my argument, I think that it is important to dwell on my method. In this study my main focus has been the *Homo Sacer* series, the first volume of which was published in Italian in 1995 and the last in 2014. Yet Agamben's writing career spans over half a century, and he has published works unconnected to the *Homo Sacer* series both earlier in his career, and after the publication of *The Use of Bodies*. Many scholars have claimed that there is a continuity in Agamben's entire corpus. Claire Colebrook and Jason Maxwell suggest that each one of Agamben's books "makes a continuing contribution to a long-term project".[8] Colby Dickinson sees Agamben as producing "a remarkably cohesive body of work" which has a consistency of thought,

DOI: 10.4324/9781315191447-1

meaning it is possible to find similar themes in a variety of publications.[9] For Sergei Prozorov, the *Homo Sacer* series takes explicit stock of Agamben's politics as they have been theorised in previous works.[10] Leland de la Durantaye sees the series as reformulating concerns that accompanied Agamben's work since his first publications.[11]

Adam Kotsko, in reviewing these perspectives on Agamben's thought, has persuasively argued that it is not possible for a writer with a career spanning just over half a century to remain as consistent as Agamben's commentators claim, and it would not be a good thing either. No author should aspire to this level of continuity.[12] Kotsko sees Agamben's work as responding to the time in which he finds himself, but not through direct political commentary. Agamben takes on new influences even as he deepens and complicates his most familiar influences.[13] This I think is what Catherine Mills alluded to when she stated that Agamben's work does not follow a systematic trajectory, but is instead a "complex recursive exercise that extends and modifies his approach to several key questions and issues that reappear in one guise or another in almost every text".[14] The same concepts and patterns of thought reappear throughout Agamben's works.[15] Agamben continually reworks and recontextualises his key insights, sometimes to the point where they have a radically different valence.[16]

This study attempts to approach Agamben in the way Kotsko recommends. For Kotsko, Agamben's body of work as the contingent and inappropriable body of work that it is.[17] This means pushing his texts beyond their limits until "the difference between what belongs to the author and what is attributable to the interpreter becomes as essential as it is difficult to grasp".[18] Agamben invites us to discover him and his tradition anew, and one way to do this is to explore what Agamben did not do.[19] It is in this spirit that I seek to continue the *Homo Sacer* project in a direction Agamben did not take.

Immanent life

One concept I do claim recurs in Agamben's thought is that of immanence, and his opposition to presuppositional transcendent relationality. Throughout Western metaphysics we see a presupposition of an unknowable and unnameable substrate (such as natural life and animality) which supports a knowable and nameable substance (such as politics and humanity).

Agamben warns of the consequences of thinking transcendence within the immanent realm. Agamben's coming politics is an immanent politics. Opposing himself to thinkers of transcendence (he explicitly identifies Emmanuel Levinas and Jacques Derrida), Agamben cautions that what threatens immanent thought is transcendence, and the consequences of holding immanent thought in relation to transcendence. This risks providing a transcendent origin for immanence,[20] an origin which, in Agamben's terms, will always already be negative.

My starting point here is the *Homo Sacer* project and Agamben's more overtly political writings. In developing my arguments I draw upon other works by Agamben which repeat the same concepts and thoughts. In short, I start by considering the position of life politically; the relation between *bios* and *zoè* places both elements in a negative functional relation. Although *bios* and *zoè* are distinct from one another, they gain their meaning, content and substance from this relation, and this unthought presupposition of life itself – they have no meaning other than that given to them in this relation. Both elements require their concrete grounding in reality for substance. This presuppositional structure *always* leads to the subjection and dominion of one part over the other and the production of bare life.[21] It is to repeat the dangers of holding immanence in relation to transcendence. Political life is defined through bare life – political existence becomes a contingent event. As Agamben puts it, man is the result of ceaseless divisions and caesurae.[22] These divisions function and are maintained through the state of exception, a zone of indeterminacy which functions like a machine, holding opposing terms in relation to each other. As Kevin Attell explains, what is produced in the exception establishes the dominion of the valourised term (*bios*) on the condition that the inferior term (*zoè*) be abandoned and produced not as pure and independent *zoè* but as bare life.[23]

The recourse to transcendence in philosophy is not deliberate. Immanence is threatened by the illusion of transcendence, in which immanence "is made to leave itself and give birth to the transcendent".[24] This, for Agamben, is a necessary illusion, which every philosopher falls prey to even as they adhere "as closely as possible to the plane of immanence".[25] Whenever immanence is interpreted as immanent *to* something, this 'something' reintroduces the transcendent, in the form of a negative relationality that divides life and creates the remainder of bare life.[26] This something can be found in the subject, or in theology, in the figure of God. It can also be found in transcendent subjectivity and appeals to an 'Other', which means that such thought is "no longer satisfied with thinking immanence as immanent to a transcendent, *we want to think transcendence within the immanent, and it is from immanence that a breach is expected*".[27] To avoid life being divided and defined through a negative transcendent relationality, Agamben theorises an immanent life – his form-of-life. This immanent life has neither a focal point nor a horizon. The only possible point of orientation is the vertigo in which outside and inside, immanence and transcendence, are absolutely indistinguishable.[28]

Agamben is a thinker of messianism, something which has guided his thought since his earliest works.[29] The path from Agamben's early works to the *Homo Sacer* project was neither smooth nor straight.[30] For example, the triad of language, potentiality and messianism came to be rearticulated in the later triad of law, life and sovereignty.[31] Form-of-life is a being of pure potentiality.[32] This is a potential which gives itself to itself, and is not reduced to a form of actualized behaviour or action. Potentiality offers a ground for the coming politics. The answers we seek are already in the world:

> [T]he art of living is … the capacity to keep ourselves in harmonious relationship with that which escapes us.[33]

Form-of-life is a *non-relational* form of existence. My study focuses on what exactly living as a form-of-life entails, and how it tries to escape the foundational relational negativity Agamben diagnoses. Agamben views relational existence suspiciously and advances a provocative thesis. Any form of life which defines itself through its relation to something will inevitably lead to the creation of the remainder of bare life. Life must instead be thought of beyond this form of relationality. I have termed this a non-relational existence and ethics here.

The transformative potential of Agamben's work has attracted scholars to engage with different aspects of it in recent years, although they have all noted that details of this coming politics have often been scarce. Notwithstanding this, each focuses on a different element of his thinking, attempting to develop and theorise it in various directions.[34] Thanos Zartaloudis has approached Agamben's work from the perspective of law, and his writings on government; the argument that political existence is divided between an immanent sphere of acting and a transcendent origin, which remains without content but without which the immanent sphere cannot ground itself.[35] Jessica Whyte has focused on the redemptive qualities of Agamben's thought, connecting them to his messianism, and Marx's economic enquiries, arguing that Agamben's writings on life is his contribution to political theory, and that his hope for the future comes from the collapse of the border between politics and life.[36] Mathew Abbott deepens this connection between politics and ontology, arguing that Agamben's coming politics requires us to rethink our relation to the question raised by Being.[37] Fundamental ontological concepts that structure our understanding of the world have direct political bearing.[38] Abbott sees Agamben's messianism as presaging a revolution of everyday life in the event of thought, a refusal of forms of domination through a non-hierarchical collectivity.[39]

Just like Abbott's claim that political ontology does not provide a blueprint for political action,[40] David Kishik, in his attempt to think a vitalistic *power of life* (as opposed to a power *over* life), posits a network without a centre, a "rhizomatic configuration" of forms of life that are "virtually ungovernable".[41] In this "*inverted biopolitics*",[42] humans are 'unredeemable'; any attempt to complete this imperfect human condition through consigning man to a universal truth, defining his essence, fitting him into a fixed narrative or directing him toward an original unity will abolish ethics and politics, as all that needs to be done is to follow the user manual for life.[43] As Kishik maintains:

> Agamben's point, therefore, is not that we need to do away with all classes and identities … by repressing or dissipating or transcending them. Since no identity is sacred, the ethical task is actually to profane it, use it, play with it, examine it, struggle for and against it, or even render it completely inoperative within our life, but without trying to resolve the matter once and for all.[44]

What each of these important studies shares is a concern over the role of agency in Agamben's work, or how exactly a form-of-life can be lived.[45] Each tries to conceive of exactly what such a non-relational existence would entail, and how it would differ from our present situation in modernity.

My argument

My study continues this investigation into agency in Agamben's thought. I contend that Agamben's form-of-life should be read as a critique of the relational ethics of Emmanuel Levinas, an ethics Agamben equates with judgment and the law. In eschewing Levinasian ethics, Agamben outlines a life, and an ethics, which appears to have the potential to markedly influence future directions in philosophical, political and legal thought.

There has been no sustained study of the relationship between Agamben's work and that of Levinas. I think such a study is necessary due to the position of Levinas in Agamben's work. Nor am I alone in making this connection. Colby Dickinson reads Agamben as trying to redefine ethics along certain 'Levinasian' lines in order to arrive at a respect for the face of form-of-life before us. For Dickinson, it is not clear how Agamben seeks to develop an ethical position in the context of form-of-life in relation to Levinas's work. He concludes that *not* citing Levinas to bring Levinas's work to light in another way may have been Agamben's intention all along.[46] Agamben's methods and insights do overlap with the philosophical project of Levinas, a connection Agamben does not point to in his work.[47]

Levinas's thought is a quest for the meaning of transcendence, which he found in ethics. Ethical experience has its foundations in an irreducible relation between oneself and other people, the Other.[48] The Other is a Stranger who disturbs and disrupts every notion of ipseity, the same, and presents an ethical demand that cannot be ignored or avoided and must be faced.[49] The Other, and our relationship to the Other, defines us. Transcendent relationality is necessary for the Levinasian subject.[50] Levinas was opposed to immanence, according to which "we would truly come into possession of being when every 'other' ... would vanish at the end of history".[51] He states:

> If transcendence has meaning, it can only signify the fact that the *event of being* ... passes over to what is other than being. ... Transcendence is passing over to being's *other,* otherwise than being. Not *to be otherwise*, but *otherwise than being*. And not to not-be; passing over is not here equivalent to dying.[52]

Levinas terms the relation to the Other as the 'infinite':

> Infinity is characteristic of a transcendent being as transcendent; the infinite is the absolutely other. The transcendent is the sole *ideatum* of which there can be only an idea in us; it is infinitely removed from its idea, that is exterior, because it is infinite ... To think the infinite, the transcendent, the Stranger, is hence not to think an object.[53]

The universality of the singular Other's singularising command is expressed as follows: *Anyone* is responsible for *any Other*. Because there is more than just one Other in the world, my infinite responsibility for the Other is not enough. Given the existence of more than one Other in the world:

> [I]t is consequently necessary to weigh, to think, to judge, in comparing the incomparable. The interpersonal relation I establish with the Other, I must establish with other men; there is thus a necessity to moderate the privilege of the Other; from whence comes justice. Justice, exercised through institutions, must always be held in check by the initial interpersonal relation.[54]

In order to attend to those whom I will never encounter face-to-face (and in order to exist in a community of more than two) I must balance and negotiate my relations with the *other* Others whom Levinas called the third party.[55] This is why the "intelligibility of a system" is required to mediate and make intelligible the relations with multiple others.[56] This system is necessary as multiple others cannot be encountered purely ethically, as if they were the only other that exists.[57] A method for making sense of multiple relations with others is needed in order to place the ethical relation within any kind of community, and explain how multiple ethical relations relate to one another and exist in common.[58] This method and system can be seen as the law.

Agamben's argument is that Levinas perpetuates a negative foundation of the self by defining the I with reference to an ungraspable Other. Agamben goes so far as to label Levinas's ethics as essentially negative in nature. This criticism is not tangential to Agamben's aim to theorise the *ethos* of the politics to come, but rather represents his attempt to found an ethics distinct from those of Levinas. Agamben specifically critiques and distances himself from Levinas's connecting of ethics and responsibility:

> Ethics is the sphere that recognises neither guilt nor responsibility. … To assume guilt and responsibility … is to leave the territory of ethics and enter that of law.[59]

Agamben's reference to law here is deliberate. Unlike for Levinas, law is not a system that makes intelligible the relations between multiple others. It is, rather, an apparatus or *dispositif.* An apparatus is anything which has capacity to "capture, orient, determine, intercept, model, control, or secure the gestures, behaviours, opinions, or discourses of living beings".[60] This is deliberately very broad. It includes juridical measures but also philosophy, modern technology and agriculture. For Agamben, living beings are incessantly captured within apparatuses, and the subject is that which results from the relation between the two.[61] Agamben's subject is dominated by these apparatuses. The law is an apparatus through which bare life is created.

What Agamben refers to by the negativity in Levinas is a charge that Levinas's subject is defined negatively, through holding itself in relation to a negative foundation. It is this negative foundation which Agamben sees embodied in the law, and how (what he sees as) legal concepts of guilt and responsibility define the self not through what it is, but through what it is not, which he ties to the notion of relational existence. By equating an ethics of responsibility with the law, he aims to decisively break not just with Levinas's ethics, but also with Levinasian influenced scholarship. This charge is provocative because for Levinasian ethics (indeed for most ethics in general), relational existence is almost a tautology. Agamben's attempt at creating a non-relational ethics *necessitates* the eschewing of all forms of judgment and responsibility.

Exploring this critique of Levinas sheds light on whether Agamben's immanent life can offer a viable alternative form of ethics and living. Levinas's influence on twentieth century philosophy and ethics cannot be understated. Agamben's reference to Levinas is surely deliberate. In critiquing Levinasian alterity, Agamben is seeking to challenge all forms of ontology that define life through reference to other beings. Levinas's ideas of responsibility, relationality and the Other have influenced approaches to issues of human rights,[62] private law[63] and judicial reasoning[64] amongst others. They have informed many studies which focus not just on what the law is, but what it can and should be.[65] Levinas's philosophy and ethics is so influential precisely because there is a predominant jurisprudential interpretation of Levinas which proceeds from his claim that judicial adjudication holds the burden of comparing and prioritising competing ethical demands to institute a representative rule or norm.[66] In other words, Levinas has been so influential in this area precisely because relationality is at the heart of his work on ethics.

Agamben's immanence aims to stand outside of the confines of representational dualistic thought. For him, any responsible ethics must be founded on these grounds, as it is the only genuine manner through which to approach a thing's alterity.[67] Apparatuses of control cannot be transcended, or rethought, only deactivated. It is Agamben's messianism, derived through his reading of Paul of Tarsus, which underpins his immanent life, and will deactivate apparatuses through living life as a use, a lived form. I read the messianic figure of form-of-life as an attempt to found a life apart from Levinas and Levinasian understandings of alterity, relationality and law. Only through this reading can the limitations to Agamben's immanent life and his ethics be properly explored.

Agamben's push beyond all structures of law and politics cannot be understood apart from Levinas's reading of the contrast between ethics and ontology – a contrast wherein he sees ethics taking priority.[68] Agamben seeks a politics free of ideology, a circulation of social relations that are not predetermined by the nexuses of power already established through traditional sovereign rubrics.[69] I argue that Agamben provides an uncharitable account of Levinasian alterity and the ethics of relation, by connecting the law and judgment to the creation of bare life. I contend that this is a deliberate move on Agamben's part to generate critical distance for his own immanent thought. Agamben attempts to open up a sphere of non-relational ethics, one which is based on 'non-responsibility', 'contact' and a monadic clinamen (a form of being-in-common) with others.[70] The figure of a form-of-life is one which Agamben makes clear involves the "becoming human of the human being",[71] and an opening to "the possibilities of life".[72] In form-of-life, living and life contract into one another,[73] in a mode of living, a "*how* I am what I am".[74] An ethical clinamen forms the basis of Agamben's non-relational ethical existence. This existence is not lived through defined identities, identity politics or relationality. Rather, through contact with other forms-of-life, and in living a life of contemplative use, we can deactivate the appropriative biopolitics that constantly divides and separates life.[75]

It is contended here that in contradistinction to Agamben's critique of Levinas's subject as negative, Agamben's own non-relational form-of-life should be understood as exhibiting its own negative relation to its other. This can be placed in contrast to Levinas's more positive view of relationality. Agamben's subject is defined negatively due to his diminishing the importance of relationality for the self. As such, the subject, whilst existing in relation with others, is not defined through that relation. In this manner, Agamben's subject can be seen as exhibiting a negative non-relation to the other. This being-with the other is not positive in the sense that the other does not directly define the subject for Agamben. Levinas's view of relationality is defended here as embodying a positive form of relationality, whereby the relation between the I and the Other positively defines the I's existence.

Agamben is seeking a small and subtle yet crucial shift in our perspective of the world we inhabit.[76] There lingers in Agamben's thought an ethical imperative to form a coming community based on one's singular encounter with others, an experience that bears more than a passing affinity to Levinas's work.[77] Grasping the thing itself is a moment of revelation, in Levinasian terms it involves beholding the face of the other before us, in its sheer nudity and exposure.[78] It is in reviewing Agamben's work that we can see a proximity between his thought and that of Levinas. What is more, our formulations of political and legal community are indebted to a particular conceptualisation of transcendence that is reflected in Levinas's thought.

It is for these reasons that I conclude that Agamben's *Homo Sacer* project should be read as a flawed attempt to present an alternative to an ethics of alterity through the figure of form-of-life and attempting to produce a new basis for political existence and belonging. This is because, despite Agamben's best efforts, there remains an aporia within the construction of this ethical form-of-life, and this aporia is better accounted for in Levinas's transcendent ethics. When Agamben's form-of-life is presented with biologically liminal figures, the *life which is lived as a form* becomes identifiable only through the exercise of a judgment; it is this judgment which Agamben sees as irrevocably connected to the law and incompatible with form-of-life. In other words – form-of-life cannot account for these figures.

These liminal figures – the unborn human in the figures of the embryo and foetus, the patient in a persistent vegetative state (PVS) and the patient lacking capacity at the end of their life – which Agamben uses as examples of 'bare life', call into question the limits of a non-relational use and form of existence.[79] It is not yet possible, in considering these forms of life, to escape the form of relationality which Agamben critiques and ties to Levinasian ethics. I show how Levinasian thought can better provide an ethical framework for making judgments in relation to these liminal figures.

I wish to pause for a moment to explain precisely why I have chosen these exemplary figures. It is not the aim of this book to apply Agamben's work to the spheres of abortion and euthanasia and assisted dying. Many scholars have taken up this task, not least because Agamben has remained quiet on matters relating to reproductive rights.[80] Rather, my choice is deliberate, based in part on Agamben's claim that life is not a biological concept, but a political one.[81] Firstly, the focus on the unborn human, and the law on abortion, illustrates a conflict between the life of the unborn human and the life of the pregnant woman. It is not possible to resolve this conflict (in terms of whether the woman has a right to abortion or the unborn has a right to life) without a judgment and decision in favour of one over the other, which is the very act Agamben's thought precludes. As such, Agamben's figure of form-of-life cannot, on its own terms, account for this situation. Secondly, the issue of the end of life. I focus here on adult figures. I exclude the case-law and examples which exist of children claiming the right to make end of life decisions. Again, this is deliberate. Agamben's construction of form-of-life presupposes, I argue, a figure of a fully competent, capable adult. Children are not treated in Agamben's thought as equivalent to form-of-life. The foetus and embryo are used in this study to show how the pregnant woman cannot be resolved into form-of-life. Likewise, adult patients lacking capacity demonstrate how their lives are governed by judgments and decisions made by others, excluding them from Agamben's conception of form-of-life.

Ultimately, I contend, the political decision-making over life seen through the examples of the unborn human and the incapable human at the end of life is what leads to the creation of bare life. I conclude that these figures show that Agamben cannot escape the spectres of the law, and judgment. The abandoned *Homo Sacer* project needs further development to resolve these aporias.

My methodology

I have tried to avoid in this work to become too attached to the proper names of the philosophers I discuss and what they have produced in terms of their works, without paying due attention to the political aims and impacts their thought can provide. In a very broad sense this work can be read as focusing on names and works, especially of Agamben and Levinas. But to accept that point without further explanation would only tell half a story.

My approach is guided by my own political beliefs, my educational background and the methodology with which I approach philosophical works. A consistent theme in my research is that of ethics, community and law. By ethics I focus upon what an ethical existence entails, and how the law can contribute (if at all) to ensuring that individuals are respected and not discriminated against or oppressed. This leads on to community, which aims to find a mode of belonging that can respect differences between individuals. Viewing law as a theme connotes a focus upon how law as an instrument of power can shape and help constitute each individual's way of being in the world as well as how the law can serve to repress and coerce.

I first encountered Agamben's work in 2005, soon after my undergraduate studies. My background is in law. My legal education was strongly influenced by the Anglo-American school of analytic philosophy. I have no formal philosophical education or training. My legal studies emphasised a focus upon the importance of defining terms as well as argumentative clarity and precision in the legal arguments that I was to make. To me, Agamben's thought presented a conception of an ethical politics focused on the singularity of the living being. It was this that led to my wish to explore Agamben's thought further and understand its (to borrow a term) potentiality. My growing interest in continental forms of thought was coupled with a growing unease with the writings on law I was familiar with. I was deeply unsatisfied with and apathetic towards many legal arguments and legal judgments that I was reading. The issues that interested me – age-old political questions first and foremost relating to how best to live one's life and how best to conceive of political belonging – appeared to be eschewed in much legal scholarship in favour of formal legal reasoning, focusing upon narrower questions of statutory interpretation or precedent. My exposure to Agamben, and then to wider continental philosophy and radical politics opened new possibilities for my thought.

Although I have tried to avoid using labels in this book as much as possible, as to do so can potentially caricature a point of view and provide an uncharitable account, labels and generalisations are impossible to avoid in a finite work, and it is necessary to have recourse to them here. My method is grounded in hermeneutics and an analytic method, paying particular attention to the coherence of the thought and claims made by thinkers I have considered. This reflects my own position within legal theory. My work aims to investigate the relation between the human condition and the law. I remain fascinated by how human life is ordered and constructed by legal and political processes, and how such processes can be used to dominate and oppress. Instead of forwarding an explicit political project, my method has been to investigate certain thinkers and aim to find connections between the insights they provide. This enables me to develop detailed arguments based upon the connections and implications I find to positions held by others. I view philosophical investigation in much the same way as an analytic philosopher such as Tyler Burge:

> Philosophy is not primarily a body of doctrine, a series of conclusions or systems or movements. Philosophy, both as product and as activity, lies in the detailed posing of questions, the clarification of meaning, the development and criticism of argument, the working out of ideas and points of view. It resides in the angles, nuances, styles, struggles, and revisions of

> individual authors. In an overview of this sort, almost all the real philosophy must be omitted. For those not initiated into these issues, the foregoing is an invitation. For those who are initiated, it is a reminder-a reminder of the grandeur, richness, and intellectual substance of our subject.[82]

The clarification of meaning, the teasing out of connections between thinkers, the development of detailed arguments and questioning of the implication of certain positions held are all necessary precursors to making sense of the political possibilities of Agamben's thought, and of deciding whether these political possibilities are worth pursuing.

It is also important to state that the main focus of this study is philosophy, and a hermeneutic examination of philosophical works, but I have drawn on law to illuminate and illustrate arguments I make. The law I rely upon is drawn from the common law, and predominantly the English legal system. This is done as my expertise and legal knowledge is based in the common law. Agamben did train to be a lawyer in Italy prior to turning to politics. He therefore has experience of how a civil law legal system operates. But it is also true that his work, and the examples he predominantly draws upon, is embedded in Western European philosophical and political traditions. To use English law to interrogate the limits of form-of-life is, in this sense, to use sources from Western Europe to test the thought of a philosopher who is enmeshed in the same tradition.

The structure

Broadly speaking, this study has three main arguments it advances. The opening two chapters present Agamben's critique of philosophical and political thought, focusing on his construction of an apparatuses which endlessly govern the living being by defining it with reference to an ungraspable transcendent sphere, and illustrating the way in which apparatuses continually trap and ensnare life, enabling it to be separated and divided. The middle three chapters develop Agamben's relationship to the work, and thought, of Levinas. These chapters present Agamben's thought as a critique of Levinasian relationality and relational politics and ethics. They engage in a detailed reading of how both philosophers construct subjectivity. They illustrate how Agamben's equation of Levinas with the apparatus of the 'law' is founded on an uncharitable reading of the nature of the subject in Levinas. I set out Agamben's non-relational form-of-life, arguing that Agamben seeks to deactivate relationality through conceiving of a life lived through a paradigmatic circle of experience. These chapters will also illustrate how Agamben attempts to use this non-relational life to present future forms of political belonging, and how these differ from forms of belonging derived from, or influenced by, Levinasian ethics and subjectivity. The final two substantive chapters engage critically with the modes and details of the figure of form-of-life. They are interested in biological liminal living figures, engaging with debates about the start and end of life, which Agamben contends is a political, not a biological, question. These chapters interrogate the limits to the concept of form-of-life, concluding that Agamben's form-of-life, and ethics, are not able to account for these liminal figures. As a result, Agamben's attempt to found a new form of politics is left flawed and incomplete.

Chapter One contends that 'life' is not a biological concept but a political one. I argue that the relationship of 'inclusive exclusion' within which life itself is caught is a theme in Agamben's thought, and I connect this to his writings in *The Open* on the division between the human and the animal. This chapter sets the scene for the book's argument – to found an immanent form of life not based on this negative relation. *Chapter Two* considers the ways in which this foundational negativity is transmitted and perpetuated. I focus here on how the sovereign decision creating *homo sacer* is exercised through the apparatus of *oikonomia*. The apparatus is a key term in Agamben's thought, constantly capturing life in relational machines of domination and submission, holding it in relation to a transcendent sphere which retains an ungraspable origin. A form-of-life can only be lived once these apparatuses are challenged.

Chapter Three introduces the relationship between Levinas and Agamben and does so through interrogating Agamben's critique of transcendent relationality. This brings into focus the relationship between Levinas and Agamben. Agamben contends that Levinas replicates the inclusive exclusion which creates *homo sacer* – Agamben equates Levinasian ethics with the apparatus of the law and the sphere of judgment. This view of Levinas is a necessary one for Agamben to take, in order to generate critical distance for his own immanent construction of life. *Chapter Four* considers the figure of form-of-life and shows how Agamben's interpretations of potentiality and messianism help construct this immanent figure. I then consider Agamben's modal ontology, which I contend is a post-Levinasian ontology, critiquing Levinas's reliance of hypostases. A modal ontology focuses on a mode of potential, and 'how' a being is. This provides an ontological and ethical alternative to Levinasian ethics. *Chapter Five* details the political possibilities of form-of-life. Form-of-life is characterised by how it lives its immanent life. My exposition of hyper-hermeneutics is discussed and connected to a theory of gestures, via slavery and Franciscan monasticism, showing how form-of-life is based on a presupposition of a capable, conscious existent.

Chapter Six lays out a critique of Agamben's modal ontology, showing how transcendence haunts his immanent thought, and the immanent figure of form-of-life cannot account for the biologically liminal figures of the embryo and foetus. I show how his work comes closest to the pro-life position of the Roman Catholic Church, and contend that Levinasian ethics provides a more coherent basis for considering the position of the unborn, as unlike Agamben, Levinas's thought accounts for issues of the law and judgment. *Chapter Seven* considers the biologically liminal figure of the PVS patient and end of life decision-making for patients lacking capacity. Agamben focuses on this figure as embodying the indeterminacy of when life ends, and as evidence for his claim that life and death are political concepts which acquire a meaning through a decision. I show again that form-of-life is not able to account for these liminal figures. I return to Levinas, arguing that he can ethically account for end-of-life decisions in a way form-of-life cannot. Ultimately, through exploring these biologically liminal figures, form-of-life discloses its own limits.

Notes

1 Agamben (2016a) xiii.
2 Vacarme (2004) 123–124.
3 Agamben (2016a) 257; Prozorov (2014) ch.1.
4 Agamben (2007b) 85–87; Agamben (2000) 3–12; Agamben (1998) 181–188.
5 Agamben (1998) 181.
6 Kotsko (2020) 83.
7 Agamben (1999h) 115; Kotsko (2020) 50.
8 Colebrook and Maxwell (2016) 31.
9 Dickinson (2011) 4.
10 Prozorov (2014) 150–151.
11 de la Durantaye (2009) 11.
12 Kotsko (2020) 6.
13 Kotsko (2020) 7.
14 Mills (2008b) 2.
15 Kotsko (2020) 8.
16 Kotsko (2020) 10.
17 Kotsko (2020) 219.
18 Agamben (2009c) 8.
19 Kotsko (2020) 220.
20 Agamben (1999a) 227–228.
21 Salzani (2020) 100.
22 Agamben (2004b) 16.
23 Attell (2015) 187.
24 Agamben (1999a) 228–229.
25 Agamben (1999a) 228–229.
26 Deleuze and Guattari (1994) 45.
27 Deleuze and Guattari (1994) 46–47.
28 Agamben (1999a) 228. Agamben (2005d) 25.
29 Agamben (1999h).
30 Kotsko (2020) 47.
31 Kotsko (2020) 66.
32 Agamben (1999a) 237.
33 Agamben (2010) 114.
34 Whyte (2013) 32, 44.
35 Zartaloudis (2010).
36 Whyte (2013) 44.
37 Abbott (2014) 1.
38 Kotsko (2020) 67.
39 Abbott (2014) 118, 138–139.
40 Abbott (2014) 188.
41 Kishik (2012) 107.
42 Kishik (2012) 35.
43 Kishik (2012) 70–71.
44 Kishik (2012) 83.
45 Whyte (2013) 138; Agamben (2007b) 85.

46 Dickinson (2015a) 68.
47 Dickinson (2015b) 21.
48 Levinas (1969) 215.
49 Levinas (1969) 39.
50 Levinas (1969) 274.
51 Levinas (1969) 52.
52 Levinas (1969) 3.
53 Levinas (1969) 49.
54 Levinas (1985) 90.
55 Guenther (2006a) 129.
56 Levinas (2008) 157.
57 Stone (2010) 109; Levinas (2008) 157–158.
58 Levinas (1985) 291–292.
59 Agamben (2002) 24.
60 Agamben (2009d) 17.
61 Agamben (2009d) 19.
62 Douzinas (2000).
63 Manderson (2007) 145–164.
64 Diamantides (2000) 167.
65 Manderson (2006); Crowe (2006) 421–433; Stone (2016).
66 Cornell (1992) 147–154; Douzinas and Warrington (1994) 184.
67 Dickinson (2015b) 35.
68 Dickinson (2015b) 36.
69 Dickinson (2015b) 37.
70 Agamben (2016a) 231–233.
71 Agamben (2016a) 208.
72 Agamben (2016a) 209.
73 Agamben (2016a) 223.
74 Agamben (2016a) 231.
75 Agamben (2016a) 228.
76 Dickinson (2015b) 36.
77 Dickinson (2015b) 22.
78 Dickinson (2015b) 31.
79 Agamben (1998) 160–165.
80 Deutscher (2008) 55–70; E Ziarek (2008) 89–106.
81 Agamben (1998) 164.
82 Burge (1992) 51.

1 An ever-divided life

Introduction

Giorgio Agamben's multi-volume *Homo Sacer* study began with *Homo Sacer: Sovereign Power and Bare Life*, where Agamben makes the claim that the conception of life in Western political thought is based on a division between a natural life and a politically ordered life which inexorably produces a remainder, bare life, cast out from the *polis*.[1] Life is not a biological concept but is a political one,[2] which is ceaselessly divided and separated through apparatuses of control.[3] This chapter considers Agamben's argument that the production of bare life is the originary activity of sovereign power.[4] It outlines how Agamben appropriates Michel Foucault's biopolitical theory to this end, as well as how this has led to criticisms of both Agamben's arguments and his method. I suggest that Agamben's reading of Foucault must be seen in the context of the relationship of *inclusive exclusion* through which life is trapped, which is a theme running through Agamben's wider philosophy. Specifically, the inclusive exclusion is connected to Agamben's writings on the division between the human and the animal. The building of human life as an addition to animal existence is contended to be the same operation as the building of political life on natural life. Ultimately, this chapter aims to set the scene for my exploration of the main goal of Agamben's philosophy – to seek a life which is not based on the continual division and separation of living beings.

Biopolitics and the division of life

Life is both a biological concept and a sacred one.[5] Yet for Giorgio Agamben, life, before it could become merely biological, had to become sacred.[6] The concept of life never is defined as such. What this means is that:

> [T]his thing that remains indeterminate gets articulated and divided time and again through a series of caesurae and oppositions that invest it with a decisive strategic function ... everything happens as if, in our culture, life were *what cannot be defined, yet, precisely for this reason, must be ceaselessly articulated and divided*.[7]

DOI: 10.4324/9781315191447-2

This has been a consistent theme in Agamben's thought.[8] In *What Is An Apparatus?* Agamben explains that:

> The event that has produced the human constitutes, for the living being, something like a division ... This division separates the living being from itself and from its immediate relationship with its environment.[9]

This division is crucial for how life is treated in modernity. The division of life, which Agamben traces to Aristotle's *De Anima*,[10] operates on several levels – vegetal and relational, organic and animal, animal and human. These divisions pass as a "mobile border" within living man, and operate as an apparatus through which the decision of what is human and what is not human is possible.[11] Thus Agamben's task in his thought is clear – to investigate the very divisions and caesurae which have separated man from non-man, the human from the animal, over and above taking positions on the so-called great issues of the day such as human rights.[12]

The result of these divisions is the creation of a remainder, the most famous of which is the figure of *homo sacer*, bare life. This figure, an "originary political element", is created as "the fundamental activity of sovereign power".[13] The figure of *homo sacer* was first mentioned by Agamben in *Language and Death*, when he mentioned that the figure is "excluded from the community, exiled, and abandoned to himself".[14] In *Homo Sacer* Agamben delves deeper into bare life's creation through an engagement with the biopolitical theory of Michel Foucault.[15] To understand the position of bare life in Agamben's thought, it is important to turn to how he appropriates Foucault's thought to explain how bare life is formed by the endless division of life.

The appropriation of Foucault

My starting point is the start of *Homo Sacer* where Agamben states that his aim is to "correct, or at least complete" Michel Foucault's hypothesis of biopower.[16] This hypothesis was forwarded by Foucault in a series of lectures at the Collège de France and published as *Society Must Be Defended*,[17] and in the first volume of *The History of Sexuality*.[18] To enter debates about the history of philosophy and focus upon a thinker's influences, particularly a specific influence such as Foucault, can certainly be a fraught affair. For instance, Agamben has openly admitted being influenced by the writings of Hannah Arendt,[19] and studied under Heidegger at Le Thor.[20] It may not seem immediately clear why such a focus on Foucault is necessary. However, much scholarship deals with the fact that many of Agamben's works owe a large debt to Foucault. If Agamben's thought is conflated too readily with Foucault's then Agamben's wider project is in danger of being effaced, or worse, missed.

Biopower for Foucault was an analytic of power that focused not on sovereign power as the central source of power within the social body but instead upon disciplinary and normalising mechanisms designed to transform and influence human life. Biopolitics refers to when life enters political calculations. In his work Foucault moved away from classical views of sovereign power as it had a negative form, being used against the populace to repress or prohibit,[21] which was ineffective for the task of biopower, that of regulating life itself.[22] For Foucault biopower was a direct combination of power and life, a juncture which when explored requires the redefinition of both terms.[23]

Agamben begins *Homo Sacer* by arguing that Foucault's death prevented him from developing his nascent concept of biopolitics.[24] Such a position is a mischaracterisation at best – biopower occupied a transitory moment in the thought of Foucault and was not a central part of Foucault's analyses of power. The reason that biopower gained so little attention from Foucault was that biopower was not a refined enough category of power, which was why governmentality and apparatuses of security began to enter his work.[25] Foucault's studies of biopower took him towards his later analyses of subjectivity – in works written after *The History of Sexuality* and *Society Must Be Defended*, although published before the latter book, Foucault argued that the subject, not power, was the overriding theme of his work.[26] In addition to what is a mischaracterisation of the prominence of biopower in Foucault's work, Agamben goes on to summarize a persistent feature of Foucault's writings as including a:

> [D]ecisive abandonment of the traditional approach to the problem of power, which is based on juridico-institutional models (the definition of sovereignty, the theory of the State), in favour of an unprejudiced analysis of the concrete ways in which power penetrates subjects' very bodies and forms of life.[27]

Whilst Foucault did move away from traditional views of sovereignty, it is ambiguous what Agamben means when he refers to a "decisive abandonment".

Agamben summarises the Foucauldian project, identifying two strands of inquiry. The first is the study of political techniques with which the State assumes and integrates the care of natural life of individuals into its very centre, which can be seen in biopower and biopolitics. Roberto Esposito correctly notes that Foucault did not invent the idea of biopolitics, as its origins can be traced to the early twentieth century.[28] However, in distinction to these earlier notions, which saw biopolitics as a direct relation between biological life and politics, biopolitics for Foucault was part of a much larger analysis of governmentality.[29] For Foucault, biopower refers to the techniques of government which transform life into an element of the economy of power. Biopower focuses on disciplinary and normalizing mechanisms designed to transform and influence human life, to optimize health and prolong life.[30] In other words, biopower strives to preserve life, even at the cost of terrible suffering.[31] Importantly, as well as the government of the living, biopower refers to the multiple practices of dying. Death is the limit to biopower for Foucault because power must invest itself in the body. The second is the examination of the technologies of the self by which processes of subjectification bring the individual to bind himself to his own identity and consciousness and, at the same time, to an external power. This can be seen clearly in disciplinary power.

It is here that Agamben tries to generate critical distance between his own project and that of Foucault's. Agamben sees his correction as necessary as Foucault failed to connect his work on biopower to Arendt's studies on totalitarianism.[32] Following this, his claim was that biopower and disciplinary power are bound together through a sovereign power that retains the right of death over the individual.[33] He is by no means alone in this view. Achille Mbembé has argued that Foucault's biopower is not able to account for the contemporary forms of subjugation of life to the power of death.[34] Agamben also claims that death is not power's limit, but rather the terrain upon which power operates.[35] While Foucault wrote of the deadly combination of biopower and sovereign power, exemplified in Nazi Germany,[36] Agamben reads this combination not as a historical aberration, but as a condition of possibility of Western politics. Agamben inverts Foucault's statement that "death is outside the power relationship" and "beyond the reach of power";[37] biopolitics is much more about sovereignty and death than Foucault contended. Bare life is the unfortunate subject of these sovereign decisions of life and death.

Agamben's biopower does not liberate individuals from the theoretical privilege of sovereignty but instead radically intensifies his work with sovereignty, a sovereignty that acts through the law to create and sustain political life.[38] He contends that if Foucault was correct and the modern State has "integrated techniques of subjective individualisation with procedures of objective totalisation to an unprecedented stage",[39] the point at which these two powers converge remains unclear. For Agamben, Foucault's contestation of the juridical model of power (including sovereignty) comes at the price of his failure to identify in the body of power the zone of indistinction where the techniques of individualisation and totalising procedures come together.[40] This invocation of a zone of indistinction can be put in better context by citing Agamben's own explanation of his methodology:

> When you take a classical distinction of the political-philosophical tradition such as public/private, then I find it much less interesting to insist on the distinction and to bemoan the diminution of one of the terms, than to question the interweaving … the system is always double; it works by means of opposition. Not only as public/private, but also the house and the city, the exception and the rule, to reign and to govern, etc., but in order to understand what is really at stake here, we must learn to see these oppositions not as "di-chotomies" but as "di-polarities", not substantial, but tensional. I mean that we need a logic of the field, as in physics, where it is impossible to draw a line clearly and separate to different substances. The polarity is present and acts at each point of the field. Then you may suddenly have zones of indecideability or indifference.[41]

The scholarship on Agamben and Foucault

Perhaps not unreasonably, given his claims, and Agamben's own statement that he sees his work as "closer to no one than to Foucault",[42] a great deal of the literature reads his thought through the lens of Foucault. There is much merit in scholarship investigating the differences and divergences between philosophers. However, there is a tendency in this scholarship to read Agamben as an heir to Foucault's philosophical project, and he has been accused of constructing a blunt account and ignoring the nuances in Foucault's thought.[43]

Katia Genel, as part of a detailed analysis of Agamben's correction of Foucault, asks whether Agamben could "legitimately reinterpret" Foucault's thought in the way he does. Questioning whether Agamben has undertaken a legitimate reinterpretation implies that Agamben has directly developed Foucault's thought. Genel, not without reason, concludes that "Agamben carries out a displacement of his interrogation onto the terrain of sovereignty and the law, a terrain Foucault had abandoned".[44] Mika Ojakangas has argued that Agamben's move to ally biopower with sovereignty misses a key thrust of Foucault's analysis:

> The original problem of Agamben's analysis is that he sees bio-power as power based upon bare life, defined in turn solely by its capacity to be killed. Foucault's bio-power has nothing to do with that kind of bare life.[45]

Both Genel and Ojakangas read Agamben's thought as a continuation or descendant of Foucault's philosophical project, and as such demands a certain fidelity to Foucault. The criticisms they level at the accuracy of Agamben's corrections are supported by the knowledge that, for Foucault, biopower is a thoroughly *modern* phenomenon.[46]

It is also true that Agamben grants primacy to a specific reading of the *Politics*; by reading Foucault's biopower as beginning with Aristotle, Agamben risks positing an extremely arbitrary basis for his reinterpretation of biopower not based upon empirical evidence.[47]

Even here though, it is necessary to note that Agamben's interpretation of biopower is not as far removed from Foucault as first appears. Despite Foucault's pronouncements on the relationship between death and power, there is nothing about Foucault's account that precludes a discrimination between lives that are worth living and lives that are not worth living, as long as this discrimination is understood to enhance the population's productivity.[48] What biopolitical practices and strategies entail is not just the ability to foster life, but also allow life to die.[49] This means that the death of any particular individual is insignificant, as life continues at the level of the population.[50] Indeed, Timothy Campbell has gone so far as to claim that much contemporary writing on biopolitics, including Agamben, Esposito and Peter Sloterdijk retain a preoccupation with how biopolitics regulates death, leading to biopolitics being reduced to a form of thanatopolitics.[51]

The orthodox view is that biopower occupies a transitory moment in Foucault's thought, as it was not a refined enough category of power for his analyses. This is the reason why governmentality and *dispositifs* of security began to enter Foucault's work.[52] In addition, Foucault does conflate biopower and governmentality, claiming the state of government is defined by the "mass of population". He then makes clear that while governmentality is pre-eminent in modernity, it does not displace sovereign power.[53] This should be understood despite the fact that Foucault's hypothesis of biopower took him towards his later analyses of the subject and subjectivity, which accords with Foucault's own claim that the subject was the overriding theme of his work.[54]

Criticisms are levied at Agamben for his interpretation of the position of sovereignty in Foucault's work. Sovereignty for Foucault is more nuanced than Agamben at first glance gives him credit for. Although Foucault separated biopower from conceptions of sovereignty tied to monarchical characterizations of law,[55] Foucault did not abandon sovereignty. Mitchell Dean has noted that sovereignty still plays a role in Foucault's thought, for example in his referring to the nature of a *coup d'état*.[56] Foucault also acknowledged that sovereignty persisted into modernity, combining with other forms of power such as biopower. This was shown to murderous effect in Nazi Germany,[57] where biopower exercised the sovereign right to kill when it was justified by racism, used to decide which populations must live and which must die.[58] Biopower, disciplinary power and sovereign power manage to cover as large a surface of the population as possible, with all three forms of power exercising themselves over different areas of the population for different reasons in different ways.[59] Power relations therefore exist at all levels of the social body and interact with one another across these levels. Power relations act on actions themselves, either existing actions of those individuals or upon actions that may arise in the future.[60]

Panu Minkkinen argues that Foucault showed how the identification of weaknesses in the classical theory of sovereignty lead to sovereignty taking on a guise that allowed it to perform its classical functions whilst at the same time overcoming the clashes that result from the incompatibilities between disciplinary, normalising and juridical rationalities.[61] For Minkkinen, sovereignty in Foucault functions as a legitimating device, an ideological veil juridifying governmental practices as well as minimising interference with government through, as Minkkinen demonstrates, redefining juridical subjectivity through new "fuzzy" rights, such as the right to be a productive member of society, at the expense of traditional political rights.[62]

In a similar manner Ben Golder and Peter Fitzpatrick have argued, from a post-structuralist standpoint, that sovereignty and law persisted in an integral relation in Foucault's thought.[63] For them, disciplinary power is dependent upon the law, a law which acts as a constituent power in relation to the disciplines.[64] The law is a restraint to disciplinary power, confirming the claim at the heart of disciplinary power to adjudicate on questions of normality and social cohesion.[65] By the law confining its jurisdiction to the periphery of the disciplines the core of disciplinary power is left reinforced, whilst at the same time the disciplines remain constituently reliant upon law to curb their abuses.[66] In this way, the law masks the disciplinary domination through offering the veil of legality; law and the disciplines exist within a relation where they are dependent on one another.

If Agamben's thought was part of a Foucauldian co-ordinate, these criticisms and readings of Foucault would be unimpeachable. However, Agamben's thought should be read as appropriating Foucauldian concepts to forward a different conception of political existence to counter the caesurae of the exception and anthropological machine, based upon both a novel reading of Foucault and an interrogation into the nature of life itself.[67] Following Michael Dillon, I wish to inquire not into "the degree of faithlessness" Agamben shows to Foucault, but as to "the worth of the betrayal".[68] It is through this questioning that Agamben allows us to explore the potential in his work.

This degree of faithlessness is illustrated through Agamben's use of paradigms to construct philosophical investigations, such as the figure of *homo sacer* which stands for bare life. A paradigm for Agamben is like an example, the significance of which he explained in *The Coming Community*:

> In any context where it exerts its force, the example is characterized by the fact that it holds for all cases of the same type, and, at the same time, it is included among these. It is one singularity among others, which, however, stands for each of them and serves them all. On one hand, every example is treated in effect as a real particular case; but on the other, it remains understood that it cannot serve its particularity. Neither particular nor universal, the example is a singular object that presents itself as such, that *shows* its singularity. Hence the pregnancy of the Greek term, for example: *para-deigma*, that which is shown alongside … Hence the proper place of the example is always beside itself, in the empty space in which its undefinable and unforgettable life unfolds.[69]

The paradigm is neither inside nor outside the group or set of phenomena that it identifies. Rather, a paradigm is the particular case that is set apart from what it is meant to exemplify.[70]

Agamben traces his paradigmatic method directly to Foucault, and Agamben has stated that this method is a "philosophical archaeology" that does not deal with origins, akin to Foucault's genealogical tradition that also quested against a search for origins.[71] Rather, philosophical archaeology searches for the point of emergence of the phenomenon, the source of its existence. Therefore, Agamben's archaeology is an ontological examination of a phenomenon which will enable "the thing itself" to be grasped.[72] A focus upon origins implies a before, presupposing an original condition that existed and split into the various phenomena being studied. This in turn represents a belief that this before was a golden age that needs to be returned to – a belief that Agamben does not share.

Agamben's paradigmatic method has been very widely criticized by philosophers and historians such as Ernesto Laclau for purveying a "distorted history" as well as a view of the present that reflects "political nihilism".[73] Laclau does not simply oppose the principle of the paradigmatic method however, but seems to misread Agamben's use of paradigms as standing for examples that must be followed. Rather, as Leland de la Durantaye observes, Agamben's paradigms are examples, albeit extreme, that explore the emancipatory possibilities that exist in modernity. To dismiss Agamben as deterministic, as Laclau does, misses the key thrust of Agamben's method.[74]

Leland de la Durantaye sees the strengths of the *Homo Sacer* project as inseparable from its weaknesses in its radicalisation of Foucault's method.[75] It is Agamben's insistence that paradigms can be both concrete historical instances as well as representing broader philosophical concepts that appears to form the biggest objection to his thought.[76] It should be realized that Agamben's use of paradigms is complex, both central to his thought and developed from that of Foucault's; any criticism of Agamben must therefore be careful not to misunderstand Agamben's aims and not implicitly call into question Foucault's own conclusions and methodology.

The inclusive exclusion of bare life

After considering the use of Foucault by Agamben, we can turn to the divided nature of life. In the first volume of *The History of Sexuality*, Michel Foucault referred to Aristotle's definition of man when he summarized the process by which life was included within the mechanisms of State power:

> For millennia, man remains what he was for Aristotle: a living animal with the additional capacity for political existence; modern man is an animal whose politics calls his existence as a living being into question.[77]

Agamben re-reads Aristotle's *Politics*, and in doing so distinguishes between *zoè*, which denoted the basic fact of living common to all living beings, be they animals, men or gods, and *bios*, which was the form or way of living proper to an individual or group:

> This [life according to the good] is certainly the chief end, both of individuals and of states. And mankind meet together and maintain the political community also for the sake of mere life [*kata to zēn auto monon*] (in which there is possibly some noble element [*kata ton bion*] so long as the evils of existence do not greatly overbalance the good). And we all see that men cling to life [*zoē*] even at the cost of enduring great misfortune, seeming to find in life a natural sweetness and happiness.[78]

Bios is seen by Aristotle as the proper end of man, how man exists as a political animal. Every *bios* is equally built upon *zoè*, natural life, just as anything we name or conceive of is presupposed in language by the fact of being named.[79] As Mathew Abbott has argued, *zoè*, the fact of living, was presupposed by the polis as its unthinkable ground, upon which *bios* rests.[80] It is this distinction that Agamben argues first brought life into the political sphere, and makes Aristotle into the father of biopolitics.[81] Thus biopolitics is not, as Foucault would have it, an invention of modernity. Rather, it is as old as modernity itself.

What is essential to grasp for our purposes is the importance of this structural relation between *bios* and *zoè*. *Bios* and *zoè* do not represent life as such. Rather, they stand for the "constant attitude" whereby life is never defined but instead is articulated and divided into *bios* and *zoè*, whereby each term is determinable only in its relation to the other.[82] Life is always decided and separated politically and singularly; the product of this constant separation is inevitably a remainder.[83]

Bios is an empty signifier. Political life does not have meaning in and of itself, as it always needs to be held in relation to what it is not in order to give substance to its content.[84] The "decisive event of modernity" in Agamben's eyes is the entry of *zoè* into the *polis*, the political sphere, the very act that allows *bios* to ground itself against a politicised *zoè*.[85] Thus the fact of living is never successfully banished, and reappears in modernity as an always ambiguous political object, bare life. This bare life is a life without the rights and duties of *bios* but is still trapped within the political realm and therefore vulnerable to the operations of power that may act against it.[86] This means that within the *polis* there exist human lives that participate in the community of *zoè* but that are constitutively excluded from the political community.[87]

Thus, the most important figure to Western politics is not the rights-imbued individual characterised by *bios*, but instead bare life. Without bare life, *bios* cannot ground itself. Our political existence *requires* this remainder. The division of life has a political meaning;[88] it is by means of this division that the human being becomes capable of a political life.[89] It is bare life that maintains political existence, yet at the same time is anathema to the very system it maintains, the very system that denies that bare life can exist.

This relation between *bios* and *zoè* places both elements in a negative functional relation. Although *bios* and *zoè* are distinct from one another, they gain their meaning, content, and substance from this relation, and this unthought presupposition of life itself – they have no meaning other than that given to them in this relation. Both elements require their concrete grounding for substance. Political life is defined through the creation of bare life – political existence becomes a contingent event.

Derrida: enter stage right

It is at this point in our analysis that we turn to the relationship between Agamben and Jacques Derrida, introduced here by which of their treatments of sovereignty. Virgil Brower has described Derrida as Agamben's "primary interlocutor".[90] Kevin Attell has stated that Agamben's "critical engagement with deconstruction can indeed be identified as the context out of which emerge almost all of his key concepts".[91] This is despite Agamben's engagement with

Derrida being conducted in passing comments or just below the surface of his texts.[92]

Defining deconstruction is hazardous at best;[93] it is a point of disagreement whether deconstruction is a method, a technique or a process based on a particular ontological vision.[94] Deconstruction claims that writing precedes speech instead of operating as a supplement to speech; that every text refers to other texts; and that discontinuities between the logic and rhetoric of texts create inevitable disparities between what the author of a text means to say and what the text is nonetheless constrained to mean.[95] Instead, a text is radically indeterminate in the sense that its meaning defies the possibility of ever being constrained. Deconstruction constantly seeks out possible meanings a text can bear, juxtaposing these to expose the incoherence and indeterminacy of every text.

The best example of how deconstruction challenges Agamben's work is through the "undecidable".[96] The undecidable is a term that does not fit comfortably within either of the two poles of a binary opposition. Derrida was careful to distinguish undecidability from radical indeterminacy, as the undecidable did not mean that *any* meaning could be imparted:

> Undecidability is always a determinate oscillation between possibilities … These possibilities are themselves highly determined in strictly defined situations … I say 'undecidability' rather than 'indeterminacy' because I am interested in relations of force, in differences of force, in everything that allows, precisely, determinations in given situations to be stabilised through a decision of writing.[97]

Every decision for Derrida necessarily involves an experience of the undecidable. There is no decision that is not structured by the experience of the undecidable.[98] Derrida traces four distinct themes of the undecidable. The first is the irreducibility of any text to a given theme, set of themes or thesis. Although texts do convey thematic meanings, every text is always more or less than those meanings. Texts therefore always have a remainder. No text can be construed as fully present to itself, and is never wholly what it is without departing from itself.[99] Secondly, the essential irreducibility of a text to a given theme has a corollary in the irreducibility of any text to pre-emptive truth.[100] Third, indecision is a necessary condition for all decision-making.[101] For a decision to be possible and necessary there must be the undecidable: the hesitation between determined choices without which there would be nothing to decide. Even when there is a decision, the undecidable never disappears. The undecidable continues to haunt every decision. Each decision is therefore never entirely final. The undecidable thus ensures decisions must be confronted time and again. The undecidable is therefore the cornerstone of ethical decision-making, asking the decision-maker each time a decision is made to justify his choice. Fourthly, the undecidable is inseparable from risk. It is closely intertwined to questions of responsibility and poses the question of how it can be possible to be responsible in the face of that which is unforeseen and therefore irreducible to established knowledge or belief.

In the past Agamben has defended Derrida against characterisations of deconstruction as a hermeneutical relativism of infinite deferral:

> [I]t would be the worst misunderstanding of Derrida's gesture to think that it could be exhausted in a deconstructive use of philosophical terms that would simply consign them to an infinite wandering or interpretation.[102]

Despite this, Derrida has seen in Agamben (and Foucault) a desire to surpass. This desire is based on Agamben and Foucault adopting a linear history in which "*epistémes* that follow on from each other … render each other obsolete".[103] In addition, Derrida argues that a "sovereignty of surpassing" is detectable in the "essential claim of sovereignty" in Agamben's prose. Specifically, the "most irrepressible gesture" repeated throughout *Homo Sacer* to be "the first to say who *will have been first*".[104] Worse, he "wants to be first twice, the first to see and announce … and also the first to recall that … it's always been like that".[105] A criticism that Derrida makes of Husserl can thus be redirected at Agamben:

> [T]he negativity of the crisis is not a mere accident. But it is then the concept of crisis that should be suspect, by virtue of what ties it to a dialectical and teleological determination of negativity.[106]

In *Beast and the Sovereign I*, Derrida reads Aristotle's *Politics* in an attempt to critique Agamben's biopolitical thesis. In relation to Agamben's distinction between *bios* and *zoè*, Derrida argues that:

> What is unfortunate [for Agamben] is that this distinction is never so clear and secure, and that Agamben himself has to admit that there are exceptions, for example in the case of God, who, says Aristotle's *Metaphysics* [1027b28, quoted in *Homo Sacer*, 11], has a *zōē aristē kai aidios*, a noble and eternal life.[107]

Kevin Attell explains that for Derrida, such an opposition implies and requires a binary difference, two poles separated by the space of alterity. Agamben engages with deconstruction and Derrida's thought in *Homo Sacer*, when discussing the inclusive exclusion of the exception, a relation he terms the ban. The distinction Derrida draws between *bios* and *zoè* is not actually a distinction, as *zoè* is not separated from *bios politikos*, "inclusively excluded" from it in a relation of ban.[108] Bare life is the materialisation of the relation of ban:

> The link between bare life and politics is the same link that the metaphysical definition of man as "the living being who has language" seeks in the relation between *phōnē* and *logos* … The living being has *logos* by taking away and conserving its own voice in it, even as it dwells in the *polis* by

> letting its own bare life be excluded, as an exception, within it. Politics therefore appears as the truly fundamental structure of Western metaphysics insofar as it occupies the threshold on which the relation between the living being and the *logos* is realised.[109]

Both Agamben and Derrida agree on the description on the ban-structure (the inclusive exclusion), the fundamental structure of the law and sovereignty, but they differ on the status that they assign to that structure.[110] For Agamben, deconstruction's limit is its inability to imagine an undoing of the sovereign-ban-structure.[111] Deconstruction pushes the aporia of sovereignty "to the limit" but cannot free itself from the ban.[112] Agamben continues:

> The prestige of deconstruction in our time lies precisely in its having conceived of the entire text of tradition as being in force without significance, a being in force whose strength lies essentially in its undecidability and in having shown that such a being in force is … absolutely impassable. But it is precisely concerning the sense of this being in force (and of the state of exception that it inaugurates) that our position distinguishes itself from deconstruction.[113]

Derrida posited the impossibility of overcoming the infinite undecidability that exists on the limit of metaphysics in every decision. For Agamben, Derrida's affirmation of an irreducible undecidability with regard to questions of law and justice entails dwelling within the limbo of the sovereign *fictio* at a sort of pure decision/indecision that has no decisive content other than the function of maintaining the law in a virtual, though empty, state.

The state of exception

At this point it is apposite to turn to the state of exception, through which the human remainder is created. This is no true exception as understood by theorists of emergency powers. The exception for Agamben is a zone of indistinction where law and fact completely coincide. A distinction is drawn by Agamben between the juridical order (*il diritto*) and the law (*la legge*). The concept of a juridical order maintains a fiction. The juridical order represents an abstract notion of Law, which applies to all of reality, to all of life itself. By contrast, the law (*la legge*) of a State may be unprincipled and contain lacunae in certain areas.[114] The juridical order maintains that there are no lacunae, in the sense that the juridical order covers all lacunae and all situations that arise.

Through the operation of the exception, the sphere of law shows its proximity to that of language. Linguistic elements exist in *langue*, in language, without any real meaning. These linguistic elements only gain meaning through their use in actual speech, *parole*. Yet equally, speech, concrete linguistic activity, only gains meaning if a language is presupposed.[115] The relationship between speech and language is not based upon any logical operation.

The only way in which a generic proposition endowed with a merely virtual reference, such as a 'tree', passes to a concrete reference that corresponds to a segment of reality is through a practical activity, presupposing what is meant when the linguistic element 'tree' is used.

As it is for language, so it is for law. The method of application of a legal norm can in no way be established through looking at the legal norm itself. Rather, it is the exception which acts as the nexus that holds the norm in relation to its application. In order to apply a norm, it is ultimately necessary to produce an exception, to suspend its application.[116] The exception exists as a zone of indistinction where the norm and application reveal their separation. A norm is defined through instances and situations in which it does not apply.[117]

For Agamben, every act of legal reasoning thus becomes an instance of the exception, trying to contain within the law that act which is neither law nor fact. In doing so it legitimises the act of bare power which has occurred in the necessary act. The law becomes completely indistinct and is exercised solely through a concrete *praxis* in the exception, a zone of indistinction. In the zone of indistinction all legal determinations are deactivated,[118] but this does not mean that there is no law in the exception. This means that potentially any action taken in the exception can gain legal force.[119]

The exception is the opening of a fictitious lacuna in the juridical order. However, the lacuna is fictitious as it suspends the legal order that is in force, "safeguarding the existence of the norm and its applicability to the normal situation".[120] There is no gap in the legal order in the sense of a lack of law. Rather, the legal order is suspended within the exception. Almost contrarily, through suspending the norm the exception guarantees the norm's pre-eminence for future cases. By delimiting when the norm does not apply in the exception this reinforces the norm's applicability in the normal situation.

The role of the exception as dispositive is emphasised further through Agamben's reference to the word's etymology, *ex-capere*, what is being excluded is captured outside. It is included through its very exclusion.[121] The exception is not, therefore, separate from the law, but operates as a zone of indeterminacy between inside and outside.[122] The law gains meaning through its own suspension, through the exception determining when the rule, the norm, does not apply. This is a relation of exception; the juridico-political order includes what is simultaneously excluded. The law's force maintains itself in relation to an exteriority, which can be seen as life itself.[123] It is this which we can call law's crisis – legal orders gain meaning through their exclusion and regulation of life.

The legal norm is suspended but still in force. In suspending the norm the norm's *force-of-law* is also separated from its application. This term has a direct relation to Derrida's essay of the same name. In this essay, Derrida uses Walter Benjamin's "Critique of Violence" to explore the mystical foundations of the law.[124] The law is necessarily applied with force. Derrida's conception of force includes physical, symbolic and hermeneutic approaches.[125]

In a similar vein, by force-of-law Agamben refers to the constitutive essence of the law, the element that literally gives laws, decrees and other measures their force. In other words, the force-of-law makes a law legal and gives it legal force. So, legal norms that remain in force yet are not applied are separated from their force. The force-of-law therefore acts as an almost floating quality. Acts that do not have legal force can acquire this floating force-of-law that has been separated from the norm that is not being applied.

The similarities to Agamben continue throughout Derrida's essay, most noticeably when Derrida states that:

> Since the origin of authority, the foundation or ground, the position of the law cannot by definition rest on anything but themselves, they are themselves a violence without ground.[126]

This force has a peculiar property – there is no just and unjust before the foundational act. The legitimation of the order is retrospectively created by this order itself.[127] The force creates law and thus its own legitimation. Derrida denies that there exists a solid foundation for the law; the law justifies its existence through a self-referential process. The founding moment of law is neither legal nor illegal, but rather it exceeds the oppositions of founded and unfounded. The origins of the law therefore will still contain the mystical remnant that provides the basis for authority.[128]

Agamben states that if an act that does not gain legal force gains this force-of-law, then it will be by definition *legal*. Such acts are characterised by Agamben as having the force-of-law (without law), or "force-of-~~law~~". More than this, the norm that has had its force-of-law separated is still being in force, but not being applied. Thus, a legal norm, through not being applied, can lead to acts that are not legal becoming legal. The force-of-law (without law) can be claimed by both the State and non-State groups not just to justify their actions, but to give them the force-of-law, to make their actions legal.[129] The exception, through suspending the law, means that:

> The normative aspect of law can … be obliterated and contradicted with impunity by a governmental violence that – whilst ignoring international law externally and producing a state of exception internally – nevertheless claims to be applying the law.[130]

Law has passed into crisis as the relation it has to life is a negative one. Without challenging this negative relationality, bare life will continue to operate as a condition of modernity. By constantly including life in its apparatus, even through exclusionary means, the figure of bare life is created – legally – as a necessary remainder for the system's operation.

The anthropological machine

It is this system which operates as an "anthropological machine". In *The Open*, Agamben embraces Martin Heidegger's insistence on animality as what is concealed about and from humanity.[131] Agamben claims, like Heidegger, that there is an abyss between man and animal, but that this abyss is not wide enough in Heidegger's thought. Heidegger's notion of *Dasein* as ek-stasis is his escape from animal captivation, dependent upon his entrance into language, an entrance closed to the animal.

Language is a way of being in the world, and a way of having access to that world through world-formation. Animals lack access to world-formation as they are poor in world – the animal is separated from man "by an abyss".[132] Animal behaviour is instinctual; humans engage in the intentional and free self-reflexive activity of comporting themselves. Animals have no true or conscious relationships with others or their environment, whereas humans comport themselves toward others and their environment in a world-forming way.[133]

Where Agamben develops Heidegger's analysis is in arguing that man's humanity is dependent upon his effacing his own animality. This means man retains a privileged position in the dichotomy of man-animal.[134] By closing himself to the closed environment of the animal, man opens himself to the world of the properly human. Humanity is dependent upon the exclusion of animality. Animality with its world-poverty is the concealed centre of humanity with its world-formation.[135] Humanity is therefore defined as not-animality. This connection means that *Dasein* cannot perform the activity essential to it, which is to let beings be. Man cannot let animals be themselves as man is dependent upon seeing animals as closed systems from whom he differs in his openness.[136] The abyss between man and animal is produced by excepting animality from the concept of humanity.

Agamben and Derrida both focus on the ontological and anthropogenetic function of the distinction and exclusion of the animal from the human. Both focus on the impact language has on this relation. Derrida draws a distinction between the lifeless, mechanical, repetitive word of the animal (which is shared with the written word) and the vital, unique, original and responsive word of the thinking and speaking human.[137]

Agamben states that what distinguishes man from animal is language – if language is removed then the difference between man and animal vanishes.[138] But this is not simply to say that Agamben thinks man has language and animals do not. In *Infancy and History* he states that:

> Animals are not in fact denied language; on the contrary, there are always and totally language.[139]

He goes on to say that man:

> [I]s not the 'animal possessing language' but instead the animal deprived of language and obliged, therefore, to receive it from outside himself.[140]

Animal voice, like vocalisations, allows the animal to communicate immediately, and as such animal language is one with nature.[141] Man must learn language and must receive it from the outside, and is therefore split in his nature.[142] But this moment of becoming a speaker marks the living being becoming human.[143] The suppression of the animal is therefore the condition of possibility for the emergence of the human,[144] as a being who have no pre-established work.[145] As Salzani states:

> [T]his structure will recur in many a founding paradigm throughout Agamben's career, as in the couplets *physis/nomos*, nature/culture, silence/witness, *zoé/bios*, etc.[146]

Agamben has been criticised for his anthropocentrism. It is true that non-human animals are absent from Agamben's reflections on animality.[147] Dominick LaCapra has maintained that Agamben "has virtually nothing specific to say about other-than-human animals or their lives".[148] Salzani has shown how Agamben demonises biology in arguing that only humans (unlike animals) are free from "any genetic prescription".[149] Going further, Matthew Calarco has argued that *The Open* focuses:

> [E]ntirely and exclusively on the effects of the anthropological machine *on human beings* and never explore[s] the impact the machine has on various forms of animal life.[150]

Despite his writings on the animal and post-humanisms, Agamben does hold on to the name of the human in his work,[151] and he does conflate ontology and anthropogenesis.[152] Yet it is also true to say that the rift between human and animal is pivotal to Agamben's wider project, and it is perhaps because of this that he stubbornly holds on to the concept of the human whilst refusing any essentially determination of the concept.[153] Western metaphysics presupposes an unknowable and unnameable substrate (such as natural life and animality) which supports a knowable and nameable substance (such as politics and humanity). This presuppositional structure always leads to the subjection and dominion of one part over the other and the production of bare life,[154] creating a false articulation between the simply living being and the human.[155]

Derrida makes the animal/man boundary a doubtful boundary, as he deconstructs the division between *the* human and *the* animal.[156] The opposition between these two terms requires a binary difference, two terms or poles separated by the space of difference.[157] Derrida attempts to render obsolete the categories of man and animal by opening ourselves up to diversities of both animal species and individual animals. The vast differences between various animals makes the category animal particularly inappropriate. The French title of *The Animal That Therefore I Am* is "*L'animal que donc je suis*". There is an indistinction between "*je suis*" (I am) and "*je suis*" (I follow).[158] This effects the troubling ambiguity that runs like a fault line through all philosophical texts on the human and animal. Every affirmation concerning the essence or being of the human is an affirmation of an essential difference between the human and all other (inferior) forms of life.

What is at stake in Derrida's survey of philosophy on the human/animal is the way the being (*être*) of the human is inextricably bound up with the human's proximity to, distinction from, and following after (*suivre*) the animal. The human is defined by an untenable othering of "the animal" in an attempt to affirm and safeguard the coherence and purity of the human sphere.[159]

For Agamben, the dividing line between the animal and the human is an internal one that passes within man:

> [M]an has always been thought of as the articulation and conjunction of a body and a soul, of a living thing and a logos, of a natural (animal) element and a supernatural or social or divine element. We must learn instead to think of man as what results from the incongruity of these two elements, and investigate not the metaphysical mystery of separation. What is man, if he is always the place – and ... the result – of ceaseless divisions and caesurae? It is more urgent to work on these divisions, to ask in what way – within man – has man been separated from non-man, and the animal from the human, then it is to take positions on the great issues, on so-called human rights and values. And perhaps even the most luminous sphere of our relations with the divine depends, in some way, on that darker one which separates us from the animal.[160]

The man-animal divide is determined not by alterity or *différance* but by the exceptional separation, the inclusive exclusion. It is a division within the human itself. All efforts to define the human are driven by the "anthropological machine of humanism".[161] The human is a fluctuating and transient being, one whose position moves up and down on the ladder of creation according to its own self-fashioning activity:

> Insofar as the production of man through the opposition man/animal, human/inhuman, is at stake here, the machine necessarily functions by means of an exclusion (which is also always an exclusion). Indeed, precisely because the human is already presupposed every time, the machine actually produces a kind of state of exception, a zone of indeterminacy in which the outside is nothing but the exclusion of an inside and the inside is in turn only the inclusion of an outside.[162]

The human is presupposed to articulate a relation with the nonhuman other. This articulation is a fiction established by the exception. The human is established by this empty space, the exception.

This is why, in the anthropological machine, man is produced through the opposition of *bios* to *zoè*, of man to animal, of human to inhuman. This machine functions through an exclusion (which is also always already a capturing) and an inclusion (which is also always already an exclusion). In modernity this machine functions by excluding as not yet human an already human being from itself, by isolating the nonhuman within the human, the animal (*zoè*) separated within the human body itself (*bios*).[163]

The state of exception is the zone of indifference at the centre of the machine. It is here that the articulation of *zoè* and *bios*, human and animal, man and non-man takes place.[164] This caesurae ceaselessly dislocates and displaces the human being which in turn obtains a bare life, whose separation and exclusion from itself grounds political existence.[165] As Attell explains, what is produced is a (fictitious) zone of exception that establishes the dominion of the valourised term (the human in this context, *bios* in others) on the condition that the inferior term (the animal, *zoè*) be subjected to the condition of ab-bandonment and be produced not as pure and independent *zoè* but as bare life.[166] In trying to produce the human, the anthropological machine ceaselessly generates a space of sovereign exception.[167]

Conclusion

This chapter has introduced Agamben's contention that life in Western political thought should be understood as a political concept which is ceaselessly articulated and divided. This division produces a remainder, bare life. *Bios*, political life, is built upon *zoè*, natural life. *Bios* and *zoè* do not represent life as such. Rather, they stand for the "constant attitude" whereby life is never defined but instead is articulated and divided into *bios* and *zoè*, whereby each term is determinable only in its relation to the other. Political life does not have meaning in and of itself, but it always needs to be held in relation to bare life, against which it grounds itself. This is a fundamentally negative relation.

Agamben claims that the production of bare life is the originary activity of sovereign power. Bare life is created through a state of exception, through a relationship of inclusive exclusion, the 'ban'. To this end, Agamben appropriates the biopolitical theory of Michel Foucault. Agamben has been criticised for his reinterpretation of Foucault, and Jacques Derrida has criticised Agamben's construction of sovereignty. I have argued that Agamben's reading of Foucault and Derrida's criticism of Agamben must be seen in the context of this relation of ban. Agamben reinterprets Foucault's work to a specific end, and both Agamben and Derrida agree on the description on the ban-structure, but they differ on the status that they assign to that structure.

Ultimately, this chapter has connected the inclusive exclusion to the division between the human and animal. An anthropological machine produces man through opposing *bios* to *zoè*, of man to animal, of human to inhuman. This division and separation will continue unless and until we found a life which is not based on this inclusive exclusion. The next chapter builds upon this analysis and considers how the negative relation which creates bare life is transmitted and perpetuated through Western political thought.

Notes

1 Agamben (1998) 1, 181.
2 Agamben (1998) 161.

3 Agamben (2011).
4 Agamben (1998) 181.
5 Anidjar (2011) 698–699.
6 Anidjar (2011) 711; Agamben (1998) 66.
7 Agamben (2004b) 13.
8 Agamben (2006).
9 Agamben (2009d) 16. For example, the "person" is a way in which the subject is divided. See Parsley (2010) 12.
10 Aristotle (1984b).
11 Agamben (2004b) 15.
12 Agamben (2004b) 16.
13 Agamben (1998) 181.
14 Agamben (2006) 105.
15 Ross (2008) 1–13; Calarco and De Caroli (2007).
16 Agamben (1998) 8.
17 Foucault (2003a).
18 Foucault (1978).
19 Agamben (2009a) 111.
20 de la Durantaye (2009) 1–2.
21 Genel (2006) 48.
22 Foucault (2003a) 249–50.
23 Genel (2006) 44.
24 Agamben (1998) 6.
25 Golder and Fitzpatrick (2009) 32, 49; Foucault (2000b) 223–51.
26 Foucault (1982a) 208; Rabinow (1991) 7–11.
27 Agamben (1998) 6.
28 Esposito (2008) 13–44.
29 de Boever (2010) 37–38.
30 Foucault (1978).
31 Noys (2005) 54.
32 Agamben (1998) 4–6.
33 Agamben (1998) 6–7.
34 Mbembé (2003) 39–40.
35 Noys (2005) 35.
36 Foucault (2003a) 259.
37 Foucault (2003a) 247–248.
38 de la Durantaye (2009) 210.
39 Agamben (1998) 6.
40 Agamben (1998) 6–7.
41 Raulff and Agamben (2004) 612.
42 de la Durantaye (2009) 209.
43 Rabinow and Rose (2006) 201–202.
44 Genel (2006) 45. Genel here comes close to the "expulsion thesis", a view that Foucault decisively expelled law from his thought in favour of other forms of power. As has been indicated elsewhere, this view is a mischaracterisation at best – see Golder and Fitzpatrick (2009).
45 Ojakangas (2005) 5.
46 Foucault (1978) 143; Ojakangas (2005) 13–15.
47 Norris (2005) 262.
48 Foucault (2003a) 260.
49 Foucault (2003a) 255.
50 See Palladino (2011) 1–20.
51 Campbell (2011) 29.
52 Golder and Fitzpatrick (2009) 32, 49; Foucault (2000b) 223–251.

53 Foucault (2007) 107–108.
54 Foucault (1982a) 208.
55 Foucault (2003a) 35.
56 Foucault (2007) 261–266.
57 Foucault (2003a) 260.
58 Foucault (2003a) 254–255.
59 Foucault (1978) 88–90.
60 Foucault (1982b) 789.
61 For an in depth analysis of how sovereignty is dealt with through Michel Foucault's various works, see Minkkinen (2009) 95–112.
62 Minkkinen (2009) 111.
63 Golder and Fitzpatrick (2009) 53–56, 58–59.
64 Golder and Fitzpatrick (2009) 64–65.
65 Golder and Fitzpatrick (2009) 64.
66 Golder and Fitzpatrick (2009) 65–67.
67 Agamben (1999a) 239.
68 Dillon (2005) 37–46.
69 Agamben (2007b) 9–10.
70 de la Durantaye (2009) 218–219.
71 Agamben (2009b) 214.
72 Agamben (2009b) 220.
73 Laclau (2007) 19–22.
74 de la Durantaye (2009) 221.
75 de la Durantaye (2009) 226.
76 de la Durantaye (2009) 220.
77 Foucault (1978) 143.
78 Aristotle (1984c) 1278b, 23–31; Agamben (1998) 1.
79 Agamben (2018d) 3.
80 Abbott (2012) 26.
81 Agamben (2004b) 80.
82 Agamben (2016a) xix.
83 Agamben (2016a) xix-xx.
84 Agamben (1998) 181.
85 Agamben (1998) 4.
86 There have been fierce critiques of the accuracy of Agamben's use of Aristotle, and the implications of his misreading and misappropriation of primary sources for the conclusions he draws in his thought. See Finlayson (2010) for an excellent example.
87 Agamben (2016a) 198.
88 Agamben (2016a) 202.
89 Agamben (2016a) 203.
90 Brower (2017) 230.
91 Attell (2015) 3.
92 Nancy and Fabbri (2007) 435.
93 Rosenfeld (1990) 1212.
94 Unger (1983) 561.
95 Rosenfeld (1990) 1212.
96 Derrida (1997) 144–145.
97 Derrida (1988) 148.
98 Derrida (1988) 116.
99 Derrida (1986) 198–199.
100 Hill (2007) 110.
101 Hill (2007) 112.
102 Agamben (1999d) 208.

103 Derrida (2009) 333.
104 Derrida (2009) 90.
105 Derrida (2009) 330.
106 Derrida (1997) 40; Brower (2017) 232.
107 Derrida (2009) 316.
108 Attell (2015) 187.
109 Agamben (1998) 7–8.
110 Agamben (1998) 18.
111 Agamben (1998) 54.
112 Agamben (1998) 48.
113 Agamben (1998) 54.
114 Agamben (2005c) 27.
115 Agamben (2005c) 36–37.
116 Agamben (2005c) 40.
117 Agamben (2005c) 26–31.
118 Agamben (2005c) 23, 50.
119 Agamben (2005c) 59; Agamben (1998) 52.
120 Agamben (2005c) 31.
121 Agamben (2000) 40.
122 Agamben (2005d) 105.
123 Agamben (1998) 18.
124 Derrida (1990) 919; Benjamin (2004) p.236. See also Cornell (1990b) 1047; LaCapra (1990) 1065; Weber (1990) 1515; Cornell (1990a) 1687.
125 Derrida (1990) 927.
126 Derrida (1990) 943.
127 Derrida (1990) 991.
128 Derrida (1990) 943.
129 Agamben (2005c) 38.
130 Agamben (2005c) 87.
131 Oliver (2007) 1, 3.
132 Heidegger (1993) 230.
133 Heidegger (1995) 237, 239.
134 Agamben (2004b) 79.
135 Agamben (2004b) 91.
136 Oliver (2007) 6.
137 Derrida (2008) 52; Attell (2015) 179.
138 Agamben (2004b) 36.
139 Agamben (2007a) 52.
140 Agamben (2007a) 57.
141 Agamben (2007a) 3.
142 Agamben (2007a) 52.
143 Agamben (2018c) 77–78.
144 Salzani (2020a) p.103; Salzani (2020b) 74.
145 Agamben (2007d) 1–10.
146 Salzani (2020a) 103.
147 Salzani (2020a) 97.
148 LaCapra (2009) 168.
149 Salzani (2020b) 75; Agamben (1995) 95.
150 Calarco (2008) 102.
151 Lagaay and Rauch (2020) 92–93.
152 Agamben (2016a) 111.
153 Lagaay and Rauch (2020) 103; Colebrook and Maxwell (2016) 167.
154 Salzani (2020a) 100.
155 Agamben (2018b) 117.

156 Attell (2015) 168.
157 Attell (2015) 189.
158 Derrida (2008) 3–4.
159 Attell (2015) 182–183.
160 Agamben (2004b) 16.
161 Agamben (2004b) 29.
162 Agamben (2004b) 37.
163 Agamben (2004b) 37.
164 Agamben (2004b) 37–38.
165 Agamben (2004b) 38; Agamben (2016a) 199, 203.
166 Attell (2015) 187.
167 Agamben (2004b) 38.

2 The transmission of negativity

Introduction

The previous chapter focused on Agamben's claim that life is a political concept which is ceaselessly articulated and divided through a series of caesurae and oppositions (man/animal, human/inhuman, *bios/zoè*). These oppositions inevitably produce a remainder in the figure of bare life. This anthropological machine presupposes what we see political life through an inclusive exclusion, a fundamentally negative relation, effected via the state of exception.

This chapter builds upon the analysis that there is a negative relation at the heart of modernity's understanding of political, rights-imbued life. This negativity is transmitted and perpetuated through Western philosophical thought, most fundamentally with the relationship between life itself and language. Understanding this places in context Agamben's contention that bare life is created through an exercise of sovereign power. Drawing upon Agamben's work in *The Kingdom and the Glory*, I show how the sovereign decision which produces bare life is ultimately and economic and managerial decision exercised through the apparatus of *oikonomia*,[1] and the relationship between sovereignty and government is in fact an empty void, and the two poles constitute each other through a negative relation. In short, government effectively produces the power which grounds it, making sovereign power operative.[2]

This chapter then considers the respective roles the apparatus, or *dispositif*, have in the thought of Agamben and Michel Foucault. Agamben connects the *dispositif* to *oikonomia* and the bipolar machine of sovereignty and government. He further contends that the subject is produced and utterly dominated by *dispositifs* in the *oikonomic* governmental machine. To support this argument, I consider Agamben's methodology, or his philosophical archaeology, and the role of the *dispositif*.[3] For Foucault, the *dispositif* and power relations constructs the human subject, but there is always the possibility for a transcendent form of resistance to this operation of power. For Agamben, in a decisive move away from the method and thought of Foucault, it is not possible for a subject to escape the control of the *dispositif*, or to utilize the *dispositif* to construct a form of freedom which transcends the individual. For Agamben, it is through these apparatuses and signatures that life, as a political concept, is continually divided

DOI: 10.4324/9781315191447-3

and separated, held in relation to a transcendent sphere which retains an ineffable and ungraspable origin.

A foundational negativity

In response to Agamben's claim that the negativity which produces the human being is riven throughout Western political and philosophical thought, his method has faced numerous criticisms. In understanding these criticisms and how they misread Agamben, we can better situate the position of negativity in his diagnoses of the fundamental problems of Western philosophy.

Agamben's methodology combines historiography and philosophy, being critical of the contemporary yet philosophically and radically open to the coming community.[4] William Watkin has summarised the common historical and philosophical criticisms of Agamben. Historically, Agamben is said to misuse his historical source material in three ways: he claims to have discovered hidden origins of modern political structures; he misreads philological material; and he makes drastic abbreviations and unacceptable emphases by concentrating on a very partial set of historical facts. Philosophically, Agamben is criticised as having a naïve dependence on a philosophy of origins, and a commitment to a messianism which has been shown to be fundamentally aporetic.[5] Watkin contends:

> These criticisms see Agamben as a thinker who is trying to use historical data to support an already discredited philosophical project of foundations and final unities, using the empirical power of historical material to gain purchase in the philosophical community, whilst applying outmoded philosophical arguments to mask what is effectively a partial and inaccurate set of historical philological observations.[6]

The fact that Agamben's works do not obviously cohere and share a common thread throughout does seem to lend weight to these critiques. As Alice Lagaay has stated:

> In attempting to describe Giorgio Agamben's philosophy I find myself confronted with a peculiar challenge, which seems to have something to do with the very experience of reading. Whilst reading Agamben's texts, much of what he writes seems to me to make immediate sense. It feels familiar and clear, yet my attempts to reconstruct his argument soon falter. This incapacity to reflect, to speak or write about Agamben's work is perhaps not, however, just one particular reader's affliction, for it also happens to be one of the recurrent themes of the texts themselves. The difficulty of re-telling his work, which may perhaps be interpreted as a kind of reaction block, corresponds precisely with what Agamben aims to highlight. It is what is interesting to him and in his work.[7]

This reaction block may have led Antonio Negri to see Agamben as tragically bifurcated. Negri states:

> There are in fact two Agambens. The one holding onto an existential, fated and horrific background, who is forced into a continuous confrontation with the idea of death; the other seizing (adding pieces, manoeuvring and building) the biopolitical horizon through an immersion into philological labour and linguistic analysis.[8]

It is Murray's position that there is never a clear sense that the two dialectical opposites that Negri posits are truly in opposition.[9] Agamben is a controversial thinker because he is proposing:

> [A] fundamental reconsideration of what constitutes the historical, our intent towards it in the contemporary moment and the means by which systems of intelligibility and ultimately suspended.[10]

He makes apparent and then renders indifferent all structures of differential opposition that lie at the root of every major Western concept or structure, like sovereignty or life.[11] As David Kishik explains:

> These are probably the most persistent tropes in his writings, and they more or less consist of the same fundamental gesture: the pitting of two concepts against each other, followed by the localisation of a sort of whirlpool in their midst, which in turn is meant to undermine the original dualism.[12]

The presupposition that humans live in between opposite poles is one of the favourite targets of the poststructuralists. Gilles Deleuze points out that "opposition is not a maximum of difference but a minimum of repetition – a repetition reduced to two, echoing and returning on itself".[13] But Agamben's strategy is to invoke the apparatus time and again, repeating it indefinitely, and trying to find a way to disable the dichotomy through the presentation of the zone of indistinction, where one pole cannot be distinguished from its opposite. The point of indifference is not a place for unity or reconciliation, or a new metaphysical truth. Agamben insists on the *noncoincidence* of every opposition. He does not let the division collapse into itself by keeping it in a state of limbo, by maintaining it as an "uncertain terrain".[14]

The unity of Agamben's thought is found through the fundamental premise that man is defined – and constantly redefined – through his faculty for language, being a living being who *knows* how to speak.[15] The faculty of speech is inseparable from being human.[16] Central to Agamben's thought is a philosophy of language. He has stated that the terrain that all his work is oriented are the questions: "What is the meaning of 'there is language'; what is the meaning of 'I speak'?"[17] The existence of life is the proper manifestation for the existence of language;[18] the production of negativity is tied to an originary division in language and the human itself – "*life is truly only what is made in speech*".[19] And it is this originary negativity which is transmitted and perpetuated through Western thought.

To define a human being as the animal that has speech places a negative foundation for language. Speech presupposes language – anything we conceive of is presupposed in language by the simple fact of its being named.[20] This structure of presupposition determines the way in which the West has thought politics.[21] This presupposition places a negative foundation for the human, leading to the capture and suspension of life, and the figure of bare life continually being produced. In *Language and Death*, Agamben traces a negativity in Heidegger's construction of *Dasein*, although he has been accused of incorrectly interpreting Heidegger and paying scant attention to his opus.[22]

In his lecture course entitled 'What is Called Thinking?' Heidegger was concerned with thinking in general, and stated that:

> *Most thought provoking is that we are still not thinking* – not even yet, although the state of the world is becoming constantly more thought-provoking.[23]

The question 'What is called thinking?' relates to anything that is to be thought about. Reflecting on "aboutness" opens a new horizon for reflecting upon the way entities are, or their Being.[24] Heidegger makes it explicit that in order for the question of Being to be grasped, it is necessary to make an entity, the inquirer, transparent in its own Being.[25] This being's mode of Being is the very asking of the question of Being, and it is this (human) being that Heidegger terms *Dasein*, which is literally "Being-there".[26]

For Heidegger, that essence of Being can only be grasped in a moment of being-in-the-world, by *Dasein*.[27] This is so because a human being has the capability to question its being (thereness) in relation to Being, the ontological structure of its existence.[28] For Heidegger, the essence of things is intimately connected to the essence of *Dasein*.[29] *Essence* is bestowed by the thinking-Being of a being. Essence means that which enables. Essence is that which lets beings be, the unfolding potentiality of the thingness of things, but which is no-thing in particular.[30]

The Being of *Dasein* is "in each case mine", and as such each *Dasein* is designated by the personal pronoun.[31] However, *Dasein* should not be thought of as simple human life. Instead, *Dasein* is intimately connected to Being, but is also never fully identified with the Being of beings or with beings.[32] *Dasein* encounters Being in a moment of insight, a moment of clearing, although *Dasein* always-already falls back into its being among other beings. Heidegger explains the relationship between Being, life and *Dasein* as follows:

> Life is a particular kind of being; but essentially it is accessible only in *Dasein*. The ontology of life is achieved only by way of a privative interpretation; it determines what must be the case if there can be anything like

> mere-aliveness (*Nur-nich-leben*), life is not a mere being-present-at-hand, nor is it *Dasein*. In turn, *Dasein* is never to be defined ontologically by regarding it as (ontologically indefinite) life plus something else.[33]

A part of the metaphysical dominance that has forgotten the question of Being is identified by Heidegger as Aristotle's definition of man as "the animal that has speech" (*zoōn logon echon*).[34] This stood for the universal essence of man. Heidegger saw this definition as thinking of man in a particular way. Specifically, Heidegger saw Aristotle's definition as thinking of man according to a certain interpretation of animality and of life. It is in this sense that Heidegger questions the necessity of humanism and humanistic thinking, which he ties to metaphysics. Humanism defines man as an animal with an ungraspable, ineffable essence. For Heidegger, metaphysics thinks of man "on the basis of *animalitas* but does not think in the direction of his *humanitas*".[35] Humanism views the essence of man as obvious, and as such it misses:

> The simple essential fact that man essentially occurs only in his essence, where he is claimed by Being.[36]

It is through *Dasein* that Heidegger aims to challenge this humanism. Humanism, by attempting to frame out a characteristic of humans, falls short of the uniqueness of human beings, and does not set human beings high enough, in their position as respondents to Being.[37] *Dasein* does not exist – rather, it "ek-sists".[38] *Dasein* is only in-the-world when it is leaping outside of self-interpreting as a being. Being-in-the-world is a moment of nearness to Being for *Dasein*, which is only as ek-sistent.[39] To ek-sist cannot be reduced to a representational quality that is found in humanism. Ek-sistence refers precisely to "standing in the clearing of Being".[40] Ek-sistence moves away from any notion of a living being.

There is no representation by which the Being of human beings can be captured in a relationship to Being.[41] The Being of human beings, the mode of being given to humans, is related to the question of Being, to the fact that Being is in question for the way that humans are as *Dasein*. Whenever *Dasein* is, it is a Fact. The factuality of such a Fact is *Dasein*'s facticity. This means that *Dasein* has Being-in-the-world in a way that it can understand both itself and the Being of the entities that it encounters in the world.[42] *Dasein*'s ek-sistence is structured temporally, with *Dasein* always-already self-interpreting what it has been.[43] In the human's relation to *Dasein* the human is not considered for its own sake, but instead for the sake of Being.

Dasein is an opening on to Being, an opening that allows Being to unfold *in* and *as* the *Da*, the there. The *Da* of *Da-sein*, the there, marks the originary human relation to Being. The *Da* opens up in relation to the human. The human is displaced as the there of Being, as *Da-sein*. Heidegger structures *Dasein* not as prior to Being but by thrownness in Being.[44] *Dasein* is thrown into the there, the *Da*, as Being-in-the-world.[45] Being-thrown reveals itself as being thrown in the direction of death, namely the direction of possibility of

Dasein. *Dasein* can experience the death of others,[46] but *Dasein*'s own death can only be experienced as an own-most, non-relational, impending possibility.[47] In a sense, death should be thought of as *Dasein*'s indefinite possibility, an impossible possibility, as *Dasein* cannot experience its own death except through an anticipation.[48] When *Dasein* becomes free for its own death, *Dasein* becomes open to the possibility of being itself. This Heidegger terms "freedom towards death".[49]

Language and death

Death is the key issue in Heidegger's thought for Agamben. Heidegger writes:

> Mortals are they who can experience death as death. Animals cannot do so. But animals cannot speak either. The essential relation between death and language flashes up before us, but remains still unthought. It can, however, beckon us toward the way in which the nature of language draws us into its concern, and so relates us to itself, in case death belongs together with what reaches out for us, touches us.[50]

Agamben reads *Dasein* as becoming the genesis of the human being out of animality, emerging from its captivation in animality. However, *Dasein*, after emerging from one kind of captivation, then gets captivated by Being.[51] As Ziarek points out, Agamben sees *Dasein* as:

> An animal that has awakened from being taken with its environment and, as a result, begins to try and master the animality from which it has awakened and of which it no longer has a "direct" experience.[52]

And it is the relation between language and death that Agamben focuses upon:

> Both the "faculty" for language and the "faculty" for death, inasmuch as they open for humanity the most proper dwelling place, reveal and disclose this same dwelling place as always already permeated by and founded in negativity. Inasmuch as he is *speaking* and *mortal*, man is … according to Heidegger, the "placeholder (*platzhalter*) of nothingness".[53]

The idea of man as both mortal and possessing language is related to the fundamental negativity of metaphysics. Metaphysics needs to create a negative space within which to base its account of the world. Agamben's analysis focuses on this place of negativity which, by his lights, man occupies in the tradition of Western metaphysics.[54] The proper understanding of being-thrown implies a fundamental disposition that is anxiety, caused by *Dasein*'s thrownness. Agamben explains:

> Anxiety that necessarily refers to anguish in the face of death, is in truth the principle auto-affection, the *Stimmung* in which the Self is constituted

> by the very act that it is 'claimed', 'called' as an individual for its own-most being-able, absolute and unsurpassable. As a principle of individuation, of absolutisation, death is charged with a capital revelatory function: it opens *Dasein* to itself as that which exists as being-thrown for an in relation to its end. Being-there is only *there* in order to exist as thrown into possibility, or inasmuch as it strikes out in that direction, anticipates it or goes ahead of it, and by so doing delivers it as such, making possibility possible. Death is not an expiration date with which *Dasein* will surely be faced one day or another, a possibility that hangs over its head and that will ultimately come true: it is not *possible* except as being itself essentially possibilising, that is to say, as that instance always to come that allows *Dasein* to set out, going ahead, defining, or, better, in defining thereby the ontological possibility of its entire being-able-to-be.[55]

This thrownness means that for Agamben *Dasein* is linked to an experience of negativity. This is a position that Agamben does not share with Levinas. For Levinas, reading about *Dasein*'s anxiety points to the possibility of death to which *Dasein* is always already compelled.[56] Death is a negation, but not a negativity.[57] Our anxiety of death becomes a fear, but death still remains a possibility "that makes all possibility possible".[58] As Zartaloudis explains, Agamben sees anxiety as a state of mind that signifies the anxiety of desubjectivisation inherent in *Dasein*'s thrownness.[59] *Dasein* is conveyed to the world before its own *Da*, its *there*. It is only because *Dasein* has its own there that it can exist. At the same time *Dasein* reveals the *Da* as a non-place, a nowhere. This relates to the nowhere of death. Agamben argues *Dasein* is structured by death, which is an (the) absolute negativity. Agamben writes:

> If *Da* faces *Dasein* like an 'inexorable enigma'... that is because in revealing *Dasein* as always-already thrown, it (*Dasein*'s mood) unveils that fact that *Dasein* is not brought into its *da* of its own accord.[60]

Agamben reads *Dasein* as negative, arguing that it should not be understood as Being-there, but rather "Being-*the*-there". Levinas saw the *Da* as a "foundation without a ground".[61] Whilst in Levinas's reading of Heidegger this structure leads to care, for Agamben the *Da* (there) is what removes the human from *Sein* (Being):

> At the point where the possibility of being *Da*, of being at home in one's own place is actualised, through the expression of death, in the most authentic word, the *Da* is finally revealed as the source from which a radical and threatening negativity emerges. There is something in the little word *Da* that nullifies and introduces negation into that entity – the human – which has to be its *Da*.[62]

The *Da* of man was read by Levinas as a manner of being-there in the world, which is to question about Being. Man is preoccupied with being and must be enlightened in advance to pose the question of being.[63] Agamben reads this passage as highlighting the fact that we are always trying to uncover *Sein* but are unable to do so because we are located ("there" names the place from which we exist).[64] In *Dasein* something is always lacking – what it can be and become. To this end belongs the end of being-in-the-world, which is death.[65] *Dasein* (as Being-the-there) is thrown to its there (*Da*) to realise that it is threatened by a radical negativity (its death). The *Da* here is characterised as the no-place of death. Instead of revealing the ontological structure that is mine,[66] *Da-sein* becomes the placeholder of nothingness.[67] The there of *Dasein* takes place in the non-place of the living human being.[68]

The next step for Agamben is the fact that the *Da* of *Da-sein* is designated by the personal pronoun, a demonstrative pronoun or a 'shifter', an indication of an utterance.[69] Demonstrative pronouns (for example, "I", "it" and "they") are empty signs which only gain meaning through discourse and their use in language, and they have no meaning outside of the very instance of discourse:

> [Pronouns] permit the reference to the very event of language, the only context in which something can only be signified.[70]

The demonstrative pronoun that shows what is always-already indicated in *Logos* or speech without being named in philosophy, namely Being. As Zartaloudis states, for Agamben *Dasein* means "to be" or "witness" the taking place of language.[71] Agamben reads Aristotle's definition of man as "the animal that has speech" as presupposing a particular understanding of human speech. This views human speech as eroding or shifting an underlying animal voice or an animal state that must be overcome for man to be a rational animal. *Dasein* is a being without a natural voice: "Being *Da*, man is in the place of language without having a voice".[72]

Zartaloudis reads Agamben as claiming that grammatical shifters articulate a passage between signification of a concept and that concept's indication.[73] In this journey towards rationality, an animal or natural voice is displaced by another Voice.[74] This Voice becomes the presupposed place of negativity of the human being in language.[75] A negativity exists as the human Voice is built upon a lack, an animal voice that does not have the capacity for language.

Agamben maintains that because *Dasein* is always-already thrown it cannot be its own *Da*, the pure event of language.[76] Transcendence only exists as the pure taking place of language as such. This point is important for Agamben's philosophy. Transcendence is not held in relation to immanence, presupposing it. It rather only occurs as such in language.

However, *Dasein* is in language and is already in its transcendence. *Dasein*'s transcendence *has* a linguistic structure, which is its shifting through the shifters.[77] Language is in *Dasein*'s *Da*, which is essentially without a voice.[78] As Zartaloudis describes, Agamben sees Heidegger as siting a voice as a nothing in the *Da* which presupposes the Voice of *Dasein* that signifies openness to Being.[79] This is not transcendence as such but a transcendence as a presupposition. Agamben claims that the articulation of the human voice within language is a pure negativity. Every shifter is structured as a Voice, with language conceived as both being and not-being the voice of man.[80] The *Da* is viewed as trapped in this limbo in relation to the human *Dasein*.[81] The split between signification and demonstration only becomes possible if it is marked by the presupposition of a Voice, which both discloses the place of language as both a no-longer animal voice or sound and as also a not-yet meaningful discourse.[82] As Agamben states in *The Use of Bodies*:

> [I]f the human being is truly such only when, in becoming *Dasein*, it is opened to Being, if the human being is essentially such only when "it is the clearing of Being", this means that there is before or beneath it a non-human being that can or must be transformed into *Dasein*.[83]

Agamben sees man as no-longer animal because he alone experiences language. Man always-already fails to grasp meaningful discourse because he cannot reach the *Da*, the pure experience of language. Linguistics, philosophy, and the very definition of man rests upon a double negativity. The unspeakable of language (in the shifter) is guarded by its being spoken. The limit of language falls within language. The human means of *having* language rests upon a negative foundation, an originary shifter as Voice that allows humans "[t]o experience the taking place of language and to ground, with it, the dimension of being in its difference with respect to the entity".[84] This is a fracture, and due to its existence we are no longer able to experience life as we ought to.

Negativity and the split between sovereignty and government

The spectre of an originary negativity haunting philosophy is returned to in *The Kingdom and the Glory* and perpetuated through the relation between sovereignty and government. Another fracture is traced in this volume. Not between life and language, or man and animal, but a fracture focused on the divided nature of power itself. In this volume, Agamben argues that political thought is the subject of an originary negative scission between transcendent and immanent poles:

> Power—every power, both human and divine – must hold these two poles together, that is, it must be, at the same time, kingdom and government, transcendent norm and immanent order.[85]

There are two main theses in *The Kingdom and the Glory*. First, modernity has two political paradigms derived from and bequeathed to it from Christian theology. The first paradigm is political theology, which provides for the theory of sovereignty and the foundations of law. This paradigm founds the transcendence of power in the unity of God. The second paradigm is that of the Divine economy or *oikonomia*, which provides the model for the governance and economic administration of human beings and things. *Oikonomia* is an immanent, economic, domestic and non-political administrative order of governance. From the first paradigm is derived Western political philosophy and theories of sovereignty; from the second derives modern biopolitics and the modern managerial economy. The second thesis Agamben posits is that these two paradigms are both separate from each other, antinomian to each other yet functionally related.[86]

Through the presupposed relation of the two paradigms, it is possible to show the general problem of power at an ontological level. This is the fracture between being and *praxis*.[87] There remains a division between transcendent and immanent realms. This division is based upon a separation, which defines the immanent sphere through being held in relation to a transcendent sphere that it cannot reach and has no part of. In this sense, the immanent sphere of existence is defined through a negativity, through being held in relation to a sphere that can neither be defined nor grasped. There exists a realm of participation and an unparticipated realm that the immanent sphere cannot reach.[88] Agamben speaks of a governmental machine which has two poles, subject to continuous separation and articulation.[89] The two poles of this machine are Kingdom and Government, which correspond to transcendent sovereignty and the immanent government of men and things. There is a "two-stroke engine", a machine with two poles. The immanent effects, carries out and realises the effusion of the transcendent.[90] In other words:

> Immanent and transcendent order once again refer back to each other in a paradoxical coincidence, which can nevertheless be understood only as a perpetual *oikonomia*, as a continuous activity of government of the world, one that implies a fracture between being and praxis and, at the same time, tries to heal it.[91]

Zartaloudis describes Agamben's argument as stating that every metaphysical or politico-theological essence and origin is negative as they assume a scission between essence and existence. Every origin presumes two realms: one existent, immanent realm and another, essential, transcendent realm that remains ineffable. The immanent realm is defined negatively by being held in relation to a transcendent realm. The immanent sphere therefore needs the transcendent sphere to ground itself and constitute itself. The relation of *oikonomia* to sovereignty repeats this scission between existence and essence.[92] It is *oikonomia* that is the key to modernity and the production and sustaining of bare life, *homo sacer*. And it is *oikonomia* which provides the connection to Agamben's method and the importance of the use of apparatuses, or *dispositifs*, in his work.

In Greek, *oikonomia* signified the administration of the home (*oikos*) and, more generally, management.[93] Aristotle referred to *oikonomia* as *techne oikonomike*, or economic art, the art of running the household.[94] Theology put forth a convincing paradigm to recuperate an Aristotelian definition of transcendence as God as the immovable mover, the origin of all things:

> Aristotle transmitted to Western politics the paradigm of the divine regime of the world as a double system, formed, on the one hand, by a transcendent *archē*, and, on the other, by a immanent concurrence of secondary actions and causes.[95]

The economical government of men and the world, found today in biopolitics and liberal economic government, can be traced to the problem of the Christian Trinity, and the question of how to resolve a monotheistic faith with the triune nature of God.[96] Christianity inherited from Judaism the doctrine of one God, the Father and Creator as the central pillar to its faith.[97] Early Church Fathers were in agreement with the idea that one God brought all things into existence from non-existence. The problem facing theology was how to integrate this Judaic belief in one God with the specifically Christian revelation. At the simplest level, this revelation involved God making Himself known in the Person of Jesus, the Messiah, raising Him from the dead and offering salvation to men through Him, and the pouring out of His Holy Spirit upon the Church. This conception of a plurality of divine persons was deeply imprinted upon the early apostolic faith.[98]

In enquiring into the relation between God the Father and God the Son, the Early Church Fathers distinguished between *theologia*, theology and *oikonomia*, economy. *Theologia* referred to the mystery of God's innermost Being within the Trinity and *oikonomia* referred to all the works by which God reveals himself and communicates his life. This included the act of giving his only Son to the world to die and redeem all sins. This can be seen in the thought of second century theologian Irenaeus, who approached the question of the Trinity from two directions. Irenaeus envisioned God both as He exists in His intrinsic being, and as He manifests Himself in the economy, *oikonomia*, the ordered process of His self-disclosure. God is ineffably "one", yet He makes Himself known through the revelation of his Son and Holy Spirit.[99]

St Paul described the relationship between God, Christ and the Holy Spirit as the *oikonomia* of the mystery, namely an activity which will reveal the Divine mystery, God's plan.[100] Agamben reads the Early Church Fathers, including Irenaeus, Tertullian and Hippolytus as ultimately reversing the Pauline syntagma into the mystery of *oikonomia*, a mystery of the economy.[101]

The crucial point to be grasped here is that this reversal resolves the mystery not through an ontological means, but by an economic-governmental one, which emphasizes its *praxis*.[102] Action, *praxis*, has no foundation in a transcendent plane.[103] This fracture between being and acting provides for a rich inheritance in Western thought. This is evident in every attempt to conceive of a reciprocal determination of being and acting in philosophical, ethical, and political principles that provide the rules according to which an individual is to act and the authority according to which this is made possible as its justification.[104] God is to be thought not through the being of the Trinity, but through its *praxis*, through the administration of His Divine plan on Earth.[105] The mystery of the Trinity is to be revealed through the stewardship of the

Earth.[106] The Trinitarian *oikonomia* bequeathed to Western politics a transcendent sovereignty that cannot act without an immanent, *oikonomic* managerial government, which in turn derives all its power from the sovereign. *Oikonomia* represents:

> [T]he attempts to articulate in a single semantic sphere … a series of levels whose reconciliation appeared problematic: non-involvement in the world and government of the world; unity in being and plurality of actions; ontology and history.[107]

Western political history has always operated according to this *oikonomic* paradigm through a bipolar machine, rather than through a sovereign transcendentalism as has been the obsession of political theology:

> The ambiguity that consists in conceiving government as executive power is an error with some of the most far-reaching consequences … What our investigation has shown is that the real problem, the central mystery of politics is not sovereignty, but government; it is not God, but the angel, it is not the king, but ministry; it is not the law, but the police – that is to say, the governmental machine that they form and support.[108]

God's transcendent sovereignty is administered through his immanent government of the Earth.[109] Sovereign power and *oikonomia* are always present to a greater or lesser degree, and power is necessarily separate from its execution. Just as God governs in the world yet remains other to it, the relationship between sovereignty and governmentality is always vicarious. It is therefore impossible to access ultimate power since it is always deferred from one realm to the other.[110] Governmental action is anarchic and not derived from sovereignty, in the same way that Christ does not derive from God, but is God. Government does not derive from sovereignty but *is* sovereignty. Government upholds the transcendent foundation of sovereignty through its immanent *praxis*.

Oikonomic government

For Foucault, the state's splendour is a residue of an archaic power which has survived through to modern liberal governmentality.[111] For Agamben, power needs glory in the form of ceremonies and acclamations.[112] There are, theologically, two elements of glory. First, the glory of God, which is unconditioned and not of the world. Second, there is the glory that we owe to God, which is glorification.[113] Agamben asks why this is the case, which provides a distinction between his work and Foucault's. Foucault places an emphasis on the how rather than the why of power.[114] So why does power need glory?

After government articulates its own foundation in sovereignty, it disguises that foundation in the insignia of glory. The true distribution of power is to be found in the articulation between *oikonomia* and glory: "between power as government … and power as ceremonial and liturgical reality".[115] The paradigms of political theology and *oikonomia* are functionally related through glory. Glory is the "secret point of contact through which theology and politics continuously communicate and exchange parts with one another".[116] Glory allows us to "bridge that fracture between theology and economy. The doctrine of the trinity was never able to completely resolve this. It is only the dazzling figure of glory that provides a possible conciliation".[117] Both poles of the bipolar machine glorify and articulate each other: "The government glorifies the kingdom and the kingdom glorifies the government. The *oikonomia* of the Trinity is, in this sense, an *oikonomia of glory*".[118] As William Watkin explains:

> Theology differentiates two trinities, the economic trinity of revelation and the immanent trinity of substance (God as he is in himself). These match the division between praxis and ontology that make up economic theology or God's operativity in the world. Immanent trinity reveals ontology and theology and economic trinity praxis and *oikonomia*. Together these have formed the basis for what [Agamben] terms the machine of the divine government of the world around the poles of transcendent and immanent order.[119]

In glory, God's *praxis* of salvation and his being – immanent trinity and economic trinity – are conjoined and move through each other.[120] But the centre of the governmental machine is empty, and it is glory that masks this emptiness:

> [T]he center of the governmental apparatus, the threshold at which Kingdom and Government ceaselessly communicate and ceaselessly distinguish themselves from one another is, in reality, empty … and, nevertheless, this inoperativity is so essential for the machine that it must at all costs be adopted and maintained at its center in the form of glory.[121]

The doxological aspect of power becomes indistinguishable from *oikonomia* and becomes essential to the nourishment of sovereignty:

> [G]lory … renders articulate and indifferent the two modalities of power, not just the sacred power of the sovereign but also the glorious power of government.[122]

Glory is the solution to the problems of the ends of economy, the end of the history of salvation from creation to redemption, the time before creation and the time after the day of judgement, the sabbatical time during which God has nothing to do, either not yet or no longer employed.[123] After redemption, no longer needs to act on the earth. What is left is inoperative. Glory then must cover with its splendour the figure of divine inoperativity.[124] Glory covers up with its splendour the God who does nothing, exerting no effect upon his creation or subjects.[125] Today glory takes the form of public opinion and consensus, driven by the media. This leads to glory exposing the empty throne of sovereignty:

> Government glorifies the Kingdom, and the Kingdom glorifies the Government. But the center of the machine is empty, and glory is nothing but the splendor that emanates from this emptiness, this inexhaustible *kahbod* that at once reveals and veils the central vacuity of the machine.[126]

Ultimately, this means that the governmental apparatus functions because it has captured in its empty centre the inoperativity of human essence, which is always already concealed through the operation of glory.[127] Glory places human inoperativity in a separate sphere. This separation generates the notion of inoperativity:

> The *oikonomia* of power places firmly at its heart, in the form of festival and glory, what appears to its eyes as the inoperativity of man and God, which cannot be looked at. Human life is inoperative and without purpose, but precisely this *argia* and this absence of aim make the incomparable operativity [*operosità*] of the human species possible.[128]

Through concealing this inoperativity *oikonomic* government can act against living beings whilst at the same time upholding sovereignty's empty justification for its actions.

What does this mean for the state of exception, the ban, and the sovereign decision on bare life? *Oikonomic* government means that government justifies its acts with reference to sovereignty and masks the empty centre of power through glorification. As Agamben states:

> [T]he world is governed through the coordination of two principles, the *auctoritas* (that is, a power without actual execution) and the *potestas* (that is, a power that can be executed); the Kingdom and the Government.[129]

This connects explicitly to Agamben's statements at the end of *State of Exception*, where he makes the argument that:

> The juridical system of the West appears as a double structure, formed by two heterogeneous yet coordinated elements: one that is normative and juridical in the strict sense (which we can for convenience inscribe under the rubric *potestas*) and one that is anomic and metajuridical (which we call by the name *auctoritas*).[130]

The *sovereign* decision which creates bare life is therefore in actuality a *governmental* decision. When Agamben argues that the exception, by suspending the legal norm, frees the norm's force-of law, the constitutive essence of the law, he is referring to the fact that the exception justifies governmental actions through recourse to transcendent schema.[131] The state of exception both articulates and holds together:

> [T]he two aspects of the juridico-political machine by instituting a threshold of undecidability … between life and law, between *auctoritas* and *potestas*.[132]

Oikonomic government is not a despotic power but is democratic government. Within the *oikonomic* paradigm *every* power has a vicarious character, acting in the place of the foundation of sovereign transcendence. There can be no substance of power, only an *oikonomia* of power. Therefore, modern forms of government can never hold one person accountable or responsible. There exists a bipolar system formed between an image-suffused transcendence and a virtual, faceless, powerless form of immanent management or *oikonomia* that is none the less effective and inherently adaptive (*an-archic* neo-governmentality).[133] Sovereign decision-making has been replaced by an administrative apparatus that manages events; this is a governing *non-power* (in the sense of no accountability).

This means that the sovereign decision will not in fact be a sovereign decision at all, but a managerial one. The sovereign decision is based upon the exception. The undecidability of decision does not mean that decisions do not take place. On the contrary, decisions between fact and law, exception and norm occur incessantly. It is this incessant decision making that constitutes the relation between transcendence and immanence and gives *oikonomic* government the justification to act. Sovereignty is in force without significance. The sovereign decision is every time an *oikonomic* decision. The creation of bare life can be undertaken by *anyone* under the guise of administrative decision-making which refers to transcendent schema to justify itself.

With this in mind, we can now turn to the strategic role *oikonomia* plays in Agamben's thought, and its connection to apparatuses of power, and how Agamben's use of *oikonomia* provides a decisive move away from the method and thought of Michel Foucault.

The *dispositif* and transcendent resistance in Foucault

The *dispositif* structures how Agamben and Foucault conceive of life, and, by extension, death. A starting point can be found in Agamben's claim that the *dispositif* is an "essential technical term" for Foucault which takes the place of universals (or, to use another vocabulary, the transcendent) within his work.[134] Foucault's use of the *dispositif* occurred at a specific time in his thought. Jeffrey Bussolini traces the first extensive usage of the term in *The History of Sexuality, Volume 1*, which allows Foucault to elucidate his genealogical approach to history, evaluating a moving field of continuities predicated on continual change.[135] Both Graham Burchell and Bussolini note that Foucault distinguishes between *dispositif* and *appareil*, both of which get translated as "apparatus".[136] As Burchell notes, Foucault uses *appareil* to refer to State mechanisms of power.[137] This is deliberate. Bussolini contends that the terms are distinguishable because the Latin, French and Italian concepts of apparatus support a peculiar meaning distinct from *dispositif*, namely a magnificent preparation, splendour, state, pomp and show.[138] This political theatricality of state apparatuses is evident in Foucault in the opening pages of *Discipline and Punish*.[139] In an interview from 1977, Foucault defined the *dispositif* as follows:

> What I'm trying to pick out with this term is, firstly, a thoroughly heterogeneous ensemble consisting of discourses, institutions, architectural forms, regulatory decisions, laws, administrative measures, scientific statements, philosophical, moral and philanthropic propositions—in short, the said as much as the unsaid. Secondly, what I am trying to identify in this apparatus is precisely the nature of the connection that can exist between these heterogeneous elements. Thirdly, I understand by the term "apparatus" [*dispositif*] a sort of—shall we say—formation which has as its major function at a given historical moment that of responding to an urgent need.[140]

The *dispositif* named the network of power that articulated how a power that was not based upon a monist conception of sovereignty manifested itself and is a key term in Foucault's thought. This network of relations between elements that responds to an emergency and which organizes, enables, orients fixes and blocks relations of force.[141] As Foucault stated, "power is employed and exercised through a net-like organisation" and "power in the substantive sense, 'le' pouvoir, doesn't exist".[142] Foucault's network of *dispositifs* is not the totality of the relationships it gathers under it, but it exists only in relation to the object of its analysis.

Foucault's approach to the *dispositif* is inextricably linked to his view of the subject. The human being is constituted as a subject by power relations and *dispositifs*,[143] which define an area of experience that manifests itself in and through the mutually constitutive interrelationships among discourses, power relationships and relationships of the self, as well as in the different practices and systems involved in those relationships. In this sense, the *dispositif* operates as a transcendent referent for the subject, organizing the field of power and knowledge as a field of experience.[144] Despite these *dispositifs* having a productive force, in that they are responsible for the creation of subjectivity and the ordering of lives, the nature of biopolitics means that those self-same *dispositifs* also have a negative side, in that they control and order which lives are worth preserving and which are not. Foucault's thought seeks to break free of this negative logic of the *dispositif*.

So how can we summarize this analysis of the *dispositif*? Foucault wished to cut off the King's head in political theory.[145] From this, Foucault makes the claim that, "the King reigns but does not govern", precisely because government, and a politics of populations, has become preeminent in modernity.[146] Foucault replaces and subsuming sovereignty with *dispositifs* of governmentality and biopower, which structure and delimit the subject. Crucially, this transcendent *dispositif* constructs genealogies of regimes of power, which opens a space for questioning by showing that our understanding of ourselves need not be dominated and defined by power. In short, the *dispositif* shows us that resistance is always possible, and that power is never totalizing.

Foucault made the point that his books were written for "users", not "readers", and that he stated that he wanted his books to be a "tool-box" for action, has led to a multitude of interpretations and readings of Foucault's thought.[147] The starting point for such a reading is a 1982 interview, in which Foucault claimed that resistance, rather than power, was the key force in the social order.[148] Resistance comes first, and remains superior to power relations, which are obliged to change in the face of that resistance.[149] Whilst the minimum form of resistance is saying "no", Foucault sees resistance not as mere negation, but as a creative process. Resistance actively changes the strategic situation which subjects find themselves in with respect to power relations and *dispositifs*.[150] Foucault's thought can be read as showing the individual as both effected by and effecting power relations. The *dispositifs* of control both define us and provide us the opportunity to break free of them at the same time. Power relations themselves depend upon resistance, which is never exterior to power.[151] Rather, a plurality of resistances is inscribed in power as an "irreducible opposite".[152]

Despite this focus upon resistance, Foucault held reservations for the politics of what I term 'mere resistance' and cautioned against the equating of resistance with liberation. Decisively, Foucault distinguishes "freedom" from "liberation". Whilst admitting that liberation does exist, for example in the colonial setting, Foucault makes clear that liberation is not sufficient to define the practices of freedom needed for individuals to define "admissible and acceptable forms of existence or political society".[153] Liberation is used to refer to forms of resistance to domination that release a pre-existing identity from an oppressive external force.[154] Freedom bears essentially on relations of power and domination – liberation from domination only gives way to new power relationships, which must be controlled by practices of freedom.[155]

It is these practices of freedom which allows the subject to practice self-construction and in turn, resist and rework the *dispositifs* that constitute them. Mere resistance to power, like liberation, has the drawback of emerging in reaction to oppression and domination by *dispositifs* of control.[156] As such it is likely to create an attachment to an identity which is formed through that oppression, and therefore will reinforce those self-same dominating biopolitical *dispositifs*.[157] More fundamentally, due to the spectre of biopolitics and the latent role of *dispositifs* in "letting die", such a resistance and attempt to escape the *dispositif* will only, almost paradoxically, end up repeating its logic of deciding and regulating life and death. This is why Foucault sees power, and the *dispositif*, as imposing on the subject "a law of truth … which he must recognise and which others have to recognise in him".[158] Instead, the practice of freedom is a "limit-experience":

> The idea of a limit-experience that wrenches the subject from itself is what was important to me … however erudite my books may be, I've always conceived of them as direct experiences aimed at pulling myself free of myself, at preventing me from being the same.[159]

Following this theme, we can read Foucault in "What is Enlightenment?" as supporting the claim that this practice of freedom should be considered as a way of being:

> We must obviously give a more positive content to what may be a philosophical ethos consisting in a critique of what we are saying, thinking, and doing, through a historical ontology of ourselves … This philosophical ethos may be characterised as a *limit-attitude* … We have to move beyond the outside-inside alternative; we have to be at the frontiers.[160]

The politics of liberation is not enough to guarantee freedom, as freedom is not mere resistance to power. Freedom is the careful and innovative deployment of power, and by extension, *dispositifs*, in the effort to constitute the free self. In other words, the *dispositif* is needed to constitute the *ethos* of freedom:

> I do not think that a society can exist without power relations … The problem, then, is … to acquire the rules of law, the management techniques, and also the morality, the *ethos*, the practice of the self, that will allow us to play these games of power with as little domination as possible.[161]

This game of power is *agonistic*. There is no essential freedom to be found, but a "permanent provocation" between the self and the *dispositifs* of power relations.[162] The key task is to "refuse what we are", to "promote new forms of subjectivity through the refusal of this kind of individuality which has been imposed on us for several centuries".[163] The creation of new forms of subjectivity involves freedom as a practice which requires the subject to self-create themselves anew, taking into account the *dispositifs* which constrain and control, and enabling the individual to discern the types of actions and interventions that are needed to effect change and create new subjectivities.

Freedom connects the *dispositif* and what is always beyond, the outside, the transcendent. I want to connect this to Foucault's last essay, and his view of error as the proper domain of life. When Foucault writes that life is that which is destined to err, such a life must contain the possibility to transcend *dispositifs* and break free of the logic of deciding who should live and who should be left to die. Freedom is experienced at the limit of power relations through their transgression, their erring, which is always-already a possibility, or destiny, for individuals to enact:

> The limit and transgression depend on each other for whatever density of being they possess: a limit could not exist if it were absolutely uncrossable

> and reciprocally, transgression would be pointless if it merely crossed a limit composed of illusions and shadows.[164]

The act of freedom constitutes itself through acting at the limit of the *dispositif*, transgressing that limit, erring, calling out to thought from the limit of the network of power relations, creating new subjectivities through the very response of the *dispositifs* to those transgressive acts. The *dispositif* thus controls life, but also is required for freedom in the form of self-creation. This transgressive freedom that brings about the self-creation of the new is a transcendent possibility, which the individual effects and which power relations and *dispositifs* must react to in response to these creative acts.

Deleuze spoke of this kind of self-relation as the "folding" of power relations back upon themselves. It is not possible to move outside of the totalizing *dispositif* in terms of liberation. However, it is possible to think from the outside, from the limit, in a manner which brings together both the inside of the *dispositif* and the outside, of which the *dispositif* is an operation. As Deleuze states:

> The outside is not a fixed limit but a moving matter animated by peristaltic movements, folds and foldings that together make up an inside: they are not something other than the outside, but precisely the inside *of* the outside ... The inside as an operation of the outside: in all his work Foucault seems haunted by this theme of an inside which is merely the fold of the outside, as if the ship were a folding of the sea.[165]

In acting on the individual, *dispositifs* produce an inside as an "interiorisation of the outside".[166] This folding allows a subject to differentiate itself from *dispositifs* and no longer has an internal dependence upon them – for Deleuze reading Foucault, there will always be a relation to oneself that resists such *dispositifs*.[167] The individual has the potential to distance themselves from the *dispositifs* that create our identity. This folding of power relations opens a space for the individual to transgress.

The question remains as to precisely how this transcendent transgressive freedom is effected. Foucault did write of the need to bring about a "historical ontology of ourselves",[168] such a questioning of current modes of existence does, on a certain reading, suggest that if we discovered the reality about how power operates in this world the individual can break free of its chains.[169] This view comes close to a Marxist view of false consciousness, and ignores the agonistic element to this reading of Foucault.[170]

Rather, following Aurelia Armstrong, I draw upon comments suggesting that it is only under the pressure of an event which makes our present identity and control problematic that we are forced to exercise our freedom.[171] Foucault suggests the following:

> [F]or a domain of action, a behaviour to enter the field of thought, it is necessary for a certain number of factors to have made it uncertain, to have

> made it lose its familiarity, or to have provoked a certain number of difficulties around it. These elements result from social, economic, or political processes … their role is instigation.[172]

These transgressions or errors of life, of action, and of existing, are the transcendent experience of events which force a questioning of the current *dispositifs* controlling the reality we inhabit. These errors allow the individual to interiorize the outside, and practice freedom as a transgressive limit-experience, agonistically questioning and forcing *dispositifs* to react to new subjectivities. These events do not have to be epochal, or revolutionary.[173] As Foucault states, different processes can instigate this process – the key is that it is the individual who responds to such instigation and practices this freedom through their actions and errors, causing the very conception of life to be changed through an "experimental mode of inquiry".[174]

Oikonomia and Agamben's philosophical archaeology

Despite Foucault tracing a genealogy of the *dispositif* to the modern age, coinciding with the development of biopolitics and governmentality, Agamben reads a much longer history to the term. Agamben also considers the *dispositif* as a transcendent referent but traces the root of *dispositif* to the Latin *dispositio*, translated the Greek word *oikonomia*, or economy.[175]

In his writings on the Christian pastorate, Foucault refers to Gregory of Nazianzus, who speaks of an *oikonomia psychōn*, an "economy of souls".[176] Foucault traced the root of *oikonomia* to the Greek *oikos*, or household, and notes the managerial sense of the word.[177] However, he contended that the term should be translated as conduct, in the sense of leading and a form of behaviour. Agamben claims that Foucault, in this move, misses an opportunity to complete his analysis of the *dispositif* because he chooses not to connect it to the economic theology of *oikonomia*.[178]

For Agamben, the machinery of modernity has inherited the internal logic of the Trinity and deployed it in a biopolitical government which is nothing other than the art of exercising power, through *dispositifs*, in the form of a liberal economy.[179] In a similar vein, connecting biopolitics to neoliberal economics more explicitly than Agamben, Maurizio Lazzarato has argued that debt has become central to liberal economics, and operates as a *dispositif* of control which produces and governs subjects.[180] The providential ordering of the world through economic government ensures freedom, but this freedom is actually only *bios*. A bipolar machine always produce a remainder, the bare life swept away by the tide of progress. Government is what emerges when *desubjects*, individuals with no rights at the mercy of power, and not subjects, are produced by the network of *dispositifs* Agamben terms *oikonomia*.[181]

The important difference with Agamben is his situating Foucault's pastorate and governmentality in an economic paradigm, where sovereign decision-making is effected through an *oikonomia*, and *dispositifs* of control. He openly abandons the context of Foucauldian philology to situate the *dispositif* in a new context.[182] Specifically, Agamben views the *dispositif* in a much more totalizing manner:

> Further expanding the already large class of Foucauldian dispositives, I shall call an apparatus literally anything that has in some way the capacity to capture, orient, determine, intercept, model, control, or secure the gestures, behaviours, opinions, or discourses of living beings. Not only, therefore, prisons, mad houses, the panopticon, schools, confession, factories, disciplines, juridical measures, and so forth (whose connection with power is in a certain sense evident), but also the pen, writing, literature, philosophy, agriculture, cigarettes, navigation, computers, cellular telephones and – why not – language itself, which is perhaps the most ancient of apparatuses.[183]

Therefore, Agamben proposes a massive (in his own words) division: on the one hand, living beings, and on the other, *dispositifs* in which living beings are incessantly captured:

> To recapitulate, we have then two great classes: living beings (or substances) and apparatuses, and between these two, as a third class, subjects. I call a subject that which results from the relation and, so to speak, from the relentless fight between living beings and apparatuses.[184]

Agamben's subject is produced and utterly dominated by *dispositifs*. Contrary to Foucault, this power is totalizing, precisely because of the operation of the *oikonomic* governmental machine. As such, it is not possible for a subject to escape the control of the *dispositif*, or to utilize the *dispositif* to construct a form of freedom which transcends the individual.

Agamben's philosophical archaeology

To understand the way forward from this totalizing *dispositif*, we turn to Agamben's method, his 'philosophical archaeology'. William Watkin has contended that there are three elements to Agamben's method: the paradigm; the signature; and the *archē*.[185] Agamben's archaeology also avoids questing for origins.[186] This lack of focus on origins is intentional. Philosophical archaeology searches for the point of emergence of the phenomenon, the moment of its arising, its *archē*. Agamben refers to Benjamin's *Jetztzeit*, "Now-time", which allows one to say of the moment of arising that one has *not* discovered something hidden about the past that has influenced us ever since and which we can now do something resistant about it.[187] A focus upon origins implies a before, presupposing an original condition that existed and split into the various phenomena being studied. For example, a pure life that split into *bios* and *zoè*. This idea of a before can lead to a yearning to rediscover a golden age that needs to be returned to. For Agamben, such a yearning is misplaced, and does not hold the answers for our current malaise. Therefore, his archaeology studiously avoids questions of origins.

The *archē* is not a chronologically localisable point which determines the present and becomes its inner grounding force. It is instead an operative force within history.[188] The *archē* is never about unearthing hidden origins but about giving historical phenomena their intelligibility and their possibility of existence.[189] The *archē* has a particular temporal structure. It is not a past in a linear historical sense, nor a lived experience. It is a moment of arising that takes place in the future, but it is also a form of the past in the future. It is "the past that will have been when the archaeologist's gesture (or the power of the imaginary) has cleared away the ghosts of the unconscious and the tight-knit fabric of tradition which blocks access to history".[190] Access to this moment can only be obtained by "returning back to the point where it was covered over and neutralised by tradition".[191] Archaeology seeks out the traditions which covered over the moment of a phenomenon's arising, which is not a historical origin. Agamben defines his archaeology as follows:

> Provisionally, we may call "archaeology" that practice which in any historical investigation has to do not with origins but with the moment of a phenomenon's arising and must therefore engage anew the sources and tradition. It cannot confront tradition without deconstructing the paradigms, techniques, and practices through which tradition regulates the forms of transmission, conditions access to sources, and in the final analysis determines the very status of the knowing subject. The moment of arising is objective and subjective at the same time and is indeed situated on a threshold of undecidability between object and subject. It is never the emergence of the fact without at the same time being the emergence of the knowing subject itself: the operation on the origin is at the same time an operation on the subject.[192]

This archaeology and paradigm differ from those used by Foucault in his work. The use of paradigms forms a key constituent element to Agamben's philosophical investigations. The paradigm is described by Agamben as a "historically singular phenomenon" comparable to Foucault's use of the Panopticon in his work.[193] However, Agamben's use of paradigms differs from Foucault in a very important way.

The force behind Foucault's genealogies and archaeologies consists in the fact that the examples Foucault uses within his work are primarily historical. Foucault's paradigm of Jeremy Bentham's Panopticon stands as an emblematic figure for a new age of power and governmental control.[194] Despite the Panopticon never being built to its original design, a number of prisons influenced by Bentham's concept were built.[195] Foucault's work thus has a historical relevance, so much so that Foucault has been characterised by some as primarily a historian rather than a philosopher.[196]

Contrary to Foucault, Agamben's uses of paradigms do not carry the same historical weight. Agamben's paradigm is drawn from history, but the paradigm is akin to an example:

> In any context where it exerts its force, the example is characterised by the fact that it holds for all cases of the same type, and, at the same time, it is included among these. It is one singularity among others, which, however, stands for each of them and serves them all. On one hand, every example is treated in effect as a real particular case; but on the other, it remains understood that it cannot serve its particularity. Neither particular nor universal, the example is a singular object that presents itself as such, that *shows* its singularity. Hence the pregnancy of the Greek term, for example: *para-deigma*, that which is shown alongside ... Hence the proper place of the example is always beside itself, in the empty space in which its undefinable and unforgettable life unfolds.[197]

Paradigms are actual historical phenomena but "constitute and make intelligible a broader historical-problematic context".[198] The paradigm is neither inside nor outside the group or set of phenomena that it identifies. Rather, a paradigm is the real particular case that is set apart from what it is meant to exemplify.[199] A term, once taken as a paradigm, is deactivated from its normal use.[200] A paradigm:

> [I]mplies the total abandonment of the particular-general couple as the model of logical inference. The rule ... is not a generality pre-existing singular cases and applicable to them, nor is it something resulting from the exhaustive enumeration of specific cases. Instead, it is the exhibition alone of the paradigmatic cases that constitute a rule.[201]

The paradigm is a mode of knowledge which moves between singularities. It does not engage in the dialectic between the general and particular. Watkin explains that it is always suspended from the group and belongs to it. The separation of exemplarity and singularity is impossible as all groups are immanent to their paradigmatic members but never presupposed by it.[202]

After the *archē* and the paradigm, the signature. A signature is "what makes a sign intelligible" by determining its existence through its actual usage.[203] In *The Signature of All Things*, Agamben outlines his theory of signatures.[204] Again showing his Foucauldian influence, Agamben begins his investigation with Foucault's account of the signature in *The Order of Things*.[205] The signature is not a concept or a sign. A sign or concept refers to a specific interpretation or a determinate sphere. As Zartaloudis describes, this allows for a movement away from a current signification and construction of a new signification of a concept.[206] Rather, a signature dislocates concepts and signs, and does not aim to resignify concepts. It is seen to sanction and organise behaviour. A signature moves concepts and signs to another sphere, without any semantic redefinition being involved.[207] This movement to another sphere is not a movement between spheres of actual and potential interpretation. Rather, the movement to another sphere can unconceal a previously hidden connection between two seemingly unconnected spheres. For example, Agamben argues that the notion of sovereignty is a signature, which in its displacement from the domain of the sacred to that of the profane identifies a relationship existing between the two spheres.[208] One of the key examples used to explain the theory of signatures is *secularisation*. Secularisation in modernity is a signature that paradoxically returns the secular world to theology. Through secularisation, the theological leaves its mark on the political whilst avoiding a direct correlation between political and theological identities.[209]

What philosophical archaeology means

How do the three elements – paradigm, signature and *archē* – interact and what does this mean for Agamben's thought? Agamben's philosophical archaeology aims at revealing the contingency of the signatures that sanction a common operativity and intelligibility of discursive structures. It then seeks to render inoperative the signatures that control the intelligibility of Western culture by tracing the moments of arising of discursive formations through the examinations of paradigms. To put it in another form of words, Walter Benjamin wrote the following on the dialectical image:

> It is not what is past casts its light on what is present, or what is present casts its light on what is past; rather, image is that wherein what has been comes together in a flash with the new to form a constellation. In other words, image is dialectics at a standstill. For while the relation of the present to the past is a purely temporal, continuous one, the relation of what-has-been to the now is dialectical: is not progression but image, suddenly emergent.[210]

For Watkin, image is an alternative description of the visibility of signatures and paradigms in Agamben's work:

> To thinking belongs the movement as well as the arrest of thoughts. Where thinking comes to a standstill in a constellation saturated with tensions – there the dialectical image appears. It is the caesura in the movement of thought. Its position is naturally not an arbitrary one. It is to be found, in a word, where the tension between the dialectical opposites is greatest.[211]

What does a dialectic at a standstill look like when dialectics is defined by movement? Agamben's project is to use paradigms to trace signatures to suspend metaphysics; to render inoperative the basic presupposition of metaphysics.[212]

For Watkin, signatures have a historical moment of arising (*archē*) when they become active in sanctioning knowledge systems, controlling how we think, speak and act. In turn the signature is actualised across a variety of different discourses through time but is kept consistent by each discourse sharing in common a series of terms all of which are meaningfully operative due to their commonality of signatory origin and continued activity – these terms are paradigms. Watkin goes on – signatures are in a mode of opposition to the very paradigms they sanction and legitimate. Signatures only exist if they make a consistent set of paradigms over time sufficient to be named, for example life. Until these paradigms are corralled under the signatory term Life, Life as a signature does not exist. Therefore, the signature life occurs *after* its paradigm – the paradigms are paradigms because they exist due to the signature in operation.[213]

The stakes of the division of life

Agamben's philosophical archaeology underpins his thesis that *dispositifs* continually divide and separate life. The paradigm of *oikonomia*, also shown by Agamben as connected to *dispositif*, had its moment of arising in early Christian thought where it bequeathed to modernity the bipolar machine of sovereignty and government. The paradigms of *dispositifs* exist due to the signature of life creating a knowledge system denoting how we think, speak and act about what life is. Life is a term which has been constructed over time:

> Life as contemplation without knowledge will have a precise correlate in thought that has freed itself of all cognition and intentionality. Theoria and the contemplative life, which the philosophical tradition has identified as its highest goal for centuries, will have to be dislocated onto a new plane of immanence. It is not certain that, in the process, political philosophy and epistemology will be able to maintain their present physiognomy and difference with respect to ontology. Today, blessed life lies in the same terrain as the biological body of the West.[214]

This is why life is not a medical or a scientific notion but a philosophical and political one.[215] The importance of this division for Agamben's work can be seen through contrasting his reading of Foucault to his own conception of a life which is not held between a transcendent/immanent relation, and the possibilities for resistance against the *dispositifs* which exist throughout the social body.

Agamben makes clear his scepticism towards the Foucauldian idea of transgressive freedom. Agamben should be read as seeing the necessary illusion of transcendence as re-entering Foucault's thought, through the notion of freedom. He makes clear that creating new subjectivities will not affect the *oikonomic* governmental machine:

> Just as the biopolitical body of the West cannot be simply given back to its natural life in the *oikos*, so it cannot be overcome in a passage to a new body … in which a different economy of pleasures and vital functions

> would once and for all resolve the interlacement of *zoē* and *bios* that seems to define the political destiny of the West.[216]

Foucault's life lived through a transgressive freedom does not go far enough for Agamben; it still has recourse to a transcendent referent, in the form of a practice of freedom that *dispositifs* respond to and inevitably attempt to order and control. In this manner, sovereignty, through the ordering of an *oikonomic* government, recovers the ability to decide upon which lives are worth living and which lives are bare life. The *dispositif* will always totalize as long as life itself holds itself out to be defined by something other than itself, which is what it does when it relies on the logic of transcendence.

Therefore a politics of rupture and language of overcoming is unsatisfactory. Politics will only begin with the "inoperative disarticulation of both *bios* and *zoē*".[217] Only in this manner, through this rendering inoperative will the thanatopolitics Agamben sees at the heart of today's biopolitical world be countered. The task Agamben sets himself is by no means straightforward. The only resistance which is effective against the totalizing power of the *dispositif* is the construction of a form-of-life, a life which is lived immanently and therefore not reliant upon *dispositifs* to be constituted, nor any form of transcendence.

Conclusion

This chapter has analysed Agamben's claim that there is a negative relation at the heart of political, rights-imbued life. This negativity is found in the very definition of man as the animal with speech, as I have traced in Agamben's critique of Heidegger. Understanding this fundamental negativity illustrates how and why Agamben traces its continuation in many other areas of Western philosophical thought. In this light the chapter then considered Agamben's work in *The Kingdom and the Glory*. Here, Agamben shows how the sovereign decision which creates bare life is in fact an economic and governmental decision, and sovereignty and government exist in a bipolar machine.

The chapter then considered the different roles *dispositif* has in the thought of Foucault and Agamben. For Agamben, the *dispositif* produces and utterly dominates the human subject. I drew upon Agamben's method – his philosophical archaeology – to support this contention. Ultimately, Agamben rejects Foucauldian resistance and contends that only an immanent philosophy can produce a form of life that is not continually divided and separated.

The next chapter seeks to connect this chapter's discussion of the *dispositif* to Agamben's critique of transcendent relationality, and his positing of a life lived on the plane of immanence – a form-of-life. It is in the next chapter that the relationship between Agamben and Emmanuel Levinas will be introduced, as will Agamben's critique of Levinas. Through this exploration I will show how Agamben's interpretation of Levinas is necessary for him to generate critical distance for his immanent form-of-life.

Notes

1 Agamben (2011).
2 Watkin (2014) 211.
3 Agamben (2009d).
4 Murray (2010) 3.
5 Watkin (2014) 5.
6 Watkin (2014) 5.
7 Lagaay and Schiffers (2009) 325–326.
8 Murray (2010) 4, quoting Negri (2003).
9 Murray (2010) 4.
10 Watkin (2014) 5.
11 Watkin (2014) xiii.
12 Kishik (2012) 67.
13 Deleuze (1994) 13.
14 Agamben (2000) 139.
15 Agamben (2018d) 12–15; Murray (2010) 5.
16 Agamben (2018d) 1.
17 Agamben (2007a) 6.
18 Kishik (2012) 5.
19 Agamben (1999g) p.81.
20 Agamben (2018d) 7.
21 Agamben (2018d) 11.
22 Agamben (2006); Colony (2007) 1.
23 Heidegger (1968) 4.
24 Ben-Dor (2007) 42.
25 Heidegger (1962) 27.
26 Heidegger (1962) 27.
27 Ben-Dor (2007) 49.
28 Zartaloudis (2002) 203.
29 Ben-Dor (2007) 121.
30 Heidegger (1993) 220; Ben-Dor (2007) 121.
31 Heidegger (1962) 67.
32 Heidegger (1962) 51.
33 Heidegger (1962) 75.
34 Aristotle (1984c) 1253a, 9.
35 Heidegger (1993) 227.
36 Heidegger (1993) 227.
37 Heidegger (1993) 234–235.
38 Heidegger (1993) 228.
39 Ben-Dor (2007) 51.
40 Heidegger (1993) 228.
41 Ben-Dor (2007) 55.
42 Heidegger (1962) 82.
43 Heidegger (1982) 276.
44 Heidegger (1962) 321.
45 Heidegger (1962) 174.
46 Heidegger (1962) 281–285.
47 Heidegger (1962) 294.
48 Heidegger (1962) 304–311.
49 Heidegger (1962) 311.
50 Heidegger (1971) 107–108.
51 Agamben (2004b) 70.
52 Ziarek (2008) 196.

53 Agamben (2006) xii.
54 Murray (2010) 14.
55 Agamben (2006) 86.
56 Levinas (2000) 47.
57 Levinas (2000) 11.
58 Levinas (2000) 48–49.
59 Zartaloudis (2010) 228.
60 Agamben (2006) 56.
61 Levinas (2000) 30.
62 Agamben (2006) 5.
63 Levinas (2000) 25.
64 Murray (2010) 14.
65 Levinas (2000) 35.
66 Levinas (2000) 39.
67 Agamben (2006) xii; Zartaloudis (2010) 230; Levinas (2000) 92–93.
68 Agamben (2016a) 180–181.
69 Agamben (2006) 25.
70 Agamben (2006) 24–25. See also Zartaloudis (2010) 231.
71 Zartaloudis (2010) 231.
72 Agamben (2006) 55.
73 Zartaloudis (2010) 233.
74 Agamben (2006) 35.
75 Agamben (2006) 35, 44–45.
76 Agamben (2006) 55–56.
77 Agamben (2006) 26.
78 Agamben (2006) 56.
79 Zartaloudis (2010) 233–235.
80 Agamben (2006) 59–60.
81 Agamben (2006) 62.
82 Agamben (2006) 33.
83 Agamben (2016a) 181.
84 Agamben (2006) 84–85.
85 Agamben (2011) 82.
86 Agamben (2011) 1.
87 Agamben (2011) 53.
88 Zartaloudis (2010) 6; Frost (2014) 211.
89 Agamben (2011) 99.
90 Agamben (2011) 126.
91 Agamben (2011) 89.
92 Zartaloudis (2010) 7.
93 Agamben (2009d) 8.
94 Aristotle (1984c) 1253b, 1259a-b.
95 Agamben (2011) 84.
96 Agamben (2011) 110–111.
97 Kelly (1977) 87.
98 Kelly (1977) 88.
99 Kelly (1977) 104–105.
100 1 Cor. 9:17; Col. 1: 25; Eph. 3:2, 1:10.
101 Agamben (2011) 18–51. For an excellent, detailed analysis of the nuances of Agamben's analysis of the theological *oikonomia*, see Zartaloudis (2010).
102 Zartaloudis (2010) 62; Dean (2013) 175.
103 Agamben (2009d) 10.
104 Zartaloudis (2010) 65–66.
105 Ephesians 1:9–10; 3:9–11; I Timothy 1:3–4.

106 Reumann (1959) 282–292.
107 Agamben (2011) 51.
108 Agamben (2011) 276.
109 Agamben (2011) 87.
110 Zartaloudis (2010) 120.
111 Foucault (2007) 303.
112 Agamben (2011) 245.
113 Agamben (2010) 101–102.
114 Dean (2013) 200.
115 Agamben (2011) vii.
116 Agamben (2011) 194.
117 Agamben (2011) 230.
118 Zartaloudis (2010) 89.
119 Watkin (2014) 229–230.
120 Agamben (2011) 208.
121 Agamben (2011) 242.
122 Watkin (2014) 229.
123 Agamben (2011) 160–161.
124 Agamben (2011) 163.
125 Agamben (2011) 245.
126 Agamben (2011) 211.
127 Agamben (2011) 246.
128 Agamben (2011) 245–246.
129 Agamben (2011) 103.
130 Agamben (2005c) 85–86.
131 Agamben (2005c) 23, 38, 50, 59; Agamben (1998) 52.
132 Agamben (2005c) 86.
133 Zartaloudis (2010) 52. See also Schütz (2009) 233.
134 Agamben (2009c) 7–9.
135 Bussolini (2010) 88.
136 Burchell (2006) xxiii; Bussolini (2010) 93.
137 Burchell (2006) xxiii.
138 Bussolini (2010) 96–97.
139 Foucault (1991a) 3–6.
140 Foucault (1980b) 194–195.
141 Dean (2013) 50.
142 Foucault (1980b) 198.
143 Foucault (1991b) 351; Esposito (2012) 17–30.
144 Eriksson (2005) 600–601.
145 Foucault (1978) 89.
146 Foucault (2007) 87.
147 Foucault (1994) 523–524.
148 Foucault (2000a) 167.
149 Foucault (2000a) 167.
150 Foucault (2000a) 167–168.
151 Foucault (1978) 95.
152 Foucault (1978) 96.
153 Foucault (2000c) 282–283.
154 Armstrong (2008) 22.
155 Foucault (2000c) 283–284.
156 Armstrong (2008) 22–23.
157 Brown (1995) 27.
158 Foucault (1982a) 212.
159 Foucault (2002a) 241–242.

160 Foucault (2000d) 315–316.
161 Foucault (2000c) 298.
162 Foucault (1982a) 221–222.
163 Foucault (1982a) 216.
164 Foucault (1998a) 73.
165 Deleuze (2006) 96–97.
166 Deleuze (2006) 103; Armstrong (2008) 26–27.
167 Deleuze (2006) 101, 103.
168 Foucault (2000d) 315.
169 Armstrong (2008) 28–29.
170 See Lukács (1999).
171 Armstrong (2008) 28–29.
172 Foucault (1991c) 388.
173 Foucault (2000b) 449–453.
174 Rabinow (1999) 174.
175 Dean (2013) 52.
176 Foucault (2007) 192–193.
177 Dean (2013) 173.
178 Zartaloudis (2010) 5.
179 There are echoes here of an "end of history" – see Fukuyama (2006).
180 Lazzarato (2012); Lazzarato (2006) 133–147.
181 Campbell (2012) 36.
182 Agamben (2009d) 13.
183 Agamben (2009d) 14.
184 Agamben (2009d) 14.
185 Watkin (2014) 4.
186 Agamben (2009c) 81.
187 Benjamin (2003) 395.
188 Agamben (2009c) 110.
189 Watkin (2014) 30.
190 Agamben (2009c) 107.
191 Agamben (2009c) 105.
192 Agamben (2009c) 89.
193 Raulff and Agamben (2004) 610.
194 de la Durantaye (2009) 215.
195 de la Durantaye (2009) 216.
196 See Gutting (2003) 49–73. For a contrary view, see Foucault (2000d) 32–50.
197 Agamben (2007b) 9–10.
198 Agamben (2009c) 9.
199 de la Durantaye (2009) 218–219.
200 Agamben (2009c) 18.
201 Agamben (2009c) 21.
202 Watkin (2014) 9.
203 Agamben (2009c) 110.
204 See Fuggle (2009) 85–87.
205 Foucault (1998) 29.
206 Agamben (2011) p.16; Zartaloudis (2010) 97–98.
207 Agamben (2009c) 46.
208 Fuggle (2009) 86.
209 Agamben (2011) 20–21.
210 Benjamin (2002) 462.
211 Benjamin (2002) 475.
212 Watkin (2014) xi.
213 Watkin (2014) xv.

214 Agamben (1999a) 239.
215 Agamben (1999a) 239.
216 Agamben (1998) 188.
217 Agamben (2011) 259.

3 Immanence, Levinas, ethics and relationality

Introduction

The first two chapters of this monograph have focused on Giorgio Agamben's critique of Western metaphysics and his argument that life has been constantly articulated and divided. This chapter starts my engagement between the thought of Agamben and the thought of Emmanuel Levinas. I connect Agamben's critique of transcendent relationality to the goal of Agamben's work to posit a life lived in the plane of immanence.[1] Levinasian ethics offers a conception of life grounded on a transcendent plane. The first part of this chapter will present Levinas's ethics of the Other. Due to this, on an Agambenian reading, Levinas replicates the inclusive exclusion which leads to the creation of bare life. Further, Agamben equates Levinasian ethics with the sphere of judgment and the apparatus of the law.[2] All judgments are equated with the notion of guilt, which is the reason why Agamben avoids reference to the law and judgment in his immanent thought.

I argue that Agamben's interpretation of Levinas is a necessary one to generate critical distance for Agamben's immanent construction of life. He eschews transcendent relationality in his work, and seeks an immanent ethics, which cannot be reduced or compared to a Levinasian coordinate. This can be seen in Agamben's critique of Levinas's use of responsibility, shame, and the face. In response to this reading of Levinas, I argue that Agamben's critique of transcendence is premised on an uncharitable reading of Levinas's construction of the self and its relationship to the Other.[3] In addition to this uncharitable reading I argue that the differences between Agamben's and Levinas's constructions of their singular being are not as far apart as Agamben makes out. Finally, this chapter considers how Agamben also distances his thought from Kantian ethics, which he conflates with duty.[4] This analysis sets the stage for the following chapter's detailed consideration of form-of-life.

Absolute immanence

In his essay, "Absolute Immanence", with a typical rhetorical flourish, Agamben maps modern post-Kantian philosophy, dividing it between two lines depending

DOI: 10.4324/9781315191447-4

upon how it thinks of life. Firstly, the line of transcendence, beginning with Kant and ending in Derrida and Levinas. Secondly, the line of immanence, beginning with Spinoza, travelling via Nietzsche, and ending with Deleuze and Foucault.[5] It is this immanent vision of life which Agamben seeks to explore, thinking against the nihilistic consequences of holding immanence in relation to transcendence. Agamben explains that this recourse to transcendence is not necessarily deliberate:

> [I]mmanence is not merely threatened by this illusion of transcendence, in which it is made to leave itself and give birth to the transcendent. This illusion is, rather, something like a necessary illusion ... to which every philosopher falls prey even as he tries to adhere as closely as possible to the plane of immanence.[6]

He goes on:

> The task that thought cannot renounce is also the most difficult one, the task in which the philosopher constantly risks going astray.[7]

Agamben's attempt to inquire into an immanent life is strongly influenced by his reading of the late Foucault, which is idiosyncratic and draws heavily on the late Deleuze. Agamben reads Deleuze as sharing both a "secret solidarity" and a "legacy" with Foucault.[8]

In Agamben's reading of Foucault's last essay: "Life: Experience and Science", which he reads with Gilles Deleuze's essay, "Immanence: A Life...".[9] Agamben reads in Foucault's text "a curious inversion of what had been Foucault's earlier understanding of the idea of life".[10] This "earlier understanding" refers to Foucault's reading of Bichat in *The Birth of the Clinic*. Bichat placed life in opposition and exposure to death, contending that to understand disease it is necessary to take the point of view of death, which life, by definition, resists.[11] Taking on board Bichat's definition of life as the totality of functions that resist death, Foucault contends that death provides the focal point for knowledge to give life its meaning – death is the opening on life's truth.[12]

It is this definition of life which Deleuze, and, following him, Agamben sees as Foucault's originary vitalism, seeing life as capacity to resist force and power.[13] This is supported by Foucault's comments regarding death being the limiting force on biopower, and his claims in *The Order of Things* in respect of nineteenth century thought that "life becomes a fundamental force" and an "untamed ontology".[14] It is this force that annihilates and overturns everything it confronts, in the form of a ruptural intervention.[15]

Building on this, Agamben reads Foucault as having changed his vitalist consideration of life to one where life is "the proper domain of error".[16] Certainly, Foucault himself wrote that the essay represented "a different way of approaching the notion of life".[17] Foucault writes:

> In a sense, life – and this is its radical feature – is that which is capable of error … [W]ith man, life has led to a living being that is never completely in the right place, that is destined to "err" and to be "wrong".[18]

Foucault continues, seemingly reversing his conclusion in *The Order of Things*:

> Should life be considered as nothing more than one of the areas that raises the general question of truth, the subject, and knowledge? Or does it oblige us to pose the question in a different way? Should not the whole theory of the subject be reformulated, seeing that knowledge, rather than opening onto the truth of the world, is deeply rooted in the "errors" of life?[19]

Agamben reads Foucault as opening an unexplored terrain for questioning life, one which "coincides with the field of biopolitics".[20] This idea of life in Foucault sees its potential errors as being able to resist and counter the strategies of biopolitics, which carry within them the latent threat to let die, casting aside the individual for the benefit of the population.

This unexplored terrain coincides with Deleuze's meditations on a plane of immanence. The aim of isolating bare life is to mark a division in the living being such that a plurality of functions and a series of oppositions can be articulated. "A life…" marks the radical impossibility of establishing hierarchies and separations.[21] "A life…" exists on the plane of immanence. The plane of immanence, like the transcendental field of which it is the final figure, has no subject. It is immanent not to something, but only to itself.[22] As Deleuze and Guattari explain, immanence must be distinguished from an immanence which is held in relation to the transcendent plane:

> Immanence is immanent only to itself and consequently captures everything, absorbs All-One, and leaves nothing remaining to which it could be immanent. In any case, whenever immanence is interpreted as immanent *to* Something, we can be sure that this Something reintroduces the transcendent.[23]

Deleuze traces a line of immanence within the history of philosophy. Starting with Husserl, immanence becomes immanent to a transcendental subjectivity – Levinas is explicitly mentioned as a thinker of transcendence:

> This is what happens in Husserl and many of his successors who discover in the Other … the mole of the transcendent within immanence itself. … In this modern moment we are no longer satisfied with thinking immanence as immanent to a transcendent, *we want to think transcendence within the immanent, and it is from immanence that a breach is expected.* … no longer satisfied with ascribing immanence to something, immanence itself is made to disgorge the transcendent everywhere.[24]

For Deleuze and Guattari, striving for this plane of immanence is:

> [T]he supreme act of philosophy: not so much to think THE plane of immanence as to show that it is there, unthought in every plane, and to think it in this way as the outside and inside of thought, as the not-external outside and the not-internal inside.[25]

Immanence has neither a focal point nor a horizon that can orient thought. The only possible point of orientation is the vertigo in which outside and inside, immanence and transcendence, are absolutely indistinguishable.[26] What does this mean for life, an immanent life which is the proper domain of error? At the end of *What is Philosophy?* life as absolute immediacy is defined as "pure contemplation without knowledge".[27] This contemplation without knowledge functions to define life.[28] "A life..." is pure contemplation beyond every subject and object of knowledge; it is pure potentiality that preserves without acting.[29] What this means is:

> A life is everywhere, in all the moments that traverse this or that living subjects and that measure lived objects ... This undefined life does not have its moments, however close to one another they might be; it has only inter-times, inter-moments. It neither follows nor succeeds, but rather presents the immensity of empty time, where one sees the event that is to come and that has already happened in the absolute of an immediate consciousness.[30]

Life is "composed of virtuality"; it is pure potentiality that coincides with Being, and potentiality, insofar as it is lacks nothing and insofar as it is desire's self-constitution as desiring, is immediately blessed.[31]

This purity – found on the immanent plane – is found throughout Agamben's thought. For example, in responding to the foundational negativity traced at the heart of *Dasein* and its relationship with language, Agamben seeks a pure experience of language beyond any negative relationality, akin to what Plato called "the thing-itself". Such a pure experience is a foundation which presupposes nothing but itself – what Heidegger termed the "Absolute".[32] The thing-itself is that by which each being is knowable and truly is.[33] Agamben states that:

> The thing itself is not a thing; it is the very sayability, the very openness at issue in language, which, in language, we always presuppose and forget, perhaps because it is at bottom its own oblivion and abandonment.[34]

The experience of language is termed infancy, the experience of the pure fact that language exists, which is an experience of transcendence within the immanent, to borrow Deleuze and Guattari's terms.[35] It is not an immanence to something, a transcendent relationality, which will end up capturing life in apparatuses of division, but immanence as a transcendence which is a continuous participation in an excess.[36]

Levinas and transcendent relationality

The connection between the works of Emmanuel Levinas and Giorgio Agamben are not clear on first viewing. Agamben's fame arose after Levinas's death, meaning that there are no references to his work in Levinas's oeuvre. The mentions of Levinas which are made in Agamben are few, but important where they exist. My analysis of the relationship between Agamben and Levinas is influenced by Agamben's own analysis of the debate between Walter Benjamin and Carl Schmitt. The exoteric dossier between the two was not large; Agamben focused his attention upon the larger, esoteric dossier which he read as existing.[37] What I conduct here is an esoteric analysis of Agamben's consideration of Levinasian thought. I argue that these mentions, and Agamben's critical engagement with them, amount to an attempt by Agamben to distance his work from Levinas's thought.

Levinas's work in ethics was characterised by Derrida as "an ethics of ethics".[38] An "ethics of ethics" implies a normative foundation of normativity – "a primordial ethical relation" from which can be derived "a system or procedure for formulating and testing the moral acceptability of certain maxims or judgments relation to social action or civic duty".[39] Levinas did write that his was a quest not for ethics, but the meaning of transcendence, which ultimately was found in ethics. Ethics was not his starting point, but it was what he found at the end of his journey.[40] As primordial, ethics is prior to politics; the command to responsibility is issued anarchically prior to the ongoing political process of balancing, calculating, and negotiating.[41] Levinas states:

> I cannot posit myself as a subject without distinguishing myself from that which I am not. I must thematise the world around me. However, it is not possible to conceptualise the world without reaching out to the Other. In affirming myself as subjectivity in the face of the Other, I posit myself as responsible.[42]

This ethics is in opposition to the concept of totality which dominates Western philosophy. In this totality individuals are reduced to being mere bearers of forces that command them unbeknown to themselves. Individuals thus derive their meaning from this totality.[43]

Ethical experience for Levinas has its foundations in an irreducible relation between oneself and other people, the Other. The Other is a Stranger who disturbs and disrupts every notion of ipseity, the same, and presents an ethical demand that cannot be ignored or avoided and must be faced.[44] Levinas's ethics are passive and non-voluntary.[45] Each individual makes the ethical relation with the other anew. It is through this ethical relation that subjectivity is constructed.[46] Levinas attempts to create a sovereign ethics, an ethics that constitutes the subject.[47] A sense of subjectivity is felt only when facing an infinite and asymmetrical debt to the Other, the absolute alterity of difference:

> The most passive, unassumable, passivity, the subjectivity or the very subjection of the subject, is due to my being obsessed with responsibility for the oppressed who is other than myself.[48]

The Other, and our relationship to the Other, defines us. In this way, it is the Other that precedes the Self, and in that way, also precedes ontological reflections upon Being. At the heart of this is responsibility. The Other acts, through an Agambenian reading, as a negative foundational ground through which and against which life is defined negatively.

This "radical heterogeneity" of the other and its effect upon the individual is only possible with respect to a term that serves as entry into the relation – for Levinas a term can only remain at the point of departure as the I, which exists in relation to the Other. Levinas views the I as "the being whose existing consists in identifying itself, in recovering its identity throughout all that happens to it".[49] The I captures that level of identity whereby the existent encounters being where being shows up as a constituted world.[50]

The Other is irreducible to the I, and to be I is to have identity as one's content. Likewise, the I is irreducible to the Other. The I's existing consists in its identifying of itself. As soon as I come-to-be, I am: I exist. As soon as I emerge as an existent, my existence is mine and mine alone; I have myself. But as soon as I have myself, I am already doubled up; I have something, even if this "something" is my own relation to general existence. It is important for Levinas to establish the originary solitude and intransitivity of existence as the initial starting-point of an existent whose challenge is to transcend its existential solitude toward an Other.[51] Only an existent who stands on its own can encounter the Other without assimilating it or being assimilated; and yet, standing on one's own is only the beginning and not the whole point of human existence.[52] Such isolation leads the subject to be absolutely for themselves.[53] Such an attitude is self-regarding, self-sufficient and cocooned from the world, as enjoyment is characterised as interiority.[54]

At this point we can see a connection between Levinas's work on the I, and Agamben's immanent life. For Agamben, an immanent life is a pure transcendent in its taking place on an immanent plane, without recourse to presuppositional foundations.[55] The I's enjoyment is an unsustainable isolation.[56] The separation of the I through enjoyment becomes a consciousness of objects around the I.[57] Such appropriation of surrounding objects aids the I's enjoyment and the awareness of objects leads to language, as objects are thematised. So far, Levinas's account is similar to Agamben's – the difference comes when Levinas argues that awareness of objects by the I leads to awareness of the Other.[58]

Initially, the I attempts to thematise other people as means to his enjoyment. Through this, the relation between the I and the Other is always-already cast in language.[59] For Levinas, "the oneself cannot form itself; it is already formed with an absolute passivity".[60] Levinas accounts for the fact that individuals do not exist in isolation (a point first made by Heidegger). As Thomas Carl Wall has eloquently described, Levinas's ethics attempt to articulate a responsibility that realises in the extreme an abandonment of the certainties of the self.[61] Levinas places the formation of the I in the relation between the Self and the Other. The self represents the *position* in existence out of which the I projects itself in intentionality. It is in this position, at the level of self, which makes possible the subjective freedom at the level of I.[62] In explaining the necessity of relationality for the subject, Levinas maintained that:

> The idea of transcendence is self-contradictory. The subject that transcends is swept away in its transcendence; it does not transcend itself.[63]

Levinas was opposed to immanence, according to which "we would truly come into possession of being when every 'other' … would vanish at the end of history".[64] Levinas characterised Western philosophy in terms of the transcendence of the limitations of human finitude.[65] According to the traditional conception, transcendence is always a taking refuge somewhere.[66] This situates elsewhere the true life to which man gains access in the privileged instants of liturgy or in dying.[67] Levinas set out to show that transcendence has not been thought radically enough by a tradition that has compromised it.[68]

The subject must exist in relation (which for Levinas is a positive relation to the Other, prior to subjectivity), otherwise the subject is swept away in the transcendence of its own immanence (the plane of existence Agamben seeks to build his philosophy on). Levinas was never in search of a position between transcendence and immanence.[69] Levinas warned against seeking the beyond as a world behind our world because this simply converts transcendence into immanence, and it therefore does not escape the order of being. Within the bipolar play of immanence and transcendence, immanence always wins out over transcendence.[70] This is reflected in Levinas's construction of ethics:

> The most passive, unassumable, passivity, the subjectivity or the very subjection of the subject, is due to my being obsessed with responsibility for the oppressed who is other than myself.[71]

This is why transcendent relationality is at the heart of the Levinasian subject, constituting its very being.[72] Levinas proposes a transcendence that "disturbs immanence without being set in the horizons of the world".[73] To illustrate this, it is important to dwell upon Levinas's construction of the I. Levinas strives to argue that this relation is in no way negative, even if it is transcendent in the sense that the relation constitutes the subject. As Levinas states, transcendence is fundamentally important to his ethics:

> If transcendence has meaning, it can only signify the fact that the *event of being* … passes over to what is other than being … Transcendence is

> passing over to being's *other*, otherwise than being. Not *to be otherwise*, but *otherwise than being*. And not to not-be; passing over is not here equivalent to dying.[74]

This transcendent relationality and responsibility are integral to the relation between the Self and the Other.

Responsibility, the Self and the Other

The relation between the Self and the Other is the primary question presented by concrete human existence and is asymmetrical: the Self remains more responsible for the Other than vice versa. Wall describes Levinas's Self-Other relation as constituting all other relations, as well as remaining essentially ethically ambiguous.[75] The other stands as a transcendent referent to whom the self is responsible. The Other exists immemorially before any sense of self. Any relation between the I and an other will always-already betray this anterior relation that orders the Self to respond to the Other. The I must always respond, as the Other is both infinite and antecedent to any I. But Levinas asks:

> How, in the alterity of a you, can I remain I, without being absorbed or losing myself in that you? How can the ego that I am remain myself in a you, without being nonetheless the ego that I am in my present – that is to say, an ego that inevitably returns to itself? How can the ego become other to itself?[76]

In this sense, Wall maintains that there are no Levinasian ethics as they are founded upon an abyss (the very type of abyss which Agamben has warned against in his work). The relation with the Other is without a purpose, a *telos*.[77] The Other does not drive the I into any particular outcome. Nor does the relation to the Other have any meaning apart from constituting the I, the Self. Levinas terms this relation the "infinite":

> Infinity is characteristic of a transcendent being as transcendent; the infinite is the absolutely other. The transcendent is the sole *ideatum* of which there can be only an idea in us; it is infinitely removed from its idea, that is exterior, because it is infinite ... To think the infinite, the transcendent, the Stranger, is hence not to think an object.[78]

What passes for ethics is no ethics as such, and what passes for the Self-Other relation is no relation as such either. The relation to the Other will always escape the I. In this sense, the Self's relation to the Other cannot help but be betrayed. The relation between Self and Other constitutes all other relations, as well as remaining essentially ethically ambiguous. Wall explains:

> This anteriority [of the Other to the Self] will be, for Levinas, a dissymmetry and a goodness without measure that (de)structures the self *as* a

> relation with a never-present Other … any relation that the *I* establishes with *an* other subject will only betray the pure anteriority that … *orders* me to the Other.[79]

At the same time, the Other will always escape others as well in the same manner. The other person is without relation in the same manner as the I. The other person obligates the I as the other person is also without relation, as is the I. What binds the I to the other person is precisely the shared nonrelation to the Other.

The universality of the singular Other's singularising command is expressed as follows: *Anyone* is responsible for *any Other.* There is a crucial distinction between any and all. If *all* subjects were responsible for the Other then there would be a totality of subjects all of whom are responsible for the Other. But this is not how responsibility works for Levinas.[80] It is the fact that the Other is ungraspable that demands that the I recognise the Other. Ethics is the very event of the Self that is defined through relations to others. It is an ethical imperative that demands the I recognises the Other as exteriority, acknowledging her rights as a Stranger.[81] The relation with the other person is a betrayal of the relation with the Other but is a reflection of the antecedent demand for acknowledgement of the Other.

Any attempt to appropriate Otherness as interior to the Self is at odds with the reality of interpersonal exchanges.[82] Attempts to thematise the Other will always conflict with the Other's "strangeness", her "very freedom".[83] It may be impossible to speak to write about alterity without resorting to expressions such as "*the* Other" or "*the* face", which at first glance seem to miss the singularity of this or that Other, reducing him or her to a particular instance of alterity in general. As Wall argues, the Other is therefore that from which I cannot distinguish myself.[84] The anonymity of the Other means that no-thing defines the I. Precisely because no-thing obligates the I, the I cannot be distanced from obligation – the I *is* obligation. Ethics becomes the very event of the self. The Self is a relational construct between transcendent and immanent planes and always has an ethical *calling*.

Because there is more than just one Other in the world, my infinite responsibility for the Other is not enough. Given the existence of more than one Other in the world:

> [I]t is consequently necessary to weigh, to think, to judge, in comparing the incomparable. The interpersonal relation I establish with the Other, I must establish with other men; there is thus a necessity to moderate the privilege of the Other; from whence comes justice. Justice, exercised through institutions, must always be held in check by the initial interpersonal relation.[85]

In order to attend to those whom I will never encounter face-to-face (and in order to exist in a community of more than two) I must balance and negotiate my relations with the *other* Others whom Levinas called the third party.[86] In a passage towards the end of *Otherwise than Being*, Levinas notes that this responsibility for the other becomes a problem when a third party arrives This presents a problem as the third party is other (and a neighbour) to both the other and the I. Levinas argues that the other stands in a relationship to the third party that the I cannot answer. The other and the third party put distance between the I and the other and the third party, the properly Other.[87] While my relation to the third is mediated by the Other, it is not for this reason subordinate to ethics:

> In no way is justice a degradation of obsession, a degeneration of the for-the-other, a diminution, a limitation of anarchic responsibility, a neutralisation of the glory of the Infinite, a degeneration that would be produced in the measure that for empirical reasons the initial duo would become a trio. But *the contemporaneousness of the multiple is tied about the diachrony of two*: justice remains justice only, in a society where there is no distinction between those close and those far off, but in which there also remains the impossibility of passing by the closest. The equality of all is borne by my inequality, the surplus of my duties over my rights.[88]

The implication of this is that one individual cannot be absolutely and uniquely responsible for more than one other. Matthew Stone develops this point, arguing that the I must compare and prioritise the appeal of others upon a plane of objectivity, and also recognise that the I is also the subject of judgment of others.[89] Stone posits that this is why Levinas states that the "intelligibility of a system" is required to mediate and make intelligible the relations with multiple others.[90] This system is necessary as multiple others cannot be encountered purely ethically, as if they were the only other that exists.[91] A method for making sense of multiple relations with others is needed in order to place the ethical relation within any kind of community, and explain how multiple ethical relations relate to one another and exist in common.

This insistence on the equality of all persons hold open the political space in which a singular ethical response might arise. As Levinas said in a 1982 interview:

> I don't at all believe that there are limits to responsibility, that there are limits to responsibility in "myself". My self, I repeat, is never absolved from responsibility towards the Other. But I think we should also say that all those who attack us with such venom have no right to do so, and that consequently, along with this feeling of unbounded responsibility, there is certainly a place for defense, for it is not always a question of "me" but of those close to me, who are also my neighbours. I'd call such a defense a politics, but a politics that's ethically necessary. Alongside ethics, there is a place for politics.[92]

An ethically necessary politics is married to responsibility, which is at the heart of the transcendent relation with the Other. It is clear from Agamben's writings in "Absolute Immanence" that Levinas has fallen prey to the illusion of transcendence and has repeated the nihilistic consequences of holding immanence in relation to transcendence – the empty throne.[93] But Agamben does go further and explicitly call into question specific elements of Levinasian philosophy.

The elision of ethics and law

Agamben's main interaction with Levinas's thought is found in *Remnants of Auschwitz*. Agamben's engagement with Levinas in *Remnants* exists as a critique of Levinasian ethics. I contend that Agamben's critique of Levinas is necessary for him to make. This is because Agamben seeks to generate critical distance between his work and Levinas's. This critical distance is illustrated in three ways. First, the charge Agamben makes that Levinas's ethics retain a juridical form. Second, Agamben criticises the relationship between shame and responsibility in Levinas's work. Third, the different positions "the face" holds in Agamben's and Levinas's philosophy. This distance allows Agamben to conceive of a politics of immanent life outside the Levinasian register. However, I follow Colby Dickinson's lead as he reads Agamben as redefining ethics along Levinasian lines to arrive at a respect for the face of the singular being before us. Agamben's methods and insights do overlap with the philosophical project of Levinas, a connection Agamben does not point to in his work.[94]

Turning to the first critique of Levinas's ethics and the law – Agamben sees the law and juridical constructions as harbouring a form of responsibility that is equated to the transmission of self-referential origins.[95] As a result of this, Levinasian ethics are indicative of the operation of the ban. Agamben therefore implies that Levinasian ethics repeat the same *dispositifs* and signatures of the law. Levinas presupposes a juridical structure in his stating that the ethical relation presupposes ontology.[96] As a result of repeating these *dispositifs* of the law such ethics would create and entrench bare life. For Agamben, Levinasian ethics imposes a negative relation between the law and life.

Agamben declares as one of the most common mistakes in political thought the tacit confusion of ethical categories and juridical categories:

> Almost all the categories that we use in moral and religious judgments are in some way contaminated by law: guilt, responsibility, innocence, judgment, pardon.[97]

Before we sketch the connection between the law and responsibility, we must ask: what is responsibility? Agamben traces its etymology to the Latin verb *spondeo*, meaning "to become the guarantor of something for someone (or for oneself) with respect to someone".[98] Agamben notes that in Roman law *spondeo* was used in a juridical sense, both to arrange the marriage of a man's daughter with the promise of compensation if the union did not occur, and to allow a free man to become a hostage to guarantee the compensation of a wrong or to fulfil an obligation.[99] He uses this evidence to claim that (in an indirect criticism of Levinas's ethics):

> The concept of responsibility is also irremediably contaminated by law. Anyone who has tried to make use of it outside the juridical sphere knows this.[100]

He goes on:

> The gesture of assuming responsibility is therefore genuinely juridical and not ethical. It expresses nothing noble or luminous, but rather simply obligation.[101]

As:

> [R]esponsibility is a juridical and not an ethical concept, the gesture that claims to dismiss it as alien to ethics as that which would like to assume it.[102]

These short statements declare that Levinasian ethics are not ethics but exist in the field of the law. The law is not directed to justice but to judgment, independent of truth and justice.[103] A *res judicata* becomes a substitute for the true and just.[104] A legal judgment as incompatible with an ethical decision. In *Remnants of Auschwitz* Agamben delivers the following lengthy passage on legal judgment that is quoted in its entirety:

> In 1983, the publisher Einaudi asked [Primo] Levi to translate Kafka's *The Trial*. Infinite interpretations of *The Trial* have been offered; some underline the novel's prophetic political character (modern bureaucracy as absolute evil) or its theological dimension (the court as the unknown God) or its biographical meaning (condemnation as the illness from which Kafka believed himself to suffer). It has been rarely noted that this book, in which law appears solely in the form of trial, contains a profound insight into the nature of law, which, contrary to common belief, is not so much rule as it is judgment and, therefore, trial. But if the essence of the law – of every law – is the trial, if all right (and morality that is contaminated by it) is only tribunal right, then execution and transgression, innocence and guilt, obedience and disobedience all become indistinct and lose their importance. "The court wants nothing from you. It welcomes you when you come; it releases you when you go." The ultimate end of the juridical regulation is to produce judgment; but judgment aims neither to punish nor to extol, neither to establish justice nor to prove the truth. Judgment is in itself the end and this, it has been said, constitutes its mystery, the mystery of the trial.[105]

At this point, it is worth recounting Agamben's understanding of *dispositifs* which was explained in the previous chapter:

> I shall call an apparatus literally anything that has in some way the capacity to capture, orient, determine, intercept, model, control, or secure the gestures,

> behaviours, opinions, or discourses of living beings … prisons, mad houses, the panopticon, schools, confession, factories, disciplines, *juridical measures*, and so forth.[106]

And is it *dispositifs* which are in relations with living beings and incessantly capture them and produce subjects.[107] The law, the realm of guilt, responsibility, judgment and punishment, is a *dispositif* that captures life. For Agamben the subject is produced and dominated by *dispositifs* like juridical measures. If we follow this line of reasoning and accept that ethics and responsibility are equivalent to the law and juridical measures, then they too must be *dispositifs* which capture life and produce subjects. It must also hold that it is not possible to use those self-same *dispositifs* to try and transcend the subject and escape their clutches. And just as the law is such a *dispositif*, so is language, and Agamben explicitly connects guilt and punishment to the apparatus of language (which in turn connects to Agamben's points about the fundamental negativity the rights-imbued human being is based upon).[108]

He goes on to state that today's crisis calls into question not only the *legality* of institutions but also their *legitimacy*.[109] A crisis that affects legitimacy cannot be resolved solely at the level of law. He continues:

> The hypertrophy of law, which presumes to legislate over everything, betrays, through an excess of formal legality, the loss of all substantive legitimacy. Modernity's attempt to make legality and legitimacy coincide, by seeking to secure through positive law the legitimacy of a power, is completely inadequate.[110]

Agamben's critique is furthered and the connections between responsibility and the law deepened when Agamben states:

> [R]esponsibility is closely intertwined with the concept of *culpa* that … indicates the imputability of damage.[111]

Culpa designates negligence in the exercise of obligatory behaviour. It indicates the threshold across which certain behaviour becomes imputable to the subject who becomes culpable.[112] Agamben associates *culpa* with the Latin term *crimen*, which is the form that human action assumes when it is imputed – intended or willed – and called into question in the order of responsibility and law.[113]

Agamben argues that the concept of *crimen*, culpable action, action that is intentional, sanctioned, imputable and productive of consequences, stands at the foundation of law, ethics, and the religious morality of the West.[114] Let me unpack this statement. Agamben tuns back to Aristotle to make the argument that there is a split between acting and being,[115] or Aristotle, acting unjustly or justly is not the same as being just or unjust. This implies not only action (and its connection to will), but a certain way of being.[116] Yet Aristotle resolves this split by unreservedly affirming the ethical primacy of action.[117] Agamben explains:

> In the tradition of Western ethical and political thought there are two paradigms, which intersect and incessantly keep separating from one another in the course of its history. The first [from Aristotle] situates the essence of the human and the proper place of politics and ethics in action and praxis; the second [from Plato] situates it instead in knowledge and contemplation (in *theoria*). The first model is tragic and predominates, at least up to a certain point, in modernity ... the second, decisively anti-tragic, prevails, albeit with some ups and downs, in ancient thought.[118]

The first looks consistently at becoming; the second holds its eyes fixed on being. The first paradigm takes primacy in Western ethics (including Levinas). Emphasising the primacy of action and connecting ethics to action means that the human being is responsible for his actions. Without this Western philosophy found it impossible to construct an ethics or politics.[119]

As a result, we can see how Agamben concludes that *crimen*, culpability and responsibility are here intertwined. Responsibility presupposes responsible actions – this form of ethics requires the subject to act. As a result of this ethics have, in Agamben's terms, become contaminated with the law and are beholden to the juridical. Human relations have been completely juridified.[120] We have focused on action to the expense of being. As Agamben states, making explicit his move away from Levinas:

> Responsibility and guilt thus express simply two aspects of legal imputability; only later were they interiorised and moved outside law. Hence the insufficiency and opacity of every ethical doctrine that claims to be founded on these two concepts. (This holds ... for Lévinas, who, in a much more complex fashion, transformed the gesture of the *sponsor* into the ethical gesture par excellence.)[121]

Crucially, what is subordinated to responsibility and action is character, or *ēthos*.[122] Character is assumed through actions, and is the "enigmatic shadow" that the ethics of action projects on the subject.[123] The subject is what results from the *crimen*, the series of responsible actions.[124] It is the definition of the relationship between being and acting that is the problem that Western ethics does not manage to solve.[125] Levinasian ethics require responsible actions. Agamben seeks to call into question the centrality of action and will to ethics.[126]

For our argument, the important point is that Agamben specifically equates the law with responsibility, and ethics with *non-responsibility*.[127] Non-responsibility:

> [S]ignifies – at least for ethics – a confrontation with a responsibility that is infinitely greater than we could ever assume. At the most, we can be faithful to it, that is, assert its unassumability.[128]

Ethics, to be properly ethical, *cannot* be based upon forms of responsibility.[129] It is a way of being, not a way of becoming. Ethics is not a question of acting.

This move means Agamben clearly aligns himself with Spinoza and Deleuzian immanence rather than Levinasian responsibility and the transcendence of the Other:

> [E]thics is the sphere that recognises neither guilt nor responsibility; it is, as Spinoza knew, the doctrine of the happy life. To assume guilt and responsibility – which can, at times, be necessary – is to leave the territory of ethics and enter that of law.[130]

The doctrine of a happy (immanent) life is coterminous with an *ēthos*, character, a way of being.

Agamben and Levinas on shame

The second critique of Levinas by Agamben focuses on the position of shame in Levinas's work. Levinas 's work could be read as a meditation on ethical shame, a feeling of remorse and responsibility for the suffering of others. Responsibility is to be thought as a feeling of "being-put-in-question, but also put to the question, having to answer—the birth of language in responsibility".[131] Levinas shows how shame is transformed into responsibility through ethical temporality and the Other opening my future.

Shame points to "a problem that remains irresolvable within its own terms".[132] Ontological shame takes the form of an inability to escape one's own relation to being, being riveted to oneself – "In the identity of the I [*moi*], the identity of being reveals its nature as enchainment, for it appears in the form of suffering and invites us to escape".[133] I can neither be what I am nor refuse to be. This is similar to Heidegger when he wrote that shame is an emotive tonality that traverses and determines man's whole Being. Shame is an ontological sentiment that has its place in the encounter between man and Being. It is in shame we find ourselves exposed in the face of Being.[134] For Levinas, as an embodied existent, the I is weighed down by its own relation to being. The I's solitary relation to being traps it in immanence:

> What appears in shame is therefore precisely the fact of being chained to oneself, the radical impossibility of fleeing oneself to hide oneself from oneself, the intolerable presence of the self to itself. Nudity is shameful when it is the obviousness of our Being, of its final intimacy. And the nudity of our body is not the nudity of a material thing that is antithetical to the spirit but the nudity of our entire Being, in all its plenitude and solidity, in its most brutal expression, of which one cannot not be aware … What is shameful is our intimacy, that is, our presence to ourselves. It reveals not our nothingness but the totality of our existence. … What shame discovers is the Being that *discovers* itself.[135]

The reference to nudity should not be taken literally. Nakedness has nothing to do with the clothes we are wearing.[136] The body can be dressed and full of shame or naked and shameless. In shame I experience my being as a weight – a burden for itself.[137] As we attempt to cover up, there is a disruption in our own being that exposes our nakedness – shame then unveils the self as visible *to others*.[138]

Shame extends interminably without interruption. The only path of escape is through a relation to the Other who opens a future that is not my own, beyond the horizon of my own being.[139] In *Totality and Infinity* shame is no longer a sign of ontological self-encumbrance but rather of ethical projection by the Other.[140] The face of the Other calls into question my spontaneous freedom and commands me to justify myself.[141] For Levinas, the process of measuring oneself against the infinite demand of the Other "is accomplished in shame where freedom is at the same time discovered in the consciousness of shame and is concealed in the shame itself".[142] In this sense, the ethical shame which the Other provokes in me does not make me feel riveted to myself; rather, it opens a way of getting un-stuck from my own suffocating relation to being. Shame is a necessary precursor to ethical dwelling with the Other.

Both Agamben and Levinas take a similar position in that shame is grounded in our being's incapacity to move away and break from itself.[143] However, Agamben makes clear that the hidden structure of subjectivity is shame:

> Shame is truly something like the hidden structure of all subjectivity and consciousness. Insofar as it consists solely in the event of enunciation, consciousness constitutively has the form of something that cannot be assumed. To be conscious means: to be consigned to something that cannot be assumed.[144]

It is not a way for an existent to escape enchainment through a relation to an Other. Agamben seeks to deepen Levinas's analysis, whilst remaining close to a Levinasian coordinate. To be ashamed is to be consigned to something that cannot be assumed. But what cannot be assumed is not something external. Rather, it originates in our own intimacy; it is what is most intimate in us. Agamben continues to state that the "I" is overcome by its own passivity, its ownmost sensibility; yet this expropriation and desubjectification is also an extreme and irreducible presence of the "I" to itself.[145]

In shame the subject has no other content than its own desubjectification; it becomes witness to its own disorder, its own oblivion as a subject. This double movement, which is both subjectification and desubjectification, is shame.[146] Agamben theorises shame as an ontological affect proper to beings who have nothing in common but the impropriety of their own death; beings who are expropriated at the very moment that they appropriate themselves.[147]

If "shame is truly something like the hidden structure of all subjectivity and consciousness",[148] then each of us are summoned to be present at our own defacement, insofar as we both appropriate being and are expropriated by it:

> The *self* is what is produced as a remainder in the double movement – active and passive – of auto-affection [in Kant, read through the lens of Heidegger (*Remnants of Auschwitz*, pp.109–112)]. This is why subjectivity constitutively has the form of subjectification and desubjectification; this is why it is, at bottom, shame. Flush is the remainder that, in every subjectification, betrays a desubjectification and that, in every desubjectification, bears witness to a subject.[149]

Shame creates subjects. Following Agamben's method, this implies that shame is a *dispositif*, an apparatus which traps human beings. Since these *dispositifs* are totalising, it simply is not an option to the living being to escape shame through the Other. Every other living being, including the Other, would be subjectified by shame in the same way.

Another difference can be found in the relation between shame and nudity. For Levinas nudity (via shame) reveals the self as visible to others. Agamben reads nudity as a theological apparatus (and again, the same logic applies about the *dispositif* capturing living beings).[150] This theological apparatus presupposes "the [corrupt] naked corporeality of human nature".[151] The nudity that the first humans saw in Paradise when their eyes were opened is the opening of truth, without which knowledge would not be possible. To see a body naked means to perceive its pure knowability beyond every secret, beyond or before its objective predicates.[152] It is a pure means, or pure immanence. After the Fall, shame was felt at naked bodies.[153] And nudity became impure because it was only accessible through the removal of clothes.[154] But in Agamben's reading, shame (and clothing) hides the light of knowability. If we experience shame in nudity, it is because we cannot hide what we would like to remove from the field of vision (the nudity itself); it is because the unrestrainable impulse to flee from oneself is confronted by an equally certain impossibility of evasion (on this point Agamben and Levinas agree).[155] Agamben privileges a "nudity without veils".[156] He urges us to "liberate nudity from the patterns of thought that permit us to conceive of it solely in a privative … manner". Striptease epitomises "the impossibility of nakedness"; he designates it as "the paradigm for our [unsatisfying] relationship with nudity", in that it is "an event that never reaches its completed form".[157] Nudity and clothing must shake themselves free of their theological signature, to open up the possibility of a certain invaluable *dwelling*, manifested in a "special trembling".[158] This a condition of nude life that precludes the abandonment of *zoè* that turns it into bare life.[159] In this sense, I could say that nudity in the thought of Agamben *and* Levinas reveals the self as knowable to others, even if Agamben reaches that position via a theological detour.

Agamben sees a common structure of shame understood as the "absolute concomitance of subjectification and desubjectification, self-loss and self-possession, servitude and sovereignty".[160] Guenther sees this as presenting an uncharitable reading of Levinasian shame, when she argues that:

> Agamben's … approach to shame effaces a crucial distinction between shame as a feeling of collective ethical responsibility, and humiliation as an instrument of political domination. It is one thing to be "constitutionally divided on account of having become speaking beings" (*Remnants of Auschwitz*, p.129), and another thing to be humiliated as part of a project of extermination.[161]

Shame is different from humiliation. Humiliation desubjectifies; shame intersubjectifies, attesting to an irreducible relation to others.[162] Shame confirms the relationality of the subject. Humiliation works by singling out this or that person as deviant, out of place, abnormal, or bad, and displaying them before real or imagined others, building a sense of unity and common identity among those who remain within the fold. Humiliation severs relations between one person or group and a larger community. Shame also individuates the subject, but in a different way: not by singling one out for negation or exclusion, but by intensifying the ambiguity of an indissoluble relation to others. What is unassumable in the feeling of shame is not an aspect of one's own being, but rather the relation to an other to whose gaze I am exposed, but whose view of myself I cannot control.[163]

For Guenther, Agamben equates the structure of shame with the structure of humiliation, and as such overlooks the ethical and political dimensions of shame as an irreducible relation to the other.[164] This does however miss the nuance in Agamben's writings on nudity and how they come close to Levinas's position on recognition by an Other. Although not a connection made by Guenther, there is a clear parallel here to shame, humiliation and the position of Adam and Eve after the Fall being ashamed of their naked bodies. Shame emphasises relations rather than acts; shame occurs because I care what others think of me. As such for Guenther shame can function as a site of resistance, confirming the root of responsibility in our relations with others, and holding open the possibility that things could be otherwise.[165] In order to desubjectify or dehumanise, individuals still have to be singled out. This process does not, like Agamben says, evidence an ontological connection between appropriation and expropriation, but rather a political connection between oppression and resistance. This means that the oppressor must, on some level, affirm the resistance they seek to overcome.[166] If shame is moved onto an ontological realm (as Agamben wants) the responsibility to which it commands each one of us may be effaced. For Guenther, this collective responsibility needs to be emphasised and developed as the condition for ethics as such.[167]

The face

The third generation of critical distance by Agamben from Levinas's work is found in "the face". There is no reference to Levinas in Agamben's works when he writes on what the face means, but the connection cannot be overlooked or ignored. This is perhaps the clearest example of Agamben redefining ethics along Levinasian lines. As Dickinson has argued, *not* citing Levinas to bring Levinas's work to light in another way may have been Agamben's intention all along.[168] For both, the face opens up the living being to other beings, but in very different ways.

Levinas locates the revelation of the Other in the "face-to-face" encounter.[169] It is the face of the other person that causes an "epiphany".[170] Recognising an other is phenomenologically different from recognising an inanimate object; it "is not an object-cognition". The sensory impression of the face is the other as we perceive him or her, yet something transcendent simultaneously:

> The transcendence of the face is at the same time its absence from this world into which it enters ...[171]

As "not an object-cognition" the relation to the face of the other exceeds or transcends the same, the grasp, the attempt of the same to (rationally) co-opt all into itself: "The face resists possession, resists my powers".[172] It transcends the same; it is "a movement of retreat and overflowing".[173] In exceeding myself and my grasp, the face of the other calls into question "my joyous possession of the world".[174] We encounter the face of the other visually and through other sensations. The face of the other also speaks. The face can be tactile. The face is both flesh and more. The face is not only the literal and the colloquial face but the entire body and embodiment of the other, as well as something that transcends all this: "what in the countenance of the other escapes our gaze when turned towards us".[175]

The entire embodiment in which the other presents themselves to us is a form of nakedness (and this should be seen as close to Agamben's formulation of nudity explained above). This expresses the openness and vulnerability in which the other presents itself to us. This is a nakedness of the face that "extends into the nakedness of the body that is cold and that is ashamed of its nakedness".[176] In Agamben's terms this shame is due to the fact that the face and body cannot hide what we would like to remove from the field of vision and that we want to flee from ourselves.[177] For Levinas, the face is at one and the same time the physical, fleshed face that the term colloquially refers to and otherness itself, that which "escapes our gaze".[178] In the face of the other, we "see" otherness, infinity, that which exceeds and resists our grasp. The face is not a metaphor for a deeper reality; it is the deeper reality itself.

The face is infinite as it hints to the I of the Other, of the fact that the other person is truly Other to the I, ungraspable. Such a connection reminds the I that its freedom is inhibited, and that in order to affirm its own subjectivity, the I is compelled to acknowledge that affirming its own subjectivity necessarily involves assuming responsibilities. These responsibilities are ethical. What is more, the encounter itself is ethical and no-one can release the I from these responsibilities which the I must encounter alone.[179] Faced with the other the I is made aware of the other person as an unpredictable, irreducible entity.

Levinas distinguishes between access to the face in terms of its (ethical) alterity and its empirical difference (which is apparently not ethically relevant):

> I wonder if one can speak of a look turned toward the face, for the look is knowledge, perception. I think rather that access to the face is straightaway ethical. You turn yourself toward the Other as toward an object when you see a nose, eyes, a forehead, a chin, and you can describe them. The best way of encountering the Other is not even to notice the colour of his eyes! When one observes the colour of the eyes one is not in social relationship with the Other.[180]

For Levinas, the relationship to the other person must involve a face-to-face ethical encounter. This encounter is ethical as it involves speaking to the other and being for the other.[181] There are key differences between the early and late Levinas. For the early Levinas subjectivity begins in the impersonal and *moves toward* ethical experience.[182] This ethical subjectivity is a being-toward-alterity: ethics is synonymous with a movement toward otherness.[183] In *Otherwise than Being*, Levinas abandoned the progressive model underlying his earlier works. There, he described the subject as lung, as exposed flesh.[184] This is designed to elucidate two things. First, the subject's exposure is inescapable. Second, that this exposure is always already a responsibility.[185] The subject *cannot not* be exposed to the other, that it *cannot not* be responsible.[186] Ethics consists in the subject's response to the fact that it is always already shouldering a responsibility.[187] The face of the Other stands as a transcendent reference through which the I assumes responsibility and affirms its own subjectivity. This is the self-same responsibility which Agamben studiously avoids in his thought.

For Agamben, just as for Levinas, the face is an opening, a threshold, to another person.[188] It is also the openness in which we are, through which the human being exposes himself and communicates. This is why Agamben sees the face as the place of politics.[189] However, there is no demand for recognition from the other subject, at least in terms of one underpinned by relationality. For Agamben, if a face is encountered by the subject, the subject experiences an exteriority, another person. It is through the face that men perceive similarity and diversity, distance and proximity.[190] This is characterised as having "an *outside* happen to me".[191] An encounter with the face involves the living being's encounter with and understanding of themselves, rather than the Other.

All living beings manifest themselves in their appearance. There is an irreparable exposure in the face for Agamben, so fundamental that it is an opening and the only location of community.[192] This can be contrasted to the exposure in Levinas, which reveals the vulnerability of the other in the experience of the face-to-face. Yet this could easily be mistaken for a description of *homo sacer* abandoned to sovereign violence.[193] Levinas writes:

> Prior to any particular expression and beneath all particular expressions, which cover over and protect with an immediately adopted face or countenance, there is the nakedness and destitution of the expression as such, that is to say extreme exposure, defencelessness, vulnerability itself. This extreme exposure – prior to any human aim – is like a shot at point blank

> range ... From the beginning there is a face to face steadfast in its exposure to invisible death, to a mysterious forsakenness.[194]

The face for Agamben remains immanent to the living being, which allows the living being to grasp its own being exposed.[195] Exposition itself becomes the location of politics. To put it another way, appearance (the very fact of being nothing other than a face) remains hidden from human beings, and politics causes appearance to appear. The focus of this politics is an immanent life which exists *as* immanent, without the need for defining itself relationally. This immanent life is given a variety of names in Agamben's work, but we will here use *being-thus*, which was used to describe a life "just as it is".[196]

Both Agamben and Levinas remain very close in how they connect exposure to the living being, but the fact that being-thus focuses on the living being's capacity for communicability, or existence such that it is, shows how far apart Agamben wishes to present them as.[197] Agamben sees the face as pure communicability, and politics as a communicative emptiness which is trying to be controlled by *dispositifs* including politicians and the media. Key to understanding the living being is taking their face's own communicability upon itself, not seeking to understand how it relates to others.[198] Being-in-common does not denote the face's encounter with others. Rather, it relates to grasping the simultaneity of the visages that constitute the face.[199] Only once I exist in this point of indifference will I be able to encounter the Other. I exist with all my properties (my being brown, tall, pale, proud, emotional) but these properties do not identify me or belong to me. The face is an immanent being through which, and only which, I encounter other immanent beings.[200]

Through the elision of law and ethics, shame, and the face, Agamben's work sketches out an immanent critique of transcendent relationality, and implicitly Levinas's thought. This is a necessary critique for Agamben. Levinas argued that within the bipolar play of immanence and transcendence, immanence always wins out over transcendence.[201] To put my own interpretation on Agamben's thought – his work is marked by a concern that transcendence will always win out over immanence. It is for this reason that Agamben has done his utmost in his critique of Western metaphysics to foreclose transcendence as the basis for a coming freedom or coming politics. However, as we will see in the next section of this chapter, Agamben's critique of Levinas and transcendent ethics is premised on an uncharitable interpretation of the I's relationship to the Other. Specifically, within substitution, and the figure of the ethical singularity, Levinasian ethics can be read as coming very close to Agamben's project of founding an immanent life.

Substitution and the ethical singularity: a defence of Levinasian ethics

Substitution

What is substitution? Substitution frees the self from itself.[202] Levinas distinguished the identity of the self from the identity of identification.[203] The identity of identification is based on "distinguishing characteristics": bodily marks, culture, a language, an accent and so on.[204] In this sense Levinas serves as a precursor to Agamben's writings on the face. The identity of identification is akin to all the features of the living being, but they fall short of identifying the being as it is because they reduce that being to those characteristics. The self for Levinas is akin to the face for Agamben, as it exists as a unity of all its properties.

The self keeps falling back into identity. The identity of the self is that of *inquietude*, unrest, being ill at ease in one's skin.[205] The self feels persecuted as it bears the weight of the world, which throws subjectivity back on itself, reinstating identity.[206] Substitution allows the self to slip away from its identity.[207] Substitution radicalises Levinas's own philosophy and transforms the tradition it criticises.[208] Substitution is not just freeing the self from itself. In *Otherwise than Being* Levinas theorises the subject as one who is always already the Other-in-the-same, anarchically affected by the alterity of the Other to the point of substituting for him or her. The self becomes *uniquely* itself, singular and irreplaceable, precisely by substituting for a singular and irreplaceable Other. Substitution works through the interplay of singularity and indeterminacy, strangeness and proximity, alterity and indifference.[209] The impossibility of escaping oneself is the impossibility of fleeing one's responsibilities.[210] Substitution thus becomes substitution for others.[211]

At this point it may appear that substitution remains distant from Agamben's immanent life due to the central position of the Other and responsibility in its construction. Yet the proximity is shown through both Agamben and Levinas critiquing the Western tradition's attempts to mystify its own origins.[212] Levinas's strategy for demystification is to reread the tradition for the opportunities it affords to exit being.[213] This proximity is echoed in Agamben's notion of religion, in which he shares a key term with Levinas, spirituality:

> Non-thingness (spirituality) means losing one-self in things, losing oneself to the point of not being able to conceive of anything but things, and only then, in the experience of the irremediable thingness of the world, bumping into a limit, touching it. (This is the meaning of the word 'exposure'.)[214]

Spirituality is Agamben's word for the kind of openness to which a non-thing is delivered by the messianic. The position of the messianic in Agamben (and its meaning for Levinas) will be developed fully in the next chapter. For our purposes here, it is enough to note that for Agamben the messianic shows the irremediable fact that the world and things simply are *thus*, and everything *else* also exists in its own being-thus.[215] Being-thus is also a singular being, akin to Levinas's uniquely singular and irreplaceable self.

Here, I follow Christopher Fox's erudite discussion of how substitution operates in Agamben's being-thus. Agamben establishes substitution as a meeting point of the religious, community, and the ethical. The archaic bases of his substitution lie in Judaism and Christianity. Agamben refers to a Talmudic theological doctrine whereby each person, pending death, has reserved two places, one in Eden and one in Gehenna.[216] At the final judgment, each person earns a place in one of the possible destinations, as well as the place reserved for another whose judgment ordained the other destination. Similarly, the one who goes elsewhere inherits the unused spot that was reserved for the first. Agamben focuses on the implications that one's theological arrival produces for being-thus:

> At the point when one reaches one's final state and fulfills one's own destiny, one finds oneself for that very reason in the place of the neighbor. What is most proper to every creature is thus its substitutability, its being in any case in the place of the other.[217]

I can hardly substitute for another if I have been totally displaced and annulled. My being-thus already refers to another (in the way the self in Levinas always refers to an Other).[218] Agamben turns to the Arabist Louis Massignon, who founded a community named *Badaliya* (the Arabic word for substitution), whose members "took a view to live *substituting themselves* for someone else, that is, to be Christians *in place of others*".[219]

Agamben spells out two possible meanings of this vow.[220] The first, which he dismisses, would turn substitution into a reciprocal economy of salvation in which one soul pays for another.[221] The second sense discloses the novelty residing within substitution as an expression of being-thus. Agamben elaborates this second sense as "*exiling oneself to the other as he or she is* in order to offer Christ's hospitality in the other's own soul, in the other's own taking place".[222] For Fox this formulation intensifies novelty to a power of three, since the capacity for surprise expressed in accepting my own taking place would be doubled through my exile to another's and tripled through the welcome I would extend to the being-thus of Christ. To go further to the level of community, substitution creates its own sort of space:

> [T]his substitution no longer knows a place of its own, but the taking-place of every single being is always already common – an empty space offered to the one, irrevocable hospitality.[223]

This one hospitality is immediately many, since substituting myself for another produces the space in which all others are free to be-thus.[224] Being-thus always means being with others and accepting their being-thus as cotemporaneous with my own. This is also reflected in *Nudities* when Agamben appears to admit of the centrality of relations with others to humanity:

> The desire to be recognised by others is inseparable from being human. Indeed, such recognition is so essential that, according to Hegel, everyone is ready to put his or her own life in jeopardy in order to obtain it. This is not merely a question of satisfaction or self-love; rather, it is only through recognition by others that man can constitute himself as a person.[225]

Like Levinas, Agamben also critiques the identity of identification. He speaks of a "new figure of the human" that is "beyond personal identity".[226] This notion of substitution effects the transition to a community founded upon being-thus, as the site in which the displacement of each is the condition of possibility for encountering the thing by which things might be displaced and novel.[227] In substitution it simply is the case that "there is no place that is not vicarious".[228]

For Fox, Levinas would not allow being-thus into his account of substitution. Levinas asserts that in substitution the subject undergoes a pre-original displacement on the way to taking its transcendental plane.[229] And yet here we can see an analysis which shows that substitution plays a central role in freeing the self from a politics of identity, and creates a place where the self can be-with others.

The ethical singularity

Agamben's immanent politics of being-thus also finds a close parallel in Levinas's ethical singularity. Singularity articulates an *ethical* relation for Levinas. It refers to an existent's (non-relating) relation to *another singular existent.* Ethical singularity involves a relation between existents who are irreducible to each other or to anything else; it arises through the ethical event of substitution, whereby I become myself in being commanded to unique responsibility for you. The self is "one and irreplaceable, one inasmuch as irreplaceable in responsibility".[230]

This unicity arises in response to an Other whom I can never quite grasp in terms of my own consciousness. I respond as someone, *anyone*, not even as "I" but as "oneself".[231] Identity and alterity are united,[232] and this uniting intertwines opposites into contact without either contradiction or fusion, in a relationship "where there is no disjunction between the terms held in relation".[233] The "singular torsion *or* contraction of the oneself"[234] is a precise formulation of this twisting – together of identity and alterity which forms a point from which "one must speak in the first person"[235] without being reduced to a solitary individual. To summarise:

> The oneself is a singularity prior to the distinction between the particular and universal. It is, if one likes, a relationship, but one where there is no disjunction between the terms held in relationship.[236]

Singularity requires and sustains plurality, for no one can be faced or encountered alone.[237] For Levinas to exist is to be one, alone, a monad with its own separate relation to existence as such.[238]

Yet for Levinas the ethical relation is asymmetrical. The singularity of the self refers to its unique responsibility for an Other. The singularity of the Other refers to its *expression* of singularity in a face which breaks with its own image to express itself on its own terms, as a unique, irreducible and unrepeatable Other.[239] It does not matter who this Other *is*; what matters is *that* she faces me, and that *a* face, any face, commands me.[240] The singularity of the Other is not incompatible with a certain universality which entitles us to use a phrase like "the Other" without contradicting or diminishing the singularity of *this* Other who faces me here and now. This universality is precisely *not* a generality which effaces distinct singularities by subsuming them all indifferently under the same category, such as "being".[241]

Levinas explains that the materialisation of a *singular* but *anonymous* self in terms of what he calls a recurrence. Recurrence refers to a contraction of the self, a retreat inward with no chance of escape or diversion, to the point where this retreat feels more like an exile or expulsion than a homecoming. The self in recurrence is "in itself already outside of itself", "expelled into itself outside of being", in "exile or refuse in itself".[242] The oneself in recurrence is a "nameless singularity".[243] For Levinas, the oneself may appear as a faceless neutrality, "on the edge of the generality characteristic of all said" but this appearance is a mask covering its nameless singularity, its recurrence as a point of identity bearing alterity. The nameless singularity is irreducible to being, but it also inscribes itself as a trace in the midst of being; it borrows a name from being in order to show itself in the said, in order to matter in the world. This name of being is only a mask that is constantly unmasked, or unsaid, in its singular exposure to the Other.[244]

In this sense the ethical singularity comes close to Agamben's being-thus, which is also a singular being.[245] Being-thus, and the face, is being such as it is, with all its properties, but not reducible to any property in particular, nor marked by an *absence* of shared properties.[246] These properties are held in relation without disjunction in the living being. Being-thus also involves being with others, so again a parallel could be drawn with Levinas stating that the singularity of the self refers to its unique responsibility for a singular Other. Agamben's philosophy and its focus upon language and grammatical shifters as examples of the very existence of language also belie this being-with-others. The entry into language through the use of personal pronouns does not only designate the position of the individual in relation to language (something Agamben argues is fundamentally negative) but also designates the position of the individual in relation to others.[247] Enunciative pronouns only gain meaning in the presence of and by the existence of other persons.

We could read this as being faced with two singularities. Both require plurality – for Levinas in the Other and for Agamben as living beings require recognition. The dividing line for Agamben appears to centre on the position of recognition in Levinas's thought, being a placeholder of transcendence and therefore leaving open the door to apparatuses of control. The distinction between a philosophy of immanence and a philosophy of transcendence (seen as an illusion to which every philosopher falls prey) is fine indeed.

But I think we can go further. Both Levinas and Agamben require an *other* with which to give meaning to the existence of the self, the singular existent, being-thus. For Levinas, this other is the Other which the self is uniquely responsible for. For Agamben, the other is *homo sacer*. Lorenzo Chiesa has argued that a formulation of a *positive* form of *homo sacer* – which is being-thus – arises from Agamben's writings.[248] *Homo sacer* stands for a life that is dominated by its relation to sovereignty and *dispositifs* of control; being-thus stands as an immanent life whose community is mediated by belonging itself.[249] Yet being-thus remains haunted by *homo sacer*; without *homo sacer* being created, there would be no need for this immanent life:

> Law that becomes indistinguishable from life in a real state of exception is confronted by life that, in a symmetrical but inverse gesture, is entirely transformed into law … Only at this point do the two terms distinguished and kept united by the relation of ban (bare life and the form of law) abolish each other and enter into a new dimension.[250]

Agamben's immanent life is, in this reading, still structured by a foundational negativity.

Ethics, Kant and duty

The final section of this chapter builds on the discussion of Agamben's critique of Levinas. Before we move onto a detailed consideration of Agamben's immanent philosophy and ethics in the coming chapters, there is one final generation of critical distance made by Agamben. Agamben conflates ethics with duty via the works of Emmanuel Kant. This sets the stage for Agamben's attempt to think ethics not as duty, but as a way of being. An excursus into Agamben's writings in *Opus Dei* can illustrate this point.[251]

In *Opus Dei*, Agamben returns to the paradigm of modern political economy to establish new parameters for thinking ethics. *Opus Dei* starts with a claim that Western ontology is dominated by an operative and practical paradigm that subordinates being to praxis.[252] This praxis has, in Agamben's view, exercised a huge influence on the way in which modernity has thought its ontology and its ethics, its politics and its economy.[253]

Opus Dei is a technical term that designates the priestly liturgy. The Greek *leitourgia* means "public work". Beyond the Pauline corpus, the terms *leitourgein* and *leitourgia* figure only twice in the Bible (Luke 1:23; Acts 13:1–2), and even in Paul's writings the term maintained a meaning of a service for the community (Romans 15:27, 2 Corinthians 9:12). The Letter to the Hebrews presupposes an identity between the actions of Christ and liturgy; Christ's sacrifice on the cross is a liturgical action that is both absolute and can be carried out only once (Hebrews 9:28, 10:12). Christ coincides completely with his liturgy, a sacrifice which must be endlessly repeated through the covenant (instituted at the Last Supper) to renew its memory (Hebrews 10:3). The *leitourgia* by the third century CE comes to acquire the characteristics of a stable and lifelong office, a special activity, a Eucharist which continuously reactualises Christ's sacrifice and renews the foundational and eternal character of Christ's priesthood.[254]

The liturgical character of Christ's sacrifice is connected by Agamben to the doctrine of the Trinity through *oikonomia*, an apparatus through which the Trinitarian dogma and the idea of a divine providential government of the world were introduced to the Christian faith.[255] Agamben argues that in liturgically celebrating the new covenant, the ministry celebrates the *oikonomia*'s memory and renews its presence.[256] The liturgy is an apparatus, and the priest acts as an "animate instrument" whose action is split in two. The early Church protected the reality of the sacrament from the subjective qualities of the person performing the office. The *opus operatum* refers to the validity and effectiveness of actions. The *opus operans* refer to the moral and physical actions of the agent.[257] This meant that any moral or ethical flaws on the part of the priest would not affect the validity of the sacrament. For Agamben this meant that the ethical connection between the subject and their action is broken.[258] What is determinative is only the function of the agent in carrying out the action, not their intent. By defining the peculiar operativity of its public praxis in this way, the Church invented the paradigm of a human activity whose effectiveness does not depend on the subject who sets it to work.[259]

Liturgy, for Agamben, is the origin of our modern ideas of office. Before the nineteenth century, we find in liturgy's place the Latin *officium*.[260] The paradigm of the office consists only in the operation by means of which it is realised. It acts independently of the qualities of the subject who officiates it.[261] Agamben explains that the term indicating the political liturgy of the Roman Empire was *munus*. *Munus* corresponded to *leitourgia* in Roman political and juridical vocabulary. There is thus a nexus between *munus*, office, liturgy, *oikonomia* and the *dispositif*. *Munus* designated the function that the officials carried out; Christ's sacrifice was a *publicum munus*, a public performance, a liturgy done for the salvation of humanity. *Munus* as *officium* carries a meaning of "an effective action" which is "appropriate to carry out" given one's social condition. An office (or *munus*) is what causes an individual to comport himself in a consistent way.[262]

The paradigm of the office is more effective than any ordinary human action because it acts *ex opere operato*, independently of the qualities of the subject who officiates it.[263] In office and duty, what a human being does and what a human being is enters into a zone of indistinction – only what is effective becomes real.[264] In an office operativity and effectiveness replace being and acting, which have no representation other than effectiveness. Only what is effective, and as such is governable and efficacious, is real.[265]

Agamben uses as a paradigmatic example of the office that of the priest. The sacraments of the communion confer grace *ex opera operato*; the priest is an instrumental cause – an animate instrument – of an act (communion) whose primary agent is Christ himself (through the transubstantiation of the bread and the wine).[266] The sacraments confer grace that proceeds from God, the principal cause. Its effect is produced by means of an element that acts as instrumental cause. The sacrament divides the one working the work (*opus operans*, the act of the instrumental agent, the celebrant) and the work worked (*opus operatum*, the sacramental effect in itself). The minister's intentions are irrelevant to the validity of the sacrament, because the latter acts *ex opere operato*.[267]

This distinction was made because in early Church liturgy, the effective reality of the sacrament had to be protected from subjective qualities of the person performing the office (*ex opera operato*). By elevating the *opus operatum* (validity and effectiveness of actions) of the priest at the expense of his *opus operans* (moral and physical qualities of the agent), the priest was transformed into an animate instrument that merely performs a function. This formulation, which "conceive[s] of human actions as an *officium*",[268] disrupted the ethical connection between the subject and his action, such that "what is determinative is no longer the right intention [or moral character] of the agent but only the function that his action carries out as *opus Dei*".[269]

The liturgy as *opus Dei* is the effectiveness that results from the articulation of these elements – the ethical connection between the subject and his action is thus broken.[270] The liturgy is connected by Agamben to office. The term indicating the political liturgy of the Roman Empire was *munus*.[271] *Munus* designated the function that the officials carried out; Christ's sacrifice was a *publicum munus*, a public performance, a liturgy done for the salvation of humanity.[272] *Munus* as *officium* carries a meaning of an effective action which is appropriate to carry out given one's social condition. An office (or *munus*) is what causes an individual to comport himself in a consistent way. This then becomes translated as duty, starting in the seventeenth century.[273]

Agamben traces in *munus* the notion of a way to conduct one's common life. The *munus* is an *officium* which renders life governable, by means of which the life of humans is "instituted" and "formed".[274] The sphere of *officium* as that in which what is in question is the distinctively human capacity to govern one's own life and those of others. The official, in carrying out their office, their *munus,* is what he has to do and has to do what he is: he is a being of command. In this way, being is transformed into having-to-be, and duty is introduced into ethics as a fundamental concept which comes to define ethics.[275]

Starting in the seventeenth century office and *munus* becomes translated as duty. Duty underlies Kantian ethics and is defined as "the necessity of an action from respect for the law".[276] Ethical duty is "to be able to do what one must".[277] *Munus* becomes coterminous with the idea of virtues and *habitus*. The goodness of a virtue is viewed as its effectiveness; an act carried out thanks to the inclination of an individual's virtuous habit is "the execution of a duty".[278] This duty is a *debitum*; in religious terms it is an infinite debt, a debt that is inexhaustible. Kantian ethics introduces the figure of a virtue that can never satisfy its debt, and the idea of an infinite task or duty.[279] Ethics therefore becomes an imperative, which decrees that one must behave a certain way.[280] In this way, *munus* (office), or duty, founds the notion of a human *habitus*. Kantian ethics collapses ethics into an action whose sole purpose is duty.[281] Such a duty operates as another apparatus attempting to divide life into those beings who follow their duty and those who do not.

There is a parallel here to be drawn to Levinas, who stated that a sense of subjectivity is felt only when facing an infinite and asymmetrical debt to the Other, the absolute alterity of difference.[282] Agamben's ethics seeks to move beyond Levinas, whose ethics are irremediably contaminated with the law, and Kant, whose ethics becomes a duty to be founded in an *oikonomia*.

Agamben makes clear that the register for ethics needs to be thought in terms of potential, not will. As the moderns speak of free will, the ancient world speaks of *potential*: human beings are not responsible for their actions because they *willed* them, but because they were *able* to carry them out.[283] The will is separate from freedom. The will acts as an apparatus which aims to render masterable what the human being can do. The being who *can* is transformed into a being who *wills*.[284] The passage from the ancient world to modernity coincides with the passage from potential to will, from the predominance of the modal verb "I can" to that of the modal verb "I will" (and later, "I must"). Ancient human beings were people who "can", who conceive their thought and their action in the dimension of potential; Christian human beings are beings that will and must act.[285] Human potential thus becomes subsumed to the will and duty.

The primacy of the concept of action and will must be questioned.[286] Agamben's coming philosophy seeks to focus on thinking an ontology of potential which is liberated from duty and will.[287] In such a philosophy Agamben does speak positively of debt, but this debt relates to being proper to oneself instead of being a duty which must be met:

> Since the being most proper to humankind is being one's own possibility or potentiality, then and only for this reason (that is, insofar as humankind's most proper being – being potential – is in a certain sense lacking, insofar as it can not-be, it is therefore devoid of foundation and humankind is not always already in possession of it), humans have and feel a debt. Humans, in their potentiality to be and to not-be, are, in other words, always already in debt; they always already have a bad conscience without having to commit any blameworthy act.[288]

Debt places one in a position that is "humankind's most proper being". Instead of Kantian or Levinasian ethics, the ethics Agamben proposes start from the contention that there is nothing to enact or realise about the living being. This is the *ethos* which ethics must adhere to, and it is this which is explored in the next chapter.

Conclusion

This chapter has made several arguments. First, it connected Agamben's critique of transcendent relationality to his goal of positing a philosophy of immanence. Second, it argued that Agamben's interpretations of Levinas (namely that Levinasian ethics are equated with the sphere of judgment, the law and guilt) are necessary ones for him to make. They allow him to generate critical distance between Levinasian transcendent philosophy and ethics and Agamben's own project. This is also why Agamben avoids reference to the law and judgment in his immanent thought – Agamben is trying to avoid his work being reduced to a Levinasian coordinate. Despite this, I have contended that Agamben's critique of Levinas is uncharitable, and the differences between their constructions of the singular being are not as far apart as first thought. The final attempt this chapter made was to introduce Agamben's move away from Kantian ethics and duty.

This leads on to the arguments of the following chapter, which will consider in detail Agamben's immanent life which stands in contrast to transcendent ethics, his form-of-life. It will discuss the messianic influences which underpin this form-of-life, and these will be contrasted to the Biblical influences on Levinas's work. Agamben's messianism is intimately connected to his post-Heideggerian political ontology. This ontology sets out a mode of potential which focuses upon *how* being is. This how is found in a singularity that bears witness to itself in its being. Through an engagement with this how, the next chapter outlines how Agamben seeks to present an ontological and ethical alternative to Levinasian philosophy, but suggest ultimately Agamben does not provide the radical break with Levinas that he seeks.

Notes

1 Agamben (1999a) 220–239.
2 See Agamben (2002) 20–22.
3 Levinas (2008).
4 Agamben (2013a) 89–125.
5 Agamben (1999a) 239.
6 Agamben (1999a) 228–229.
7 Agamben (1999a) 227–228.
8 Agamben (1999a) 220.
9 Agamben (1999a) 220; Deleuze (2001).
10 Agamben (1999a) 220.
11 Foucault (2003b) 177–178.
12 Foucault (2003b) 191, 243.
13 Deleuze (2006) 77; Agamben (1999a) 220.
14 Foucault (1998c) 303.
15 Foucault (1998c) 303.
16 Agamben (1999a) 220. For a detailed and insightful essay on this issue, see Palladino (2013) 207–222.
17 Foucault (1998b) 477.
18 Foucault (1998b) 476.
19 Foucault (1998b) 477.
20 Agamben (1999a) 221.
21 Agamben (1999a) 233.
22 Agamben (1999a) 227.
23 Deleuze and Guattari (1994) 45.
24 Deleuze and Guattari (1994) 46–47.
25 Deleuze and Guattari (1994) 59–60.

26 Agamben (1999a) 228. Agamben (2005d) 25.
27 Agamben (1999a) 233.
28 Agamben (1999a) 233–234.
29 Agamben (1999a) 234.
30 Deleuze (2001) 6.
31 Agamben (1999a) 237.
32 Heidegger (1994) 32.
33 Agamben (1999f) 32.
34 Agamben (1999f) 35.
35 Agamben (2007a) 8–9.
36 Zartaloudis (2010) 250.
37 Agamben (2005c) 52.
38 Derrida (1978) 4.
39 Critchley (1992) 3.
40 Levinas (1998b) 200n.23.
41 Guenther (2006a) 128.
42 Levinas (1969) 215.
43 Levinas (1969).21–22.
44 Levinas (1969) 39.
45 Levinas (2008) 15.
46 Levinas (1969) 245.
47 Levinas (2008) 50, 136–140.
48 Levinas (2008) 55.
49 Levinas (1969).36.
50 Sealey (2010) 366.
51 Levinas (1969) 117.
52 Guenther (2009) 172.
53 Levinas (1969) 134.
54 Levinas (1969).118.
55 Agamben (2007b) 15.
56 Levinas (1969) 120.
57 Levinas (1969) 139.
58 Levinas (1969) 148.
59 Levinas (1969) 69.
60 Levinas (2008) 104.
61 Wall (1999) 31.
62 Sealey (2010) 366.
63 Levinas (1969) 274.
64 Levinas (1969) 52.
65 Levinas (2003b) 69.
66 Levinas (2003b) 53.
67 Levinas (1969) 274.
68 Bernasconi (2005) 110.
69 Levinas (1969) 23.
70 Levinas (2003a) 40.
71 Levinas (2008) 55.
72 Robert Bernasconi has written that Levinas tried to leave transcendence behind in his work, but found it impossible to do so –Bernasconi (2005) 104.
73 Levinas (2003a) 39.
74 Levinas (1969) 3.
75 Wall (1999) 32.
76 Levinas (1987) 91.
77 Levinas (1996d) 23.
78 Levinas (1969) 49.

79 Wall (1999) 32.
80 Guenther (2009) 170.
81 Levinas (2008) 77.
82 Levinas (1969) 73.
83 Levinas (1969) 73.
84 Wall (1999) 37.
85 Levinas (1985) 90.
86 Guenther (2006a) 129.
87 Levinas (2008) 157.
88 Levinas (2008) 159.
89 Stone (2010) 109.
90 Levinas (2008) 157.
91 Stone (2010) 109; Levinas (2008) 157–158.
92 Levinas (1985) 291–292.
93 Agamben (1999a) 228–229.
94 Dickinson (2015b) 21.
95 Agamben (2002) 19.
96 Agamben (2002) 22.
97 Agamben (2002) 18.
98 Agamben (2002) 21.
99 Agamben (2002) 21–22.
100 Agamben (2002) 20–21.
101 Agamben (2002) 22.
102 Agamben (2018c) 13.
103 Agamben (2018a) 13; Romans 7:7–10.
104 Agamben (2002) 18; Agamben (2015a) 53.
105 Agamben (2002) 18–19.
106 Agamben (2009d) 14 (my emphasis).
107 Agamben (2009d) 14-15.
108 Agamben (2017b) 16–18.
109 Agamben (2017c) 2.
110 Agamben (2017c) 3.
111 Agamben (2002) 22.
112 Agamben (2018a) 6.
113 Agamben (2018a) 25.
114 Agamben (2018a) 29.
115 Aristotle (1984d) 1450a35–41.
116 Aristotle (1984e) 1137a5–25.
117 Agamben (2018a) 38–39.
118 Agamben (2018a) 35.
119 Agamben (2018a) 3.
120 Agamben (2012) 40–41.
121 Agamben (2002) 22.
122 Aristotle (1984d) 1450b7.
123 Agamben (2018a) 39.
124 Agamben (2018a) 84.
125 Agamben (2018a) 38.
126 Agamben (2018a) 60.
127 Agamben (2002) 24.
128 Agamben (2002) 20–21.
129 Agamben (2002) 21.
130 Agamben (2002) 24.
131 Levinas (1998a) 124.
132 Guenther (2011) 33.

133 Levinas (2003b) 55.
134 Heidegger (1992) 74–75.
135 Levinas (2003b) 65–66.
136 Levinas (2003b) 65.
137 Critchley (2010) 54.
138 Levinas (2003b) 64–65.
139 Levinas (1978) 58–67; Guenther (2011) 30.
140 Levinas (1989b) 170.
141 Guenther (2011) 23.
142 Levinas (1969) 84.
143 Agamben (2002) 104–105.
144 Agamben (2002) 128.
145 Agamben (2002) 105–106.
146 Agamben (2002) p.106.
147 Guenther (2012) 63.
148 Agamben (2002).128.
149 Agamben (2002) 112.
150 Agamben (2010) 67.
151 Agamben (2010) 64.
152 Agamben (2010) 81.
153 Agamben (2010) 71.
154 Agamben (2010) 69.
155 Agamben (2010) 81.
156 Agamben (2010) 88.
157 Agamben (2010) 65.
158 Agamben (2010).90.
159 Restuccia (2017) 256.
160 Agamben (2002) 107.
161 Guenther (2012) 60–61.
162 Guenther (2012) 61–62.
163 Guenther (2012) 61.
164 Guenther (2012) 62.
165 Guenther (2012) 64.
166 Guenther (2012) 70.
167 Guenther (2012) 71–72.
168 Dickinson (2015a) 68.
169 Levinas (1969) 202.
170 Levinas (1969) 194.
171 Levinas (1969).75.
172 Levinas (1969) 197.
173 Burggraeve (1999) 30.
174 Levinas (1969).76.
175 Burggraeve (1999) 29.
176 Levinas (1969) 75.
177 Agamben (2010) 81.
178 Burggraeve (1999) 29.
179 Levinas (1969) 205.
180 Levinas (1985) 85; cf. Derrida (1991).
181 Levinas (1996a) 7, 9.
182 Levinas (1987) 42.
183 Abbott (2014) 93.
184 Levinas (2008) 180.
185 Abbott (2014) 93.
186 Abbott (2014) 94.

187 Levinas (2008)7 163.
188 Agamben (2000) 91.
189 Agamben (2020e).
190 Agamben (2020g).
191 Agamben (2000) 100.
192 Agamben (2000) 91.
193 Abbott (2014) 92–93.
194 Levinas (1989a) 83.
195 Agamben (2000) 92.
196 Agamben (2007b) 39.
197 Fox (2011) 145–146.
198 Agamben (2000) 96.
199 Agamben (2000) 99.
200 Agamben (2000) 99–100.
201 Levinas (2003a) 40.
202 Levinas (1996c) 90.
203 Levinas (1996c) 80–82.
204 Levinas (1996c) 84.
205 Levinas (1996c) 85–86.
206 Levinas (1996c) 88.
207 Levinas (1996c) 90.
208 Fox (2011) 131.
209 Guenther (2009) 176.
210 Levinas (2003a) 74.
211 Levinas (1996c) 90.
212 Fox (2011) 139.
213 Fox (2011) 140.
214 Agamben (2007b) 103.
215 Fox (2011) 146.
216 Fox (2011) 147.
217 Agamben (2007b).23.
218 Fox (2011) 147.
219 Agamben (2007b) 23.
220 Fox (2011) 147.
221 Fox (2011) 148.
222 Agamben (2007b) 24.
223 Agamben (2007b) 24.
224 Fox (2011) 148.
225 Agamben (2010) 46; see also Agamben (1995) 81–82; Kishik (2020) 295.
226 Agamben (2010) 54.
227 Agamben (2007b) 1; Fox (2011) 148–149.
228 Agamben (2007b) 24.
229 Fox (2011) 149.
230 Guenther (2009) 178; Levinas (2008) 103.
231 Levinas (2008) 106.
232 Levinas (2008) 118.
233 Levinas (2008) 108.
234 Levinas (2008) 104.
235 Levinas (2008) 82.
236 Levinas (2008) 108.
237 Guenther (2009) 169.
238 Levinas (1987) 42.
239 Guenther (2009) 169.
240 Guenther (2009) 182.

241 Guenther (2009) 170.
242 Guenther (2009) 177–178; Levinas (2008) 104, 105.
243 Levinas (2008) 106.
244 Guenther (2009) 181.
245 Agamben (2007b) 15.
246 Agamben (2007b) 86.
247 Agamben (2002) 104.
248 Chiesa (2009) 108.
249 Agamben (2007b) 85.
250 Agamben (1998) 55.
251 See Agamben (2013a) 89–125.
252 Agamben (2013a) 44.
253 Agamben (2013a) xii.
254 Agamben (2013a) 15.
255 Agamben (2009d) 10.
256 Agamben (2013a) 22.
257 Agamben (2013a) 23–25.
258 Agamben (2013a) 25.
259 Agamben (2013a) 28.
260 Agamben (2013a) xi.
261 Agamben (2013a) xiii.
262 Agamben (2013a) 65–66.
263 Agamben (2013a) xiii.
264 Agamben (2013a) xii.
265 Agamben (2013a) xiii.
266 Agamben (2013a) 22. I will return to this term – an animate instrument – in Chapter Five in discussing Agamben's form-of-life.
267 Agamben (2016a) 75.
268 Agamben (2013a) 91.
269 Agamben (2013a) 25.
270 Agamben (2013a) 24–25.
271 There is a clear connection to be made here with Roberto Esposito's treatment of *munus* and his connecting it to immunity and community, but this is outside the scope of this study. See Esposito (2009) and Esposito (2011).
272 Agamben (2013a) 65–66.
273 Agamben (2013a) 71–75.
274 Agamben (2013a) 75.
275 Agamben (2013a) 87.
276 Agamben (2013a) 112.
277 Agamben (2013a) 115.
278 Agamben (2013a) 101–103.
279 Agamben (2013a) 107.
280 Agamben (2013a) 124–126.
281 Agamben (2013a) 111–112.
282 Levinas (2008) 55.
283 Agamben (2018a).31.
284 Agamben (2018a) 44.
285 Agamben (2018a) 49.
286 Agamben (2018a) 60.
287 Agamben (2013a) 129.
288 Agamben (2007b) 43–44.

4 The inoperative potential of a messianic life

Introduction

The chapter turns its attention to a detailed consideration of the nature of Agamben's immanent life, its attempt to eschew transcendent ethics, and its messianism. It is this messianism which also underscores Agamben's attempt to deactivate the *dispositifs* which trap the living being, such as the law. Our starting point is the figure of immanent life itself. This has been given a variety of names by Agamben – being-thus, whatever-being, form-of-life. This form-of-life is presented as an alternative *ethos* to Levinasian ethics. Its qualities and properties are explained and explored before I then turn to perhaps its most important aspect – form-of-life is a being of *potential*, understood in a specific way as a being capable of impotentiality. This potential can render *dispositifs* of control inoperative, opening the world to a new possible use and a coming politics. It is this specific interpretation of potentiality which girds his immanent thought.

In the next section, I turn to what Agamben terms his modal ontology. This is, in my reading, a post-Levinasian ontology (whilst acknowledging the move Levinas's ontology makes from Heidegger's ontological difference). A modal ontology seeks to resolve aporias found in a hypostatic ontology, which sees existence or beings as an outcome of the activity of Being or essence, and in which Agamben traces a negative ground in the thought of Heidegger and Levinas.[1] Agamben's modal ontology does not repeat a scission between existence and essence but focuses on a "mode of potential" rather than an essence;[2] existence is thus conceived as a demand, which does not focus upon what being is but *how* being is.[3]

The how is, in my reading, is an attempt to posit an ontological and ethical alternative to Levinasian ethics.[4] To illustrate this, I use the final part of the chapter to consider Agamben's messianism, based on the Epistles of Paul, which underpins his immanent thought and modal ontology. This messianism involves a transformation of the ways in which we conceive of time, the law and justice, helping us determine how the coming politics can be actualised. Agamben views messianic time as immediate. As a result of this, Agamben devotes attention in his work to criticising Jacques Derrida's messianic without

DOI: 10.4324/9781315191447-5

messianism, stating that it is always to come and this continually defers the messianic, leading to it being thwarted.[5] I detail Agamben's criticisms of Derrida, which have received critical attention, but I mainly focus on the messianism of Levinas. Both Agamben and Levinas seek to bring about an ethical life. Like Agamben, Levinas's messianism disturbs the present time of subjectivity, but is projected into the future. Whilst many of the criticisms Agamben levels at Derrida may be made against Levinas, I contend that the two thinkers' conceptions of the messianic share qualities. Ultimately, this chapter lays the groundwork for understanding what Agamben's immanent life is, allowing me in the next chapter to conduct a detailed investigation into the political possibilities of form-of-life, asking how we can conceive of the how of form-of-life in concrete political terms.

Form-of-life

Agamben has explored his immanent life under a variety of different names: being-thus, whatever-being, form-of-life. This is a life which is not defined through transcendent relationality and it lives on the plane of immanence itself. This figure therefore stands in opposition to the Levinasian subject and its relationship with the Other. The figure of the immanent life is the way in which living beings can come to deactivate the totalising *dispositifs* which create subjects and bare life. But this task does not involve thinking a better or more authentic form of life.[6]

Agamben's thought is anti-strategic, rejecting any attempt to find the locus of radical transformation in the State, the law, or social praxis.[7] This approach is drawn from Michel Foucault. For Foucault, strategising involved the sublimation of the individual to the common good, a programmatic theorisation of resistance, revolt and subjectivity which must be avoided. An "anti-strategic" approach, on the other hand, is:

> [T]o be respectful when a singularity revolts, intransigent as soon as power violates the universal. A simple choice, a difficult job: for one must at the same time look closely, a bit beneath history, at what cleaves it and stirs it, and keep watch, a bit behind politics, over what must unconditionally limit it.[8]

Yet this is no ordinary revolution. Agamben refuses to construct his thought in terms of a traditional political project.[9] Agamben's critics emphasise his shunning of the "dirty work" of revolutionary politics.[10] Sergei Prozorov has grouped criticisms of Agamben's political thought into two categories. The first group critiques Agamben from the position of constituted power, arguing that Agamben is not sufficiently appreciative of the capacity of the institutions of the state, the law, the public sphere, and communicative action, to deal with the problems of sovereignty and biopolitics which he highlights.[11] The second critiques Agamben from the position of constituent power. This group argues that Agamben is not sufficiently appreciative of the capacity of the political subject to depose and dismantle the structures of sovereign biopolitics and replace them with an alternative form of sovereignty, or order, or state.[12] For Alain Badiou, for example, Agamben is a "Franciscan of ontology [who] prefers, to the affirmative becoming of truths, the delicate almost secret persistence of life, what remains to one who no longer has anything".[13]

Agamben has sought to disarm these criticisms. Agamben's community subtracts itself from every determinate aspect of belonging and simply exists with no essence.[14] He has been wary of being identified with many key terms of the Western political tradition, such as:

> [S]overeignty, right, nation, people, democracy and general will [which] refer to a reality that no longer has anything to do with what these concepts used to designate – and those who continue to use these concepts uncritically literally do not know what they are talking about.[15]

Immanent life, a form-of-life, is "a being that is its own bare existence, [a] life that, being its own form, remains inseparable from it".[16] This form-of-life is encountered throughout Agamben's works: the "glorious body" that is nothing but the earthly body divested of its functions and open to a new use,[17] objects of profanation and play,[18] and Franciscan monasticism.[19] All these figures have in common is their subtraction from every particular predicate and their exposure in the bare facticity of their existence or being-thus.[20] Being-thus is "neither this not that, neither thus nor thus, but *thus*, as it is, with all its predicates (all its predicates is not a predicate)", on the plane of immanence itself.[21] Form-of-life lives "the thus", the exhibition of the being itself, rather than a determined aspect. It is a matter of investigating not the articulation that keeps the two terms related but the division that has separated them.[22]

Such a life is one which does not rely upon the *dispositif*, or a transcendent transgression at its limit. In a sense, form-of-life is a *bare life*, but understood as a form of life that affirms in every being its manner of existence, reappropriating human existence from its biopolitical confinement.[23] Agamben states:

> [T]his biopolitical body that is bare life must itself be transformed into the site for the constitution and installation of a form-of-life that is wholly exhausted in bare life and a *bios* that is only its own *zoē*.[24]

What does this mean for the prospect of revolution, or even resistance? One clue can be found in an interview in 1999, where Agamben was asked why, when he clearly identifies the adversaries we must face today, his response is to take flight and evade, rather than to stand up and resist.[25] He answered:

> I think everything depends on what one understands by flight ... The notion of flight does not imply an elsewhere one might go. No, it's a very particular flight: a flight with no elsewhere ... For me, it's a question of thinking a flight which would not imply evasion: a movement on the spot, in the situation itself.[26]

The coming community must be a community of singularities who share nothing more than their singularity, their being-such. Agamben's philosophy refuses the label of universalism.[27] Form-of-life, or whatever-being, is a being freed from the dilemma of the universal and, remaining "constantly hidden in the condition of belonging".[28] This community's politics is one of *radical indifference*. As Agamben explains, form-of-life:

> [H]as no identity, it is not determinate with respect to a concept, but neither is it simply indeterminate; rather it is determined only through its relation to an *idea*, that is, to the totality of its possibilities. Through this relation ...singularity borders all possibility and thus receives its *omnimoda determinatio* not from its participation in a determinate concept of some actual property (being Red, Italian, Communist) but *only by means of this bordering* ... the relation to an empty and indeterminate totality ... Whatever adds to singularity only an emptiness ... Whatever is singularity plus an empty space, a singularity that is *finite* ... Whatever is the event of an outside.[29]

Specifically, this is a call to be radically indifferent towards the *dispositifs* which structure and delimit our existence. Given the breadth of Agamben's formulation of the *dispositif*, this could be an impossible task, given he includes language as one such *dispositif*. Yet Agamben notes that despite the pervasive nature of *dispositifs*, there will remain an "elusive element" which escapes the grasp of *oikonomic* government the more it docilely submits to it. The passage from the worst to the best takes a single step.[30] This elusive element is the heart of immanent life – form-of-life is a being of *potential*. Agamben questions whether such docility can "even threaten the governmental machine", but it is with this docility that hope for the future lies.[31] The key is to "think an *Ungovernable*", which is "the beginning and, at the same time, the vanishing point of every politics".[32]

Immanent potentiality

Form-of-life is a life in which singular modes, acts and processes of living are never simply *facts* but are always *possibilities* of life, and potential. Man is essentially *argōs*, inoperative, which means no work or vocation can define man, and it is not possible to assign a nature or essence to man, nor define his happiness and his politics.[33] Inoperativity cannot be thought of as:

> [I]dleness or inactivity but as a praxis or potentiality of a special kind, which maintains a constitutive relation with its own inoperativity.[34]

Inoperativity does not mean that the individual does nothing, but that the individual has nothing to do.[35] There is no task or purpose to be fulfilled. This inoperativity consists of contemplating one's own potentiality to act:

> [I]t is a matter of … an inoperativity internal to the operation itself, a *sui generis* praxis that, in the work, first and foremost, exposes and contemplates potentiality, a potentiality that does not precede the work, but accompanies it, makes it live, and opens it to possibilities. The life that contemplates its own potentiality to act and not to act becomes inoperative in all its operations, lives only in its livableness.[36]

Agamben's argument concerning potentiality rests on a reading of Aristotle's *Metaphysics*, and his use of *dunamis*. In Book Theta Aristotle states:

> *esti de dunaton touto hōi ean huparxēi hē energeia hou legetai ekhein tēn dunamin, outhen estai adunaton* [A thing is capable of which it is said to have the potentiality].[37]

Dunamis is an ambiguous term in Aristotle. Kevin Attell argues that two senses of the term are relevant for Agamben: possibility and capacity. The former indicates something like pure logical possibility. The second sense indicates that someone can realise a potentiality or capability if external conditions do not prevent the exercise of that potentiality.[38] I can exercise a capacity if nothing prevents me from doing so. While external conditions of possibility may determine whether I can exercise certain capacities, they do not determine the *existence* of these capacities. Agamben's reading of Aristotle argues that potentialities persist even when they are not in act.[39]

Dunamis's counterpart is *adunamia*. This is "potentiality not to" or "impotentiality". Without *adunamia, dunamis* or potentiality would immediately lead to actuality. The two form an indissoluble pair.[40] Kevin Attell has translated a long passage from Agamben's essay "La potenza del pensiero" which explains his defence of potentiality, and which has not otherwise been translated into English:

> [T]he impotentiality of which it is said that in the moment of the act will be nothing cannot be anything but that *adunamia* which, according to Aristotle, belongs to every *dunamis*: the potentiality not to (be or do). The correct translation would thus be "What is potential is that for which, if the act of which it is said to have the potential come about, nothing will be of the potential not to (be or do)" […] But how are we then to understand "nothing will be of the potential not to (be or do)"? How can potentiality neutralise the impotentiality that co-belongs with it? A passage from *De interpretatione* provides us with some precious indications. With regard to the negation of modal statements, Aristotle distinguishes and, at the same time, puts in relation the problems of potentiality and modal enunciations. While the negation of a modal statement must negate the mode and not the *dictum* (thus the negation of "it is possible for it to be" is "it is not possible for it to be" and the negation of "it is possible for it not to be" is "it is not possible for it not to be"), on the plane of potentiality

> things are different and negation and affirmation do not exclude one another. "Since that which is potential is not always in act", writes Aristotle, "even the negation belongs to it: indeed, one who is capable of walking can also not walk, and one who can see can not see" (21b 14–16). Thus, as we have seen, in book *Theta* and in *De Anima*, the negation of potentiality (or better, its privation) always has the form: "can not" (and never "cannot"). "For this reason it seems that the expressions 'it is possible for it to be' follow each other, since the same thing can and can not be. Enunciations of this type are therefore not contradictory. However, 'it is possible for it to be' and 'it is not possible for it to be' never go together" (21b 35–22a2). If we call the status of the negation of potentiality "privation", how should we understand in a privative mode the double negation contained in the phrase: "nothing will be of the potential not to (be or do)"? Insofar as it is not contradictory with respect to the potentiality to be, the potentiality not to be must not simply be annulled, but, turning itself on itself, it must assume the form of a potentiality not to not be. The privative negation of "potentiality not to be" is therefore "potential not to not be" (and not "not potential not to be"). What Aristotle then says is … If a potentiality not to be originally belongs to every potentiality, one is truly capable only if, at the moment of the passage to the act, one neither simply annuls one's own potentiality not to, nor leaves it behind with respect to the act, but lets it pass wholly into it as such, that is, is able not to not pass to the act.[41]

Actuality must be the precipitate of the self-suspension of impotentiality.[42] In becoming actualised impotentiality is exhausted and preserved in actualisation so that potentiality does not have to be sacrificed. An existence *as* potentiality is not the potential to do something but also the potential to *not-do*, the potential not to pass into actuality.[43]

Being-able is an essential having, *hexis*, a way of being of potentiality, constitutive of the living being.[44] To be human is to be consigned to a potential to not be or do.[45] Freedom is not a question of will or status, but it is a way of being in a relation to privation. Man is therefore capable of mastering his potentiality and accessing it only through his impotentiality:

> Only a potentiality that is capable of both potentiality and impotentiality is then a supreme potentiality. If every potentiality is both potentiality to be and potentiality not to be, the passage to the act can only take place by transferring one's own potentiality-not-to in the act.[46]

This potential not to be is capable of being and not being. Being or doing is founded on both the potentiality toward being or doing, and on a modification of the potentiality not to be or do.[47]

Agamben's thought is an affirmation of the possibilities already at work in the present, an injunction to seize them and warning about the dangers of not doing so.[48] Yet the difficulty in identifying how potentiality can be translated into a practical political project is compounded by Agamben pronouncing the negation of potentiality "evil":

> [The] only ethical experience (which, as such, cannot be a task or a subjective decision) is the experience of being (one's own) potentiality, of being (one's own) possibility – exposing, that is, in every form one's own amorphousness and in every act one's own inactuality. The only evil consists instead in the decision to remain in a deficit of existence, to appropriate the power to not-be as a substance and a foundation beyond existence or to regard potentiality itself, which is the most proper mode of human existence, as a fault that must always be repressed.[49]

As Prozorov states:

> One's subtraction from the apparatuses is ethical and one's dwelling within them is evil, yet the … passage from the evil to the ethical ends up extremely problematic, perpetually at the risk of relapsing back into the evil it ventures to leave behind.[50]

Agamben also has recognised the paradox of formulating as a matter of injunction, demand or duty precisely the freedom from any essence, identity or vocation:

> [T]here is in effect something that humans *are and have to be*, but this … is the simple fact of one's own existence as possibility or potentiality. But precisely because of this things get complicated.[51]

It does not make sense to ask whether the subjects of biopolitical societies would prefer to continue dwelling in them. Potentiality is separate from the question of will, as we considered in the last chapter in relation to Kantian ethics.[52] If one's subtraction from the contemporary apparatuses were something which could be *willed*, it would pose a limit to potentiality. Raising the question of why subjects of contemporary societies would *want* to subtract themselves from biopolitical apparatuses would contradict the basic tenor of Agamben's philosophy.[53] Inoperativity seeks to found human actions on their impotentiality:

> [P]otentiality is not will, and impotentiality is not necessity. To believe that will has power over potentiality, that the passage to actuality is the result of a decision that puts an end to the ambiguity of potentiality (which is always potentiality to do and not to do) – this is the perpetual illusion of morality.[54]

Inoperativity consists of contemplating one's own potentiality to act and not to act, a life lived in its own livableness.[55] Agamben states:

> Potentiality (in its double appearance as potentiality and potentiality not to) is that through which Being founds itself sovereignly, which is to say, without anything preceding or determining it … other than its own ability not to be. And an act is sovereign when it realizes itself by simply taking away its own potentiality not to be, letting itself be, giving itself to itself.[56]

Here I wish to draw a parallel between this inoperativity and letting being be and the anthropological machine, which, through the state of exception at the centre of the machine, articulated *zoè* and *bios*, human and animal, man and non-man, displacing the human being and creating bare life.[57] This connection is made because the structure of inoperative potentiality undoes all of the *dispositifs* which capture the living being. As Agamben states:

> [I]noperativity is not another action alongside and in addition to all other actions, not another work beyond all works: It is the space – provisional and at the same time non-temporal, localised and at the same time extra-territorial – that is opened when the apparatuses that link human actions in the connection of means and ends, of imputation and fault, of merit and demerit, are rendered inoperative.[58]

To render the anthropological machine inoperative means halting the machine. What does this look like? Agamben turns to Walter Benjamin who had produced an image in which the anthropological machine is deactivated.[59] Benjamin argued that nature is a world of closedness, and ascribed ideas and works of art to this closed sphere of nature. Works of art are defined:

> [A]s models of nature that awaits no day, and thus no Judgement Day; they are models of a nature that is neither the theatre of history nor the dwelling place of man. The saved night.[60]

The "saved night" is the name given to a nature that has given back to itself.[61] The figure of life in the saved night is "serenely in relation with its own proper nature … as a zone of nonknowledge", neither human nor animal. A zone of nonknowledge – or better of a-knowledge (*ignoscenza*) – means in this sense not simply to let something be, but to leave something outside of being, to render it unsavable.[62] In a passage like those above which talk of letting being be, Agamben concludes:

> To render inoperative the machine that governs our conception of man will therefore mean no longer to seek new – more effective or more authentic – articulations, but rather to show the central emptiness, the hiatus that – within man – separates man and animal, and to risk ourselves in this emptiness: the suspension of the suspension, Shabbat of both animal and man.[63]

One must decide to enter the state of whatever-being, but this decision cannot be a matter of will. It is a meta-decision in favour of potentiality *as such*, in favour of actualising the potentiality *for* potentiality, setting aside the potentiality not to be.[64] It remains up to each of us whether and how to act on this belief.[65]

Modal ontology

Agamben's immanent thought is a *modal* ontology, founding a way of being not grounded in a transcendent relationality. This is also, I argue, a post-Levinasian (and post-Heideggerian) ontology. To understand modal ontology, we first must turn to Agamben's critique of hypostatic ontology. A hypostatic ontology sees existence or beings as an outcome or residue of the activity of Being or essence. It involves the division of Being. This is the origin of every ontological difference; Western philosophy interrogates being with the division that traverses it (namely essence and existence).[66]

The ontological difference in Heidegger was the difference between essence and existence, Being and beings, and it became the crucial problem of philosophy.[67] For Heidegger: "*The essence of Dasein lies in its existence*".[68] Heidegger emphasised that the concept of existence in question is not one of traditional ontology. He spoke, regarding *Dasein*, of a "priority of existence".[69] Heidegger's ontological difference is indicative of his hypostatic ontology.

Hypostasis as a term appears around the second or third century CE in Stoic ontology. It only appears in Aristotle in the originary sense of "sediment" or "remainder",[70] and more completely "to produce a solid remainder", "to reach the solid state, to be given a real consistency".[71] Hypostasis became the key term used to express the concept of existence. The Stoics made use of the term to define the passage from being to existence. Hypostasis was an operation by means of which being is actualised in existence. Being exhausts itself and disappears, leaving in its place the residual pure effectiveness of hypostasis, bare existence as such,[72] the material remainder and sediment of that transcendent process.[73] Being is distinct from existence, but existence is something that being produces and moreover necessarily belongs to it. There is no other foundation of existence than an operation, an emanation, or an effectuation of being.[74] Existence is thus held in a relation with a negative ground. The claim here should be familiar – it is a similar charge that Agamben has made in relation to man's relation to language, law, and the animal, amongst others. It is also why Agamben states:

> Singular existence remains the *experimentum crucis* of philosophy, which it cannot avoid and in which it unceasingly threatens to make shipwreck.[75]

In Neoplatonism existence (a hypostasis) becomes a performance of the essence.[76] This doctrine finds itself reproduced in trinitarian theology, the one God who produces not three realities but three realisations of Himself. The three hypostases refer to one sole substance.[77] Today there is a priority of existence, with a divine substance manifesting itself in an individuated existence through an *oikonomia*. Singular existence must be achieved or effectuated.[78] Yet in the modern era, God is dead, so if we retain this hypostatic ontology (which Agamben claims that we do), all that is left is existence as a residue of something that was never there:

> [O]ntology now becomes a field or forces held in tension between essence and existence, in which the two concepts, whilst theoretically inseparable, tend to pull apart and draw back together according to as rhythm that corresponds to the growing opacity of their relation. The problem of individuation – which is the problem of singular existence –is the place where these tensions reach their greatest point of stretching apart.[79]

In Heidegger's later works, metaphysics is defined by the forgetting of the ontological difference and the priority of beings over Being. It is:

> [T]he thinking that thinks Being as the Being of beings, departing *from beings* and returning *back to them.*[80]

Agamben reads the final phase of the history of metaphysics as being characterised by the retreat from and abandonment by being (leaving an empty and unreachable ground for existence):

> Beings then appear in that way, namely as objects and as things objectively present, as if Being were not … the abandonment of beings by being means that Being conceals itself in the manifestness of beings. And Being itself is essentially determined as this self-withdrawing concealment. … Abandonment by Being: the fact that being is abandoning beings, is leaving them to themselves, and thus is allowing them to become objects of machination.[81]

Beings, abandoned by Being, are something like a Neoplatonic or Gnostic hypostasis that now occupies the stage of the world alone. Heidegger's thought is the unsuccessful attempt to reconstruct a possible unity and, at the same time, to think beyond it.[82]

Both Levinas and Agamben try to open a way to what lies beyond the bounds of a metaphysics inherited from Heidegger.[83] There was a conversation between the two philosophers regarding Heidegger, recounted by Leland de la Durantaye:

> Agamben has recounted on several occasions a conversation he had with Emmanuel Levinas about the teacher they had known at different periods. The image of an 'extraordinarily hard' man that Levinas had retained of Heidegger in 1928 and 1929 was offset by Agamben's recollection of a

> man who, nearly forty years later, singled himself out for what Agamben called the "gentleness" of his demeanor.[84]

Without falling into pop-psychoanalysis I could claim that this is indicative of the two men's approaches to the ontological difference. Whereas Agamben sees Heidegger's work as a failed attempt to find a unity between Being and beings (which is why modal ontology is forwarded), Levinas seeks to ethicise the ontological difference.

Agamben reads Levinas as developing Heideggerian ontology coherently and explicitly in a hypostatic direction. Agamben states:

> In *De l'existance à l'existant,* forcing the concept of Dasein, he defines as a hypostasis the passage from the impersonality of the "there is" (*il y a*) to the emergence of a simple individual existence, which is not yet a subject or a consciousness.[85]

This is not strictly speaking the case. Levinas makes clear that "through taking position in the anonymous *there is* a subject is affirmed".[86] A subject – not simple individual existence. Nevertheless, a being arises on the ground of the *il y a*, the *there is*. This entity exercises a mastery over the fatality of Being, which has become its attribute. In this way Levinas attempts to resolve the ontological difference.[87] At the base of Levinas's hypostases is an effectuation of being, first found through God.

The Hebrew Bible plays a key role in Levinas's thought.[88] In Judaism, God does not create out of nothingness, but extracts light from darkness, and darkness has its being too. The stars separate the *being* of the light from the *being* of the darkness. This is a heritage of a Being that is full. Rather than situating the dark principle as coeval with creation, Levinas reframes it ontologically, with the *there is* as the neutral ground of Being.[89] The thought of the *there is* "consists in promoting a notion of being without nothingness, which leaves no hole and permits no escape".[90] There is no beginning or end to the *there is*, only the monotonous persistence of emptied existence.[91] Agamben makes an esoteric connection to the *there is* when he speaks of the possibility of the world's appearing "as a good that absolutely cannot be appropriated".[92]

Someone exists who assumes Being, which henceforth is *his* being. Though it is there, the *there is* is neutral Being, and consciousness emerges from it like light out of darkness. Consciousness *emerges from itself* by fully waking up, out of insomnia. An existent is a consciousness because consciousness is posited, and through the act of taking a position it comes to being out of itself.[93] The existent's struggle for its existence is a struggle for its very *position* in existence.[94] It is an effort, exerted at the level of the Self, directed toward *beginning*, or toward the obligation to be a self.[95]

Furthermore to experience the *ethical* claim of the other is to undergo an experience of radical responsibility and to be granted *salvation* from the clutches of the *there is*.[96] The early Levinas thinks pure being as an anonymous force that must be evaded for an experience of and relation to alterity to become possible.[97] Likewise Simon Critchley understands the *there is* as a space of alterity.[98] The event of the salvation of the subject by the other is also the event of the subject's realisation of its utter indebtedness to it.[99] To be saved from being is to be responsible for the other; to be responsible for the other is to be saved from being.[100] Levinas's *Da* is a here, not a there, *my* body or my self, a condition of my transcendence and of my suspending the "there" of the "there is".[101] This structure is indicative of Levinas's hypostases, with the distinction being made between existence and the subject or Self. Agamben reads this as a process of subjectification, which leaves behind the subject as a kind of sediment. This ends up repeating the dialectic of grounding by which bare life is separated for political life to be assigned to subjects as a property.[102]

Agamben distinguishes his position from Levinas and Heidegger by claiming that the *zoè/bios* distinction should be thought of as relating to Heidegger's ontological difference.[103] Existence and essence, *zoè* and *bios* have completely collapsed into one another, and the historical task for their articulation seems impossible to carry out.[104] Agamben makes clear in *Homo Sacer*:

> Today *bios* lies in *zoè* exactly as essence, in the Heideggerian definition of *Dasein*, lies (*liegt*) in existence. Schelling expressed the outermost figure of his thought in the idea of a being that is only what is purely existent. Yet how can a *bios* be only its own *zoè*, how can a form of life seize hold of the very *haplos* that constitutes both the task and the enigma of Western metaphysics?[105]

The *haplos* which needs seizing is pure Being, or pure existence as such, not constituted by an unreachable essence:

> In the syntagm 'bare life', 'bare' corresponds to the Greek *haplōs*, the term by which first philosophy defines pure Being. The isolation of the sphere of pure Being, which constitutes the fundamental activity of Western metaphysics, is not without analogies with the isolation of bare life in the realm of Western politics. … the problem is to isolate pure Being (*on haplōs*) from the many readings of the term 'Being' (which, according to Aristotle, 'is said in many ways').[106]

This is the task of modal ontology. This modal ontology is an attempt to found an ethics which is not grounded in negative transcendence. The mode and modal existence define the peculiar status of singular existence.[107] A mode is an affection of the thing which determines its ultimate state and its reason for existing without adding a new essence to it but only modifying it.[108]

This ontology thinks the question of being in terms of a singular existence.[109] Mode expresses not what but *how* being is.[110] The whole problem of the relation between existence and essence appears in a new light if it is placed in the context of a modal ontology. Essence cannot be without the relative nor being without the entity, as the modal relation passes between the entity and its identity with itself, between the singularity and its being-named.[111] Singular existence does not add anything to the common form other than a haecceity or ecceity. In a mode there is not a principle *by virtue* of which it is individuated. One only has only an ultimacy *of* form, the extreme modification that allows one to say: behold the man, or else; this is my body.[112] Existing is not a mode of essence, it is a demand.[113] And living a life as a form is an ethical existence.

Agamben argues that rethinking the categories of modality is not possible without defining the concept of demand.[114] Demand separates existence and essence and corresponds neither to language nor to the world but to their articulation.[115] This articulation is a pure sayability. Being is a pure demand held in tension between language and world. Existence is a demand contained in essence.[116] If existence becomes a demand for possibility, then possibility becomes a demand for existence. Being itself is a demand which neutralises and renders inoperative both essence and existence, potential and act. Being does not pre-exist the modes but constitutes itself in being modified, is nothing other than its modifications. Being is a demand of the modes; the modes are a demand of being.[117]

The modes are the figures in which substance preserves its demand (its *ductus*). In a mode (a certain human face) human nature crosses over into existence in a continuous way and precisely this incessant emergence constitutes its expressivity. Singular existence – the mode – is neither a substance nor a precise fact but an infinite series of modal oscillations but means of which substance always constitutes and expresses itself.[118] Thinking the concept of mode involves conceiving it as a threshold of indifference between ontology and ethics. Agamben explains:

> Just as in ethics character (*ethos*) expresses the irreducible being-thus of an individual, so also in ontology, what is in question in mode is the "as" of being, the mode in which substance is its modifications.[119]

Being demands its modifications; they are its *ethos*: its being irreparably consigned to its own modes of being, to its "thus". The mode (being-thus) in which something is, is a category belonging irreducibly to ontology and to ethics. The claim of modal ontology should be terminologically integrated: a modal ontology is no longer an ontology but an ethics; an ethics of modes is no longer an ethics but an ontology.[120]

The *how*

That Agamben is deaf to Levinas's claim of ethics as first philosophy is apparent whenever his thought encounters it.[121] Adam Thurschwell contends:

> How can one account for such an apparent failure of understanding in a thinker of Agamben's brilliance? It ought to be said in this regard that

> Agamben is hardly alone in being deaf to the philosophical implications of Levinas's discourse on the otherness of the Other. Whatever the characteristics that governs the distinction between those who find Levinas's thought attractive and those who do not, philosophical astuteness does not seem to be it.[122]

If, as Levinas would have it, philosophy is indelibly tainted by its Other, then traces of this Other ought to be found wherever philosophy makes its claims. One can detect in Agamben traces of the ostensible Other in the form of a Levinasian ethics of responsibility.[123]

Such a trace can be found in the how of mode, standing as it does in opposition to Levinas's hypostatic ontology. The mode of existence of form-of-life is the how. It is a singularity bearing witness to itself in its being.[124] Form-of-life is generated by the very act of living.[125] Living, or being, for own's one *zoè* means rendering inoperative the bipolar *zoè/bios* apparatus, "so form-of-life appears as the *tertium* thinkable only starting from this inoperativity, the coinciding of *bios* and *zoè*".[126] This form-of-life is a monad. The relationship between monad and monad is complex. The more form-of-life becomes monadic, the more it isolates itself from other monads (in a non-relation). However, each monad always already communicates with the others, by representing them in itself, "as in a living mirror".[127] Every body is affected by its form-of-life as by a *clinamen*. The ethical subject is that subject which constitutes-itself in contact (the moment in which two entities are united only by an absence of representation) to this clinamen, and focuses on *how* it lives its life.[128]

Contact is a reference point for Levinas. We encounter the Other through the command, and the subject endures a latent birth from this encounter which carries with it the burden of responsibility. Levinas's subject is in contact in its exposure to the other.[129] The subject comes to himself in his proximity to the other, and this contact between the subject and the other is unavoidable. One can detect the trace of Levinas's contact with the other in Agamben's monad which communicates with others by representing them in themselves as in a living mirror.

This clinamen presupposes a capacity for being, and a capacity for realising this how. To live life as a form, as pure means, indicates that one *must* actively act to bring about this condition, it is not something that can be passively accepted. This means that the ethical subject must constitute itself. I can support this claim through reference to "tastes". A form-of-life is the most idiosyncratic aspect of everyone; their tastes, which safeguards its secret in the most impenetrable and insignificant way:

> If every body is affected by its form-of-life as by a clinamen or a taste, the ethical subject is that subject that constitutes-itself in relation to this clinamen, the subject who bears witness to its tastes, takes responsibility for the mode in which it is affected by its inclinations. Modal ontology, the ontology of the *how*, coincides with an ethics.[130]

This is not to take the notion of tastes too literally. Taste is another form of knowledge.[131] Tastes – "the fact [individuals] like coffee granita, the sea at summertime, this certain shape of lips, this certain smell" – are ontological in character. Agamben continues:

> It is not a matter of attributes or properties of a subject who judges but of the mode in which each person, in losing himself as subject, constitutes himself as form-of-life.[132]

This is a clear indication that form-of-life applies to an already existing being *with the capacity for living ethically.* This is supported by Agamben claiming that form-of-life is its own mode of being which is continually generated by its manner of being.[133] In this sense, the community to come will be akin to a life grasped by the living beings and lived through its mode or manner of being.[134] These relations between forms-of-life are non-relational, and for my argument, operate as a trace of the other.

Compassion is a key aspect of an existential, pre-reflexive human ethical vocation for infinite ethical responsibility towards the other-*as*-other.[135] Levinas speaks of an existential drama that involves ethically demanded anarchic compassion *and* infinite personal responsibility for directing this compassion to some but not others. The Levinasian idea of compassion as persecution maintains the asymmetry and distance constitutive of the non-totalising relation to the other. Agamben would say that the drama of anarchic compassion and infinite responsibility has been appropriated by impersonal, anomic, *oikonomic* management.[136] Levinas's appeal to a universal ethics of anarchic compassion refers to a fundamental, pre-political, anarchic, ethical right to show compassion on the understanding that, without such ethical proximity, there could be no politics or law.

Considering Agamben's genealogy of Christian government, the said ethical right appears compromised, since law and politics are substituted by biopolitical processes of social control and management of populations that include the manipulation of compassion.[137] In biopolitical settings the remembering and forgetting of compassion occurs incessantly, their controversy kept alive, *so as* to provide us with the widest imaginable margin of freedom *to manage* human populations.[138] Agamben's own non-relational form-of-life (which has rendered relations non-relational) should be understood as exhibiting its own negative relation to its other, which can be placed in contrast to Levinas's more positive view of relationality.[139]

Messianism in Agamben, Derrida, Levinas

Agamben's red secret

Messianism is closely related to the law.[140] In Judaism, as well as in Early Christianity and Shi'ite contexts, the messianic event marks a "radical transformation" of the religious legal order.[141] The Messiah's arrival brings about the fulfilment, deactivation and inoperativity of the law – the law is fulfilled and gains another use.[142] For our purposes it is important to bear in mind that the Messiah is "the figure through which religion confronts the problem of the Law, decisively reckoning with it".[143] Dealing with the law is *already* dealing with philosophy, as "philosophy is always already constitutively related to the law, and every philosophical work is always, quite literally, a *decision* on this relationship".[144]

It was Ernst Bloch who stated that "messianism is the red secret of every revolutionary".[145] What underpins Agamben's inoperative, potential form-of-life is this red secret. It is messianism which opens a space for human action called politics, which corresponds to the essential inoperability of humankind. This politics is an action of "pure means", without any connection to an end, and an exposition of humankind's creative semi-indifference to any task.[146] Agamben's messianic fulfilment should be understood as properly *profane*. What is profaned returns to common use the spaces that power had seized, opening a space for new forms of political intervention.[147] The messianic presents itself as another world that demands to exist in this world.[148] Agamben relies on a passage written by Bloch relating to the messianic kingdom in Hassidic Judaism to explain that the messianic kingdom is very similar to the current world, and requires only a slight shift in thinking:

> The Hassidim tell a story about the world to come that says everything there will be just as it is here. Just as our room is now, so it will be in the world to come; where our baby sleeps now, there too it will sleep in the other world. And the clothes we wear in this world, those too we will wear there. Everything will be as it is now, just a little different.[149]

The tiny displacement of the world is a small difference,[150] but it is "in every way, a decisive one".[151] Messianism does not provide a seismic revolution, but a subtle one. It is through exploring the writings of St Paul that the boundaries of this modest difference can be explored.

The readings of Paul by contemporary philosophers are made within the context of their own postmodern questionings. But, as Tom Wright cautions, they seem little concerned with exegesis.[152] Agamben's analysis is best understood as using the first few verses of the Letter to the Romans as a jumping-off point for wider reflections.[153] I read Agamben's study not as exegesis but as an eisegesis – putting a fresh meaning on a text the author (Paul) did not intend. Walter Benjamin wrote that to get at the truth of a work required "the most precise immersion into the individual details of a given subject".[154] But if one does not pay constant attention to the one being retrieved, the Paul being invoked is not a Paul of historical study.[155] Agamben's Paul is more a Paul of cultural memory, for whom faith is the existence of the things we hope for, trying to bring about a world which does not yet exist and which presents itself as a demand or beatitude – the kingdom of heaven is *here* and *now* for those who are farthest from it.[156] Agamben is ultimately preaching – soaking himself in the Pauline texts on the one hand and offering his own critical contemporary reflection on the other, providing a fresh fusion of ideas.[157] Agamben uses Paul to construct a messianic form-of-life. Man is the living being that has been expelled from his own dwelling place, and messianism can help man find his place again.[158]

Messianic time

Agamben focuses on Paul's stress on living in a new kind of time, messianic time, a time of the now, which transforms both time and the life of the faithful.[159] Ultimately, for Paul the truly messianic event was the death and resurrection of Jesus of Nazareth, and all time since the resurrection of Jesus would be messianic time.[160] The early Christian communities expected the imminent arrival of the messiah, but there was an unexpected delay in the Second Coming of Jesus. In response to this the Church's institutional and juridical organisation was stabilised. For Agamben this means that the Church has lost the messianic experience of time that defines it.[161] In the Judaic tradition there is a distinction between two times and two worlds: the *olam hazzeh*, the time stretching from the creation of the world to its end, and the *olam habba*, the time that begins after the end of time.[162] Messianic time is the time between these two times, a time divided by the messianic event. To live the time that remains means a radical transformation of our experience of time.[163] It is a space that escapes the grasp of power and its laws.[164] To experience this messianic time implies an integral transformation of ourselves and of our ways of living.[165]

Messianic time is about immediacy. It is about grasping the potentialities of our current situation, the now.[166] This is a time when one is to live as not, *hōs mē*. This *hōs mē* is a crucial referent for Agamben's messianic thought. It does not involve living as if the redemption was at hand, but as not, since:

> The coming of the Messiah means that all things, even the subjects who contemplate it, are caught up in the *as not*, called and revoked at one and the same time.[167]

The *hōs mē*, the as not, is the ultimate meaning of the messianic vocation, the revocation of every vocation, at once voiding and transforming every vocation and tradition so as to free them for a new usage.[168] In explaining the nature of messianic time, Agamben states that:

> [E]ach time the prophets announce the coming of the Messiah, the message is always about a time to come, a time not yet present. This is what marks the difference between the prophet and the apostle. The apostle speaks forth from the arrival of the Messiah. At this point prophecy must keep silent, for now prophecy is truly fulfilled ... The word passes on to the apostle, to the emissary of the Messiah, whose time is no longer the future, but the present. This is why Paul's technical term for the messianic event is *ho nun kairos*, "the time of the now"; this is why Paul is an apostle and not a prophet.[169]

Paul's present time, *kairos*, is not a time yet to come. It is also distinguished from *chronos,* chronological time as usually understood. Ephesians 1:10 offers a summary of this *kairos*, focusing as it does on Paul's notion of recapitulation:

> Having just laid out the divine project of messianic redemption, Paul writes, 'as for the economy of the *pleroma* of times, all things are recapitulated in him, things in heaven and things on earth'.[170]

Agamben picks up the notion of the fulfilment of time and stresses the coming together of the *temporal*:

> Insofar as messianic time toward the fulfillment of time … it effects a recapitulation, a kind of summation of all things … of all that has transpired from creation to the messianic 'now', meaning of the past as a whole. Messianic time is a summary recapitulation of the past …[171]

Messianic time is not concerned with the future but is already here.[172] Agamben then borrows Paul's idea of the remnant, which he holds stands for a people who embody resistance to the prevailing systems.[173] This being said, in Romans 9, the remnant has been understood as a single point, the Messiah himself, who would be cast away so that the world might be redeemed.[174] Nevertheless, Agamben redefines the remnant, stating that messianic time is "a remnant, the time that remains between these two times, when the division of time is itself divided".[175] Agamben articulates this time as a moment to be taken hold of, to be bought up or redeemed, to be seized:

> Messianic time is *the time that time takes to come to an end*, or, more precisely, the time we take to bring to an end, to achieve our representation of time. This is not the line of chronological time (which was representable but unthinkable), nor the instant of its end (which was just as unthinkable); nor is it a segment cut from chronological time; rather it is operational time pressing within the chronological time, working and transforming it from within; it is the time we need to make time end: *the time that is left us*.[176]

Just as Paul expounded the messianic time of the gospel, so in the present day Agamben seeks to discern a sabbatical moment.[177] Messianic time renders the works of the law fulfilled and inoperative: not non-existent but suspended from within the law itself and powerless.[178]

The Derridean messianic to come

The structure of the messianic is temporal. Agamben focuses on a messianic now, whereas Derrida insists on the messianic to come. As Martin Hägglund explains, "more than any other term in Derrida's vocabulary, the messianic has invited the misconception that Derrida harbors a religious hope for salvation".[179] This is why Agamben describes Paul as an apostle, rather than a prophet. Every time the prophets announce the coming of the Messiah, the message is about a time to come, a time not yet present.[180] For Paul, the messianic event in the resurrection had already happened and his role was to negotiate the interstitial time *between* the messianic event and the future end.[181] This is why Agamben argues that "the widespread view of messianic time as oriented solely toward the future is fallacious".[182]

Agamben's charge against Derrida is that he, or rather deconstruction, is the false Messiah. Derrida's political messianic without messianism does not bring an end to law, the state, or (political) history, but comprises a structural openness inscribed in every historical moment of the traditions that open onto what is beyond that tradition and constitutes an ever-available opportunity for the tradition's radical revision, whether in the form of new interpretations or new actions of a more material kind that transform the tradition's institutions, practices and so on.[183]

To provide a (very brief) summary – deconstruction is justice, and justice is transcendent:

> Justice in itself, if such a thing exists, outside or beyond law, is not deconstructible. No more than deconstruction itself, if such a thing exists. Deconstruction is justice.[184]

Deconstruction takes place in the interval that separates the undeconstructibility of justice from the deconstructibility of *droit* (authority, legitimacy, and so on).[185] In so taking place, deconstruction exposes the violence, the force, the *Gewalt* that masquerades itself within the law with reference to sacral origins.

Justice for Derrida is a non-juridical formula, constantly compromised by its very legal form and the fact that it cannot be found other than through the law.[186] Justice cannot be reduced to any general rule as it is infinite and incalculable, and always escapes any chance to contain it to anything other than a unique singularity that is held in relation to the individual Other.[187] Justice is always to come for Derrida, a fact that underlines the very practical and political nature of deconstruction.[188] The Other as a unique individual will always remain elusive as the Other will always-already escape the grasp of any representation made to capture it. Deconstruction assumes that the level of representation is irreducible.[189] Any representation will always-already be a generalisation.[190] General rules cannot do justice to the real world of particular entities. This reflects Derrida's objection to representational philosophy in that concepts and theoretical constructions do violence to things. Respect for the Other is the means of escaping this violence, especially as regards human beings.[191]

In *Specters of Marx* Derrida sought to outline a messianic thought that would assume the structure of messianic thought, but it would be "a messianism without religion".[192] Derrida described it as follows:

> The effectivity or actuality of the democratic promise, like that of the communist promise, will always keep within it, and it must do so, this absolutely undetermined messianic hope at its heart, this eschatological relation to the to-come of an event *and* of a singularity, of an alterity that cannot be anticipated.[193]

Specters of Marx is organised around a reading of Marx and of *Hamlet*. Derrida chooses Hamlet's assertion that "the time is out of joint" as the epigraph to the book. Even after time, "the time is out of joint".[194] The spacing that opens and breaches that joint is the same futurity and promissory structure of *différance* (the difference and deferral of meaning) that here bears that nickname "the messianic".[195] For Hägglund:

> Derrida can thus be seen to invert the logic of religious eschatology. Instead of promoting the end of time, Derrida emphasises that the coming of time exceeds any given end.[196]

Derrida identifies and affirms a breach in the supposed closure and completion of the Hegelo-Marxist dialectic and the end of history.[197] Kojève makes certain prescriptive utterances about what posthistorical man must continue to do. The prescription and futurity of this must do constitutes a disjointedness in Kojève's supposedly posthistorical condition. There is some future and some history.[198] The historical dialectic, even after it has supposedly come to rest, has a temporal fissure. The messianic *is* that fissure.[199] To put it another way:

> [T]here is necessarily … some historicity as future-to-come. It is what we are nicknaming the messianic without messianism.[200]

Agamben does not suggest that Derrida promotes the end of time; he argues that deconstruction places an injunction on conceiving time differently, and thus bars the arrival or experience of what he calls, in contradistinction to the deconstructive messianic, messianic time.[201] For Derrida, we are always too late to experience the now; Derrida reads the Western tradition's concept of time as absolutely valorising the present.[202] Derrida states:

> [T]he privilege of the present has never been put into question. It could not have been. It is what is self-evident itself, and no thought seems possible outside its element. Nonpresence is always thought in the form of presence … or as a modalization of presence. The past and the future are always determined as past presents or as future presents.[203]

The now is "the form from which time cannot ever depart".[204] Because the now is what eludes presence, Kevin Attell argues that Aristotle's conception of time as nonbeing is the necessary consequence of his having defined it as constructed as an infinite series of nows. The fleeting *present instant* is what can never actually *be* present and always experienced as nonbeing.[205] Time is composed of infinitely self-negating moments and outside the realm of beings, it "belongs to nonbeings". There is nothing there to be experienced in the first place. Herein lies the originary paradox within the Western reflection on time, out of which Derrida derives the messianic futurity of the *à-venir*.[206] Derrida's philosophy "issues an identification of an *existing* crack or rupture in the edifice in question … a flaw that represents, one might say, not a messianic future task so much as an opportunity for thought and for politics in the here-and-now".[207]

The law and the katechon

Paul produced a critique of Judaism from within his Jewish context.[208] Keeping the law within Judaism always functioned within a covenantal scheme. The Jew keeps the law out of gratitude, as the proper response to grace – to stay in the covenant.[209] Paul understood the scriptures as a story in search of an ending that he would himself bring about.[210] The resurrection had shown that Jesus the Messiah was descended from the seed of David according to the flesh, and marked out as the Son of God by the Spirit of holiness through the resurrection of the dead.[211] Jesus's death was the covenant-fulfilling act, the moment when God executed judicial sentence on sin itself,[212] the moment when God's love was unveiled in all its glory.[213] The reign of sin and death is replaced with the reign of grace and righteousness.[214]

For Tom Wright, Paul showed the way for contemporary protests against the whole construct of an immanent or positivistic law as discussed by Carl Schmitt and others, in which the removal of any concept of divine right has meant "a secularisation of theological authorising of absolute rule".[215] He explains:

> Getting rid of the divine legitimation from above … has not resulted in a lasting atheism, but in the implicit theism-from-below of *vox populi, vox Dei*. 'The law' has become a way of speaking about the civil society of the western world, sustained as it were from below through the modern democratic process, in which capitalism and bourgeois values are held in place by one another under a veneer of self-congratulatory, post-Enlightenment rhetoric: *we* have discovered at last how to run the world, by voting every few years and by dropping bombs on faraway people who do things differently! In other words, because *we*, the Enlightened western world, have developed a kind of Social Darwinism into the fullest expression of a political system justified 'from below', we are in a position to justify our actions even where they constitute an apparent exception to rules that might normally apply.[216]

Wright makes the point that it will simply not do to say that Paul would have nothing to do with matters of *Realpolitik* because he writes about the gospel of Jesus. Paul's gospel was designed to transform every aspect of human existence, inner and outer, solitary and corporate, the personal, social, cultural and political included.[217]

Agamben's thought follows this *Realpolitik* and also places a gloss on the position of the law in the Epistles. Messianism suspends and renders inoperative the existing law, placing it into a non-relation with the individual. This then leads to the rendering inoperative of *dispositifs* which are currently restraining the coming politics. This is why Agamben states that "Deconstruction is a thwarted messianism, a suspension of the messianic".[218] What is crucial here is to understand the specific historicity of Paul's life. The messianic event was not in the future but had already happened. Derrida's messianic event to come can instead be characterised as an infinite deferral. Derridean deconstruction is a "petrified or paralysed messianism" that "nullifies the law, but then maintains it as the Nothing of Revelation in a perpetual and interminable state of exception, 'the "state of exception" in which we live'".[219] For Agamben, there is no point to a Derridean deconstructive subversion of sovereignty in the name of the undeconstructible justice and democracy to come, which serves only to highlight the undecidability at the heart of the law, which is essential to the latter's existence.[220] Derrida's legal thought is not messianic, as it endlessly "negotiat[ing] with the law";[221] when the Messiah is meant to "cut the Gordian knot" of the law and neutralises it.[222]

It is with this background that we can approach Agamben's interpretation of the *katechon*. Agamben turns to a reading of Paul's Second Letter to the Thessalonians, where Paul responds to the audience's concern regarding the imminence of the Second Coming and explains how it will take place:

> Let no one deceive you in any way. Because it will not be unless the apostasy shall have come first, and the man of lawlessness, the son of destruction, is revealed. He opposes and exalts himself above every so-called god and object of worship. As a result, he seats himself in the sanctuary of God and declares himself to be God. Don't you remember that I repeatedly told you about these things when I was still with you? You know what it is that is now holding him back [*ho katechon*], so that he will be revealed when his time comes. For the mystery of anomy (*anomia*) is already at work, but only until the person now holding him back [*ho katechon*] is removed. Then the lawless one [*anomos*] will be revealed, whom the Lord will abolish with the breath of his mouth, rendering him inoperative by the manifestation of his presence [*Parousia*]. The presence [*Parousia*] of the former is according to the working of Satan in every power [*dynamis*].[223]

This passage has garnered a lot of attention from scholars. The mystery of anomie or lawlessness is a *mysterium iniquitatis*, and, for Agamben, to grasp the meaning of this is to understand how Paul conceived of messianic time and the nature of the coming politics.[224] Paul never identified the *katechon*, or the one which restrains. But to give it its orthodox interpretation, the target of Paul's ire (the figure of the *katechon*) in 2 Thessalonians 2 is the Roman Empire:

> The second letter to the Thessalonians has long been regarded with suspicion, not least (we may suppose) because the vision of Paul which inspired an earlier generation of liberal or existentialist theologians did not include apocalyptic or imperial elements. But actually 2:1–12 is best read as a classic piece of counter-imperial rhetoric, not least for one who had fresh memories of the attempt of the emperor Gaius to erect a huge statue of himself in the Temple in Jerusalem, demanding that the Jews worship it. However we understand the rest of this difficult passage, there should be no doubt about its principal polemical target.[225]

The Emperor Gaius Caesar Augustus Germanicus, to provide his full name, is commonly known by his boyhood nickname, Caligula, and he attempted to build his statue in around 40CE. Agamben contrarily claims (a necessary claim for his argument as we will see), that as the term *katechon* does not appear elsewhere in the Scriptures, the interpretation of this passage remains ambiguous.

The *katechon*'s nature and relation has been connected to the Antichrist, whose revelation and elimination paves the way for the divine *Parousia.*[226] In Carl Schmitt's reading of 2 Thessalonians 2, the *katechon*'s function has been fulfilled by sovereign power, starting from the Roman Empire, and leading to Rome-centred Christianity. For Schmitt, the *katechon* is the worldly that delays the advent of the Antichrist.[227] Yet the Antichrist's arrival is what presages the arrival of the Messiah and the messianic redemption. As a result, the *katechon* is incompatible with messianism. For Agamben, the belief in the *katechon* characterises:

> [E]very theory of the state … which thinks of it as a power destined to block or delay catastrophe – [and also] can be taken as a secularisation of this interpretation of 2 Thessalonians 2.[228]

The messiah inaugurates a zone of lawlessness that coincides with messianic time and frees the *anomos*, the outlaw. Agamben has made clear that the *katechon* refers to any constituted authority (including the Church today, and the law, all acting as *dispositifs*),[229] whose function is to restrain social anomie while simultaneously withholding a radical redemption from it:

> [T]he katechon is the force – the Roman Empire as well as every constituted authority – that clashes with and hides … the state of tendential lawlessness that characterises the messianic, and in this sense delays unveiling the "mystery of lawlessness".[230]

This includes deconstruction. Agamben makes an explicit connection between Derrida's deferred messianism, *différance*, and the *katechon*:

> The *katekhōn*, suspending and holding back the end, inaugurates a time in which nothing can truly happen [*avvenire*], because the sense [*senso*, also "direction"] of historical becoming, which has its truth only in the *eskhaton*, is now indefinitely deferred. What happens [*avvenire*] in the suspended time of the *katekhōn* is, in this sense, an undecidable, which happens, so to speak, without truly happening because its coming [*avvenire*], the *eskhaton* that alone could give it sense [*senso*], is ceaselessly deferred and adjourned. Schmitt's katekhontic time is a thwarted messianism: but this thwarted messianism shows itself to be the theological paradigm of the time in which we live, the structure of which is none other than Derridean *différance*. Christian eschatology has introduced a sense and a direction in time: *katekhōn* and *différance*, suspending and delaying this sense, render it undeciable.[231]

To put it in Kevin Attell's words:

> The thwarted messianic may indeed see the irreducible displacement and futurity of the punctual instant on the timeline, but the true messianic also gazes "backward" upon the kairological "now" that is always already happening in the production of *khronos*. This incorporation of *Kairos*/operational time into our *experimentum temporis* is the messianic operation itself. Without this "apostolic" point of view, we are left with the "homogenous, infinite, quantified time" … of *khronos*, and messianism is thwarted.[232]

Only when the *katechon* is removed (through messianic deactivation) will "the life that begins on earth after the last day [be] simply human life".[233]

The messianic law and justice

There are correspondences between the main features of the exception and Paul's account of the deactivated law. In the suspension of the law, everything is the same, albeit a little different. Thus, given the suspension of the law, one does not know how to execute the law (which is also an issue in the exception).[234] The link between the messianic vocation and the state of exception has been described as follows:

> The messianic vocation is a not a right, nor does it furnish an identity; rather, it is a generic potentiality [*potenza*] that can be used without ever being owned. To be messianic, to live in the Messiah, signifies the expropriation of each and every juridical-factical property (circumcised/uncircumcised; free/slave; man/woman) under the form of the *as not*. This expropriation does not, however, found a new identity.[235]

Expropriation means a different way of experiencing properties by means of the filter of the *hōs mē*.[236] The state of exception and the messianic *hōs mē* both deactivate the normal juridical situation: the law is suspended and not executed.[237] Messianic life is revolutionary because it gives up any attempt to destroy the established order of social and political relationships. It maintains them and deactivates them by means of the *hōs mē*.[238] This can be illustrated through the fact that the fulfilment of the law does not produce a new identity for the subject.[239]

Agamben does not read Paul as offering a truth for all. Given Agamben's eschewing of universalism, it may be no surprise that he rejects Badiou's designation of Pauline messianism as universalist.[240] Instead, on his reading, Paul affirms the non-coincidence of all with themselves, whereby the particularistic division into Jews and Greeks, men and women etc., is divided once more according to a new criterion, the distinction between "flesh" (apparent, superficial belonging valid only in the eyes of the law) and "breath" (genuine belonging on the basis of fidelity).[241] The division between those who were inside the law (the Jews) and those who are outside of the law (non-Jews) (which is the fundamental division of the Jewish law) does not hold.[242] We end up with the figure of the remnant. The remnant is not any kind of numerical portion or substantial positive residue. It consists in cutting the polarised Jew/non-Jew partition,[243] a non-non-Jew who is not under the positive law of the community but the law of the Messiah.[244]

In Romans 2 Paul sets up a running contrast between two categories of people. The first consists of Jews who do not keep the law.[245] The second is the gentile Christian who keeps or fulfils the law. Agamben's description of the non-non-Jew applies to a paradoxical category of persons: gentiles who, despite remaining uncircumcised, seem to have a highly positive relation to the Jewish law.[246] Paul does not mean that these gentiles have now become law-observant.[247] Those who are members of the new covenant fulfil the law.[248] The new members have not been, and do not need to be, circumcised. As a matter of logic, uncircumcised gentile Christians do "keep the statutes of the law". The fulfilment is one of status; the Gentiles must be fulfilling the law by their very existence. What is more, Paul nowhere works out in detail what keeping the law involves. He refers to Christians as "law keepers" because, as he says Roman 8:3, that which the law intended but could not do has been brought to fulfilment in them.[249]

What of this fulfilled law? Agamben refers to Paul's use of the verb *katargeō*, which he identifies as etymologically connected to *argōs*, inoperativity.[250] The law, which had been in existence to bring about the Messiah's coming, is transformed to a new use in the messianic kingdom. The messianic *katargēsis* simultaneously suspends and fulfils the law, meaning that the negative relation that the law has to life is severed. The law is no longer negatively related to life.[251] Whereas bare life, *bios* and *zoē* are forms of life lived through the law, messianic *katargēsis* enables form-of-life to define its own way of living, to other itself:

> [There] is often nothing reprehensible about the individual behaviour in itself, and it can, indeed, express a liberatory intent. What is disgraceful –

> both politically and morally – are the apparatuses which have diverted it from their possible use. We must always wrest from the apparatuses – from all apparatuses – the possibility of use that they have captured.[252]

We read in Agamben that the messianic fulfilment of the law is justice itself. Justice without law is the law's fulfilment, and not a juridical notion (in a nod to his criticism of Levinas, responsibility and the law).[253] Messianic time is an unsovereign mode of temporality in which sovereign juridical conditions are transformed so that justice performs without the law, yet without abolishing it.[254] Sketching out these ideas of justice can help us understand the contours of form-of-life. Agamben sees justice as "the handing on of the Forgotten".[255] Here, the "Forgotten" are embodied in the figure of those souls in Purgatory, or limbo. This connection is deliberate on Agamben's part; God's forgetfulness, the greatest punishment that a creature can meet with, is not a punishment in Purgatory, nor is it an affliction. As those souls only have natural knowledge and not supernatural knowledge, they do not know that God has forgotten them, and so the greatest punishment becomes "a natural felicity".[256] Just like form-of-life, the souls in Purgatory as *argōs*, without tasks or work, or ends. If we see the remnant as a cipher of the deactivation of law, and in turn, if we see the deactivation or fulfilment of law as justice, then the figure of form-of-life is the cipher of justice. The experience of justice can then only be experienced by whatever-being as a vocation, as a way of being.[257] From this discussion of justice, Catherine Mills notes two key features. First, justice is not opposed to the law, but is found *within* the messianic law. It is only because justice is found within the law that the law can contribute towards the attaining of justice. In Agamben's terms, the law is not justice, but the gate that leads to it.[258] Justice is a condition of possibility of the law, brought into realisation through its deactivation. Second, justice requires the transmission of the Forgotten.[259] That implies that justice, as an experience, occurs in the very handing on of form-of-life. Relationality exists even in Purgatory, as the Forgotten are held in a (non) relation to God. They are not negatively defined through being held in relation to a transcendent referent – God. Instead, they remain in relation to God, but are not defined through that relation. Likewise, the law, in its deactivation, maintains a relation between subjects in the form of a nonrelation.

Messianism and the trace in Levinas

In considering Levinas's own writings on messianism, I endeavour to draw connections to Agamben's own work. Like Agamben, Levinasian messianism centres on the subject. Central to my analysis here is that Levinas proposes a "messianism of the trace", marking the messianic to come. This ethical experience is one in which the infinite, in the form of a trace, withdraws from presence to signify the interruption of one realm by another.[260] This meaning poses the trace as a noninterface between distinct orders of transcendence and immanence, remaining compatible with a traditional sense of religion (or, as I posit, God).[261] Levinas elaborates the paradoxes by which an ethical command, that as a trace both arrives and withdraws, disrupts the time and the self-presence of its addressee. He writes:

> [T]his trace does not belong to the assembling of essence. … It is the trace of a relationship with *illeity* that no unity of apperception grasps, ordering me to responsibility. This relationship is religion, exceeding the psychology of faith and of the loss of faith.[262]

The mention of *illeity* shows that religion is honorific and structural, as *illeity* names the nonevent by which the infinite approaches me by withdrawing so that I may turn to the other and to the others. Agamben notes the importance of this term for Levinas's thought, but notes it merely founds another negative ground:

> Lévinas's critique of ontology … really only brings to light the *fundamental* negative structure of metaphysics, attempting to think the immemorial having-been beyond all being and presence, the *ille* that is before every *I* and every *this*, the *saying* that is beyond every *said*.[263]

The face is always a trace of an absolute absence, of *illeity*. The face "proceeds from the absolutely Absent" but its relationship "*does not indicate, does not reveal,* this *Absent*; and yet the *Absent* has a meaning in the face".[264] The face in which "the manifestation of the height in which God is revealed",[265] promises the subject his infinite messianic sensibility vocation.[266] The face does not point beyond itself to something transcendent or absolute that it signifies. For the face to have the force it does, there must be a beyond or an absolute ground – either face must be a ground, or each must point itself to a ground. The beyond from which the face comes signifies as a trace. The face is not a thing or an appearance of a thing, and the Absent is not an entity. The beyond is *illeity*.[267]

Illeity signifies a retreat from and abandonment by being leaving an empty and unreachable ground for existence. *Illeity* holds the same position as the *there is* – a presupposition of pure being. If pure being is presupposed, it can only be presupposed as a negativity. Pure being, once it has been set up as that which must be transcended or escaped for the ethical experience of the other to become possible, has a tendency to return where we least expect: on the face of the other who was supposed to represent my salvation from it.[268]

In this sense, following Agamben's critique, the negative hypostases cannot be escaped. *Illeity* is the otherness of the other that is present in that other as a trace. It is a relationship that bears on responsibility and obligation. The other person's otherness is constitutive of ethical force. The trace disturbs the order of the world. Levinas calls *illeity* divinity, and he quotes Plotinus's account of the One (a Neoplatonist account) when he says that "the trace of the One gives birth to essence, and being is only the trace of the One".[269] *Illeity* or divinity is in the face of the other person as a trace of what is never present: "The Infinite passes in saying".[270] For Levinas, the face-to-face is the way God is present or effective in human existence. The trace underscores a hypostatic ontology where all that is left is existence as a residue of something that was not there (God or the trace).

Levinas's messianism and the responsibility of the Self

Despite this there is a proximity between Agamben and Levinas in their conceptions of the messianic. For Levinas, the mode of messianism and the political meaning of messianism are addressed through its passage into subjective responsibility.[271] Judaic messianism has not forgotten the "intersubjective experience that leads to [the] social experience and endows it with meaning".[272] It is a "personal vocation among men".[273] Levinas suggests that "the very subjectivity of the subject" is the "messianic sensibility inseparable from the knowledge of being chosen".[274] Messianism is drawn onto the plane of subjectivity:

> The subject is therefore never a pure activity, but is always placed in question. The subject is not in possession of himself in a relaxed and inalienable way. He always has more asked of him.[275]

The event of messianism is a rehabilitation of subjectivity.[276] Subjectivity is prefigured by the movement of messianism into the deep interior of the self.[277] To paraphrase Levinas, he (like Agamben) sees the messianic life marked by a way of being. Messianism is "no more than this apogee in being, a centralizing, concentration or twisting back on itself of the Self [*Moi*]. And in concrete terms this means that each person acts as though he were the Messiah".[278] Exteriority is the revelation through which infinity ruptures ordinary experience;[279] this rupture is accomplished by the idea of infinity in the *Moi*.[280]

Messianic temporality is not a central focus of Levinasian ethics, but it is present behind the scenes in all Levinas's writings.[281] The future is meaningful for Levinas in the present; sensibility is conditioned by being directed toward messianic futurity.[282] This temporally places Levinas closer to Derrida's to come than Agamben's messianic now. However, Levinas's focus is the intersubjective relation, rather than Derrida's aim to inscribe a structural openness in every historical moment, which is an important distinction for me. Levinasian futurity is part of a process that inflects the monotony of flowing, repetitive time, characterised by our drive to escape immanence. The messianic coming is an event from the outside which enters history and time.[283] Without focusing on the futurity of the messianic, subjectivity is empty and lacking content.[284] Subjectivity is ethically transformed by the alterity of death:

> The relationship with the Other is absence of the other; not absence pure and simple, not the absence of nothingness, but absence in a horizon of the

> future, an absence that is time. This is the horizon where a personal life can be constituted in the heart of the transcendent event, what I called above the "victory over death".[285]

Messianism is distributed beyond a single entity and heralds a form of existence whose individuation is not located in a single being.[286] Robert Bernasconi calls attention to this nonteleological way in which Levinas takes the messianic to interrupt history:

> The 'beyond history' is … that which interrupts history. … Eschatology in Levinas is not a question of the future, but a disturbance or interruption of the present.[287]

Levinas elaborates on this reading of messianism in *Totality and Infinity* with a question:

> [I]s this eternity a new structure of time, or an extreme vigilance of the messianic consciousness?[288]

This messianic time is an event of an individualised ethical call that breaks through the monologue of history.[289] Levinas views history as constantly interrupted by the messianic instant that makes an appeal for responsibility. The content of messianic temporality is the experience of being responsible. Levinas's messianism involves the rethinking of the ethical becoming of subjectivity. Levinas's eschatology is a vision *in* the overflowing infinity which "makes possible *existents*" and *of* absolute alterity in the face of the other.[290] It institutes a relation with being beyond the totality or beyond history.[291] It is not a doctrine of the last things, so it is not to be confused with Christian (and Pauline) eschatology.[292]

For Levinas, like Agamben, messianism is interpreted as an instant that affects the temporal flow of consciousness. It is a time to be seized. Consciousness directs itself toward something other than itself ("consciousness *of*"), so it is disposed to a recognition of messianic interiority and responsibility.[293] Consciousness *of* is emboldened and completed by a transposition to messianic consciousness *of* messianic responsibility. From Agamben's writings we know he is deeply suspicious of the juridical nature of responsibility. On this point we can see a clear divergence between the two thinkers' positions. However, I think it is legitimate to borrow Agamben's vocabulary and state that messianism for Levinas allows subjectivity to be experienced as an ethical vocation. The distinction is that instead of Agamben's singular way of being, Levinas places responsibility for the Other as a foundation for the messianic. Levinas has taken the transcendent weight of eschatology and invested it in the ontological and ethical condition of the *Moi*. The categorisation of the messianic event is instantiated in moments of asymmetrical social responsibility.[294] Messianic politics demands action as "not to build the world is to destroy it".[295]

The self is the point of convergence for messianic interiority, suffering and responsibility.[296] Levinas's messianism is "my power to bear the suffering of all. It is the moment when I recognise this power and my universal responsibility".[297] Levinas concludes that "the fact of not evading the burden imposed by the suffering of others defines ipseity itself. All persons are the Messiah".[298] The messianic moment for Levinas is found in the radical thought of the Other, manifested in the renewable movement of giving, which appears as a non-rational morality founded in messianic participation.[299] The immediate agent of this messianic ethics is the person who reaches out to accept and care for another person, the Other.[300] The appeal of the other regulates the subject's sensibility – it is vulnerable and exposed and open to all wounds.[301] This form of suffering has a very special place:

> [I]t is not yet moral initiative, but it is through suffering that *a freedom may be aroused.* Man receives suffering, but in this suffering he emerges as a moral freedom.[302]

Messianism is acts of responsibility in response to the suffering of others.[303] Messianic futurity initiates my relation with the other's call upon me: "The very relation with the other is the relation with the future".[304] One must welcome the event of the relationship with the other revealed to us in death, and this welcoming is an expectation.[305]

Levinas's messianic call is without specific content – like the way Agamben states that the messianic call is "essentially and above all *a call of the call, appeal of the appeal*".[306] The messianic subject is called out through a recognition which exceeds political identity; he is response-able; he suffers; his giving and solidarity are infinite; this posture corresponds with the apologetic position to which the subject is recalled upon the revelation of the face.[307] The messianic sense of time is never completed: the act aimed at futurity is not fulfilled. The future is confined within the intersubjective relation:

> Relationship with the future, the presence of the future in the present, seems all the same accomplished in the face-to-face with the Other. The situation of the face-to-face would be the very accomplishment of time; the encroachment of the present on the future is not the feat of the subject alone, but the intersubjective relationship.[308]

The future is messianic because the future is explored only from the standpoint of the face-to-face relation with the other. The other is always to come and who appeals to subjectivity from the future evokes the ethical sense of the present for subjectivity. The impossibility of conceptualising and foreseeing the future event of the other brings us to the very secret of the revelation of responsibility: subjectivity becomes essentially open, sensitive, and vulnerable in a state of "waiting for".[309] Here I wish to make another connection. For Agamben, justice requires the transmission of the Forgotten, the handing on of form-of-life. The Forgotten are those souls in limbo without tasks or ends. Agamben sets up a negative nonrelation between form-of-life and the Forgotten – there is a connection between the singular being and an other (even if not an Other). Both Levinas and Agamben are seeking to ground an ethical messianism here through different routes – one embracing the transcendent, the other trying its best to avoid falling into the transcendent.

Conclusion

In this chapter I have attempted to construct the terms of Agamben's immanent life. Immanent life – form-of-life – exists as a messianic figure. It is through that messianism that Agamben seeks to deactivate the *dispositifs* that constantly ensnare the living being. What is more, form-of-life is a being of potential. This reading of potentiality is drawn from Aristotle and is idiosyncratic – Agamben defines true potentiality as the potentiality-not-to, the potential not to pass into actuality. This prevents immanent life from being bound by a means-end logic, and from being beholden to transcendent relationality.

I have investigated Agamben's messianism through his reading of the Pauline epistles. I have shown how this reading is unorthodox, but also that Agamben's messianism is distinguishable from the messianism relied upon by Jacques Derrida and Emmanuel Levinas. Agamben's messianism seeks to suspend and render inoperative the law, opening it for a new use. Agamben's immanent ontology is a modal ontology. This is a post-Heideggerian, and post-Levinasian ontology. Agamben traces in the ontological difference a form of hypostatic ontology, shared by Heidegger and Levinas. This hypostatic ontology is a negative ontology. It has aporias – existence is the outcome of the activity of an unreachable and ungraspable essence. Ultimately this is the negative ground for philosophy which Agamben has opposed throughout his work, for example with animality as we saw in the first chapter. For Agamben, modal ontology does not repeat the aporias of hypostases, as can be seen in Levinas's messianism. It focuses upon *how* being is, as a demand. This *how* is an ontological alternative to Levinasian ethics. Modal ontology does raise important questions – namely, how are we to effect the *how*? It is to this question that the remaining chapters turn.

Notes

1 Levinas (1985) 17–18, 115, 117.
2 Agamben (2016a) 146–175, 170.
3 Agamben (2016a) 157, 164; Agamben (2018d) 30.
4 Levinas (1969) 49, 55, 66, 202–203.
5 Agamben (2005d).
6 Agamben (2016a) 277.
7 Prozorov (2010) 1056.
8 Foucault (2002b) 453.
9 Agamben (1998) 46–7; Prozorov (2014) 183; Prozorov (2017) 172–173.
10 Prozorov (2014) 178.

11 Mills (2008b).
12 Chiesa and Ruda (2011) 163–180.
13 Badiou (2009) 559.
14 Agamben (2007b) 1–3, 17–21; Agamben (2000) 94–95.
15 Agamben (2000) 110.
16 Agamben (1998) 188.
17 Agamben (2010) 91–103.
18 Agamben (2007c) 73–91.
19 Agamben (2013b) 122.
20 Prozorov (2017) 180.
21 Agamben (2007b) 93–94.
22 Agamben (2018b) 127.
23 Agamben (2005d) 26–29, 134–137; Agamben (2007c) 73–92.
24 Agamben (1998) 188.
25 Vacarme (2004) 120.
26 Vacarme (2004) 121.
27 Agamben (2007b) 9.
28 Agamben (2007b) 2.
29 Agamben (2007b) 67.
30 Prozorov (2010)1054.
31 Agamben (2009d) 23.
32 Agamben (2009d) 31; Agamben (2011) 65.
33 Agamben (2017b) 52; Prozorov (2009a) 530.
34 Agamben (2017b) 53.
35 Agamben (2017b) 51; Aristotle (1984e) 1097b22–30.
36 Agamben (2017b) 54.
37 Aristotle (1984f) 1047a 24–26.
38 Attell (2009) 39–40.
39 Attell (2009) 40.
40 Attell (2009) 41.
41 Agamben (2005b) 284–285; Attell (2009) 41.
42 Attell (2009) 44.
43 Agamben (1999c) 180.
44 Seshadri (2014) 475; Agamben (2017b) 37–38.
45 Seshadri (2014) 478.
46 Agamben (2017b) 41.
47 Attell (2009) 42.
48 Agamben (2007b) 64.
49 Agamben (2007b) 44; Prozorov (2014) 184–185.
50 Prozorov (2014) 185.
51 Agamben (2007b) 43.
52 Prozorov (2010) 1064.
53 Prozorov (2010) 1066.
54 Agamben (1999b) 254.
55 Agamben (2017b) 54.
56 Agamben (1998) 46.
57 Agamben (2004b) 37–38.
58 Agamben (2018a) 85.
59 Agamben (2004b) 81.
60 Benjamin (1996) 389.
61 Agamben (2004b) 82.
62 Agamben (2004b) 91. In addition to meaning “not knowing”, the word *ignoscenza* also carries the sense of “forgiveness” or “pardon” and might best be understood as a sort of “forgetful forgiveness”.

63 Agamben (2004b) 92.
64 Prozorov (2010) 1068.
65 Prozorov (2014) 187.
66 Agamben (2016a) 115.
67 Agamben (2016a) 144.
68 Heidegger (1962) 67.
69 Heidegger (1962) 68.
70 Aristotle (1984a) 677a15, 647b28, 671b20, 677a15.
71 Agamben (2016a) 136.
72 Agamben (2016a) 135–136.
73 Agamben (2016a) 136.
74 Agamben (2016a) 137.
75 Agamben (2016a) 151.
76 Agamben (2016a) 139.
77 Agamben (2016a) 140–141.
78 Agamben (2016a) 142.
79 Agamben (2016a) 143.
80 Heidegger (2012) 336.
81 Heidegger (2012) 88–91.
82 Agamben (2016a) 145.
83 Fox (2011) 132.
84 de la Durantaye (2009) 307.
85 Agamben (2016a) 145.
86 Levinas (1978) 82.
87 Levinas (1978) 83.
88 Levinas (2001b) 133.
89 Bergo (2005) 155.
90 Levinas (1987) 50.
91 Guenther (2009) 172.
92 Agamben (2005c) 64.
93 Levinas (1978) 83.
94 Sealey (2010) 369.
95 Levinas (1978) 10.
96 Levinas (1987) 75.
97 Levinas (1987) 46–47; Levinas (2003b) 73.
98 Critchley (2004) 91.
99 Abbott (2014) 89–90.
100 Abbott (2014) 90.
101 Levinas (1978) 39.
102 Agamben (2002) 158.
103 Abbott (2014) 19.
104 Agamben (2016a) 133.
105 Agamben (1998) 188.
106 Agamben (1998) 182.
107 Agamben (2016a) 152.
108 Agamben (2016a) 155.
109 Abbott (2014) 17.
110 Agamben (2016a) 164.
111 Agamben (2016a) 167.
112 Agamben (2016a) 156.
113 Agamben (2016a) 159.
114 Agamben (2016a) 168.
115 Agamben (2016a) 169.
116 Agamben (2018d) 30.

117 Agamben (2016a) 170.
118 Agamben (2016a) 172.
119 Agamben (2016a) 174.
120 Agamben (2016a) 174.
121 Thurschwell (2005) 185.
122 Thurschwell (2005) 186.
123 Thurschwell (2005) 186.
124 Agamben (2016a) 233.
125 Agamben (2016a) 221.
126 Agamben (2016a) 227.
127 Agamben (2016a) 232.
128 Agamben (2016a) 231; Agamben (2018d) 27.
129 Levinas (2008) 139.
130 Agamben (2016a) 231.
131 Agamben (2017a) 5–6.
132 Agamben (2016a) 231.
133 Agamben (2016a) 224.
134 Agamben (2016a) 228.
135 Diamantides (2017) 197; Wilkinson (2017) 212–224.
136 Diamantides (2017) 208.
137 Diamantides (2017) 208.
138 Diamantides (2017) 209.
139 Agamben (2016a) 232.
140 Agamben (1999e) 160.
141 Agamben (2000) 135.
142 Agamben (1999e) 163; Agamben (2005c) 64.
143 Agamben (1999e) 163.
144 Agamben (1999e) 161.
145 Bloch (1972) 317.
146 Agamben (2000) 141–142.
147 Agamben (2007c) 77.
148 Agamben (2018b) 33.
149 Agamben (2007b) 43.
150 Agamben (2007b) 56.
151 Agamben (2005d) 69.
152 Wright (2013b) 485–486.
153 Wright (2015) 315.
154 Benjamin, quoted in Agamben (2012) 50.
155 Wright (2015) 311.
156 Agamben (2018d) 32, 34
157 Wright (2015) 320.
158 Agamben (2020h) 14.
159 Wright (2015) 315; Agamben (2017c) 14.
160 Wright (2015)321.
161 Agamben (2012) 3.
162 Agamben (2012) 8.
163 Agamben (2012) 9.
164 Agamben (2005d) 27.
165 Agamben (2012) 12–13; 1 Corinthians 7:29–31.
166 Agamben (2012) 59.
167 Agamben (2005d) 41.
168 Agamben (2012) 13–18.
169 Agamben (2005d) 61.
170 Agamben (2005d) 75.

171 Agamben (2005d) 75.
172 Agamben (2005d) 78.
173 Agamben (2005d) 57.
174 Wright (2013d) 1208.
175 Agamben (2005d) 62.
176 Agamben (2005d) 67f.
177 Wright (2015) 319.
178 Agamben (2005d) 97–98; Chiesa (2009) 111.
179 Hägglund (2008) 132.
180 Attell (2015) 232.
181 Agamben (2005d) 61–62.
182 Agamben (2005d) 77–78.
183 Thurschwell (2005) 192.
184 Derrida (1990) 945.
185 Derrida (1990) 945.
186 Zartaloudis (2010) 279.
187 Derrida (1990) 961.
188 Derrida (1980).
189 Attell (2015) 244.
190 Derrida (1978) 164.
191 Derrida (1978) 203.
192 Derrida (1994) 59.
193 Derrida (1994) 65.
194 Attell (2015) 233.
195 Attell (2015) 233–234.
196 Hägglund (2008) 134.
197 Attell (2015) 232; Kojève (1969) 162.
198 Derrida (1994) 73.
199 Attell (2015) 233.
200 Derrida (1994) 73.
201 Attell (2015) 234.
202 Attell (2015) 218.
203 Derrida (1982) 34.
204 Derrida (1982) 39.
205 Attell (2015) 220.
206 Attell (2015) 234.
207 Thurschwell (2003) 1234.
208 Wright (1997) 17.
209 Wright (1997) 19.
210 Wright (1997) 31.
211 Wright (1997) 36; Romans 1:4.
212 Wright (1997) 48; Romans 3:24–26, 8:3; Romans 5:6–11; 8:31–39.
213 Wright (1997) 48.
214 Romans 5:12–21.
215 Wright (2015) 320.
216 Wright (2015) 320.
217 Wright (2015) 322.
218 Agamben (2005d) 103.
219 Agamben (1999e) 171.
220 Agamben (2006) 39–40; Agamben (2005c) 63–64.
221 Agamben (2005c) 88.
222 Agamben (1998) 48; Attell (2015) 246.
223 2 Thessalonians 2: 3–9.
224 Agamben (2017c) 27.

225 Wright (2013a) 449.
226 Prozorov (2014) 146.
227 Schmitt (2003) 59–60.
228 Agamben (2005d) 110.
229 Agamben (2012) 35–40.
230 Agamben (2005d) 111.
231 Agamben (2005a) 16–17, translated and quoted by Attell (2015) 251.
232 Attell (2015) 245.
233 Agamben (2007b) 7.
234 Agamben (2005d) 106.
235 Agamben (2005d) 26.
236 Cimino (2016) 108.
237 Agamben (1998) 18.
238 Cimino (2016) 112.
239 Agamben (2005d) 106.
240 Badiou (2001) 14; Badiou (2005) 39–40.
241 Prozorov (2017) 168.
242 Agamben (2005d) 48.
243 Agamben (2005d) 52–53; see also Kaufman (2008) 37–54.
244 Agamben (2005d) 50; Romans 9:6; Romans 9:25.
245 Romans 2:25, 2:27, 2:28.
246 Wright (2013c) 139.
247 Wright (2013c) 139.
248 Wright (2013c) 140–141.
249 Wright (2013c) 141.
250 Agamben (2005d) 95.
251 Agamben (2012) 19. Wright argues that this is perhaps an overstatement: Agamben cites the use of *argeō* in 2 Macc. 5.25, but this is not the verb used in e.g. Gen. 2.2f. or Ex. 20.11, or indeed Heb. 4.10 (though Heb. 3 and 4 is knocking on the door of this discussion).
252 Agamben (2007c) 92.
253 Agamben (2005d) 107.
254 Biddick (2016) 82.
255 Agamben (1995) 79.
256 Agamben (1995) 78.
257 Agamben (1995) 79.
258 Agamben (2005c) 64.
259 Mills (2008b) 26.
260 Fox (2011) 132.
261 Levinas (1969) 101.
262 Levinas (2008) 168.
263 Agamben (2006) 40.
264 Levinas (1996b) 60.
265 Levinas (1969) 79.
266 Yates (2011) 172.
267 Levinas (1996b) 61, 64.
268 Abbott (2014) 92.
269 Levinas (1996b) 63.
270 Levinas (2008) 147.
271 Yates (2011) 164.
272 Levinas (1969) 53.
273 Levinas (2001b) 88.
274 Levinas (2001b) 96; Levinas (1969) 135.
275 Levinas (2001b) 78.

276 Levinas (2001b) 87.
277 Levinas (1969) 26;Yates (2011) 168.
278 Levinas (2001b) 90.
279 Levinas (1969) 102f, 277.
280 Levinas (1969) 117; Levinas (1994a) 143.
281 Poleshchuk (2014) 56.
282 Levinas (2001b) 96.
283 Yates (2011) 164.
284 Levinas (1999) 157–168.
285 Levinas (1987) 90. Whilst it is tempting to ascribe the same negativity here to Levinas as Agamben does to Heidegger when he conceived of *Dasein*'s being-toward-death, it is important to distinguish that here death is an opening to a relationship to the Other, not a placeholder of nothingness for the living being – see Agamben (2006) xii.
286 Levinas (2001b) 87.
287 Bernasconi (1998) 7; Levinas (1969) 22.
288 Levinas (1969) 285.
289 Levinas (1969) .21–23, 241–244.
290 Levinas (1969) 23.
291 Levinas (1969) 22.
292 Levinas (1969) 23.
293 Yates (2011) 166–167.
294 Yates (2011) 167.
295 Levinas (1990) 112.
296 Yates (2011) 166.
297 Levinas (2001b) 90.
298 Levinas (2001b) 89.
299 Yates (2011) 167.
300 Morgan (2014) 195; Bergo (2009) 246.
301 Levinas (2008) 49.
302 Levinas (2001b) 71.
303 Morgan (2014) 200.
304 Levinas (1987) 79.
305 Levinas (1987) 78.
306 Agamben (2005d) 43.
307 Levinas (1969) .252, 293.
308 Levinas (1987) 79.
309 Levinas (1987) 76–77.

5 Agamben's hyper-hermeneutics

Introduction

The previous two chapters have explored Agamben's immanent life, its messianic basis, and importantly, interpreted his thought as responding to and distancing itself from a Levinasian form of ethics which is based in a transcendent relationality. I have attempted to show how – through explicit and implicit mentions in his work – Agamben's immanent life (his form-of-life) is constructed in a way so as to try and make it irreducible to a transcendent coordinate. This form-of-life is a being of potential, which will deactivate the *dispositifs* that have constantly created the human subject – language, sovereignty, law (and others besides). I have also shown, through a hermeneutic method, that Agamben has provided an uncharitable reading of transcendent Levinasian ethics to ensure critical distance for form-of-life, which constitutes itself through a modal ontology. The last chapter provided a schematic of this modal ontology. It argued that the position of the how in Agamben's thought retains a trace of the relation with the Other, leaving form-of-life proximate in construction to the Levinasian subject.

This chapter focuses on the political possibilities of form-of-life. To be more precise, I turn to the details of how a life of pure immanence can be lived, without falling into the traps of outlining a programmatic politics or philosophy, nor sliding into a reliance on a transcendent, ungraspable ground. Human action and agency is central to the coming politics. It is through understanding Agamben's interpretations of thought and poiesis that the ground is laid for such action. Following this, I argue that the construction of form-of-life itself should be read as hyper-hermeneutic. This is my own neologism. Form-of-life retains a hermeneutic structure but is constructed through singular paradigmatic examples. Agamben's paradigm stands as a real particular case set apart from what it is meant to exemplify.[1] Agamben reads these paradigms as constructing a "paradigmatic circle",[2] which allows form-of-life to exist as a mode of being outside of the hermeneutic circle, through which Heidegger constructed the experiences of *Dasein*.[3] By stepping outside of this hermeneutic circle, form-of-life can exist non-relationally, deactivating apparatuses of control.[4] These paradigms are gestural.[5] Such gestures reveal the possibility of a new way of being that does not require a revolutionary "zero hour" to be brought about. These

DOI: 10.4324/9781315191447-6

gestures are compared favourably to the position of "repetition" in the thought of Søren Kierkegaard – repetitive acts can create the being (and the world) anew. What is more, these gestures are contended to be coterminous with the "use of oneself", which Agamben argues is a contemplative life,[6] a form generated by living itself, a style of living.[7] This is exemplified by Agamben's writings on slavery and Franciscan ontology.

As a conclusion to this hyper-hermeneutic study, I will argue that form-of-life does provide a basis for reimagining political modes of being. Even though form-of-life ostensibly presupposes nothing but itself, that presupposition is actually based on an assumption that the living being is a fully capable, conscious existent. Form-of-life retains a key aporia when faced with liminal figures of living that it cannot yet account for. It is to these forms of life that this book turns to in its last two chapters.

An immanent politics of agency

Agamben has asked: "what could be the politics of whatever singularity?"[8] I follow Gavin Rae who argues that Agamben's politics depends upon individual political action.[9] Rae notes that recent scholarship on Agamben is split between those who claim he offers no reconstructive political project,[10] and those persons who accept that there is a project, but disagree on whether to affirm,[11] or reject it.[12] It is true that on first viewing there appears to be a deficiency in Agamben's work in relation to human agency. Jess Whyte has contended that Agamben appears to exclude agency – for example, in his treatment of pornography he leaves no room for the roles of political movements in challenging assumptions about the roles of women and the possibilities for sex.[13] Whyte also identifies that Agamben has paid insufficient attention to the role of past political struggles in resisting the forms of domination that have existed, especially in relation to human labour.[14]

Rae has crystallised a position that the debate over whether to affirm or reject Agamben's project misses a key point as proponents of both options depend upon, but do not engage with, whether or not Agamben permits individual action to bring his project about.[15] The focus of form-of-life is potentiality, which will render inoperative *dispositifs* of control. Form-of-life communicates by contact, in a void of representation that is also a care for the inappropriable – a care for opacity. This contact participates in an ontology of nonrelation and use from which derives, in the final instance, a politics of intimacy in which life is inappropriable and inseparable from its form – a life that actively preserves its sense of nonknowledge and the generative limits of its own mystery.[16] What is at issue is agency. Agamben does state that "[t]he potential welcomes non-Being, and this welcoming of non-Being *is potentiality*, fundamental passivity".[17] This fundamental passivity is distinct from a passivity to be found in the opposition of activity to passivity. What is more, Rae contends correctly in my view, that the fundamental passivity of potentiality arises from the act of *welcoming* non-Being, and so is dependent on a form of action.[18] It describes the indeterminate contingency between activity and passivity that gives rise to the active-passive opposition.[19] If we place too much emphasis upon a *passive* interpretation to Agamben's messianism, this gives the impression that there is nothing that agents can and need to do to bring about the coming politics.[20] This is compounded by the way Agamben has written on will (and which we have explored in relation to ethics in earlier chapters), arguing that:

> The problem of the coming philosophy is that of thinking an ontology beyond operativity and command and an ethics and a politics entirely liberated from the concepts of duty and will.[21]

The agential aspect has to be excavated from Agamben's thinking. Whilst willing may be absent from the coming politics, it is not claimed that it is absent from the *transition* to the coming politics. Rae also draws a key distinction between activity understood as praxis, work and poiesis to argue that each term is dependent upon a different form of willing. A command-orientated willing of praxis and work is tied to a means-end schema, whereas poiesis is tied to the production of truth which is then connected to contemplation and the openness of potentiality.[22]

This does not create a binary opposition between poiesis and will. Agamben relies on a reductionist conception of will that does not distinguish between will-as-instrument and will-as-impetus. Rae defines will-as-instrument as an intention actualised by a form of action which is undertaken in relation to a means-end logic. Will-as-impetus only entails an intention actualised by a form of action. Poiesis depends on will-as-impetus. Agamben's rejection of the relationship between the coming politics and willing is a rejection of will-as-instrument.[23] This distinction does allow us to sketch out a form of agency in Agamben's work, but it is equally important to state that Agamben does not make this distinction himself.[24]

Poiesis depends upon the intention to participate in poietic activity. It requires a willed intention to affirm contemplation, which makes inoperative the means-end logic and liberates the potentials to allow a different use of them.[25] A decision must be made to affirm the potentiality not-to, or impotentiality. Will-as-impetus does not disappear once the coming politics has been effected; the coming politics must be continuously affirmed to avoid regression. The biopolitical substance of each individual is their relation with the inappropriable. This can (and has been) violently appropriated by others as a property (which can lead to totalitarianism).[26] This means that the coming politics, and the road to the coming politics, remain dependent upon a specific form of agential willing.[27]

The distinction between praxis, work and poiesis is made clear in *The Man Without Content*. Central to Agamben's task is to understand what is meant by man's productive activity. Modernity understands this activity as praxis, a "manifestation of a will that produces a concrete effect".[28] Praxis is a movement whereby an individual wills a particular end that is brought into effect by a concrete act. Agamben does not have a problem with this form of activity.[29] The problem which has arisen is that modernity has become so accustomed to understanding all of man's doing as praxis that we are unable to "recognize that it could be, and in other eras has been, conceived differently".[30] Agamben goes on:

> [C]entral to praxis was the idea of the will that finds its immediate expression in an act, while, by contrast, central to poiesis was the experience of pro-duction into presence, the fact that something passed from nonbeing to being, from concealment into the full light of the work.[31]

In contrast, poiesis is not a practical and voluntary process but a mode of being understood as unveiling, *aletheia*, a process of freedom. It was because of this that Agamben argues that Aristotle assigned a higher position to poiesis to praxis. The roots of praxis lay in the condition of man as an animal, a living being, and it was defined in terms of a voluntarist will. To work was to submit to necessity and had an immediate relation to the biological processes of life. Work is distinct from poiesis and is the willed satisfactions of bodily need.[32]

In his later works Agamben follows Arendt in arguing that Aristotle prioritised praxis over poiesis, associating the former with human freedom and the latter with biological necessity and slavery. His goal in *The Man Without Content* is to maintain a distinction between artistic labour and utilitarian labour in Greek society, although he will later reject this distinction stating that the Greeks used the same term, *technē*, for both.[33] Yet in this work Agamben states that this distinction between the three types of human doing – poiesis, praxis and work – has been obscured. We have lost the chance to distinguish praxis from poiesis. At the same time, work, "which used to occupy the lowest rank in the hierarchy of active life", has climbed to be the common denominator of human activity.[34] All human doing becomes to be interpreted as praxis, and praxis is conceived in turn as starting from work, from the production of material life that corresponds to life's biological cycle.[35] This means all activity is associated with the biological processes that underpin work.[36] All attempts made in the modern era to found man's doing differently have remained anchored to this interpretation of praxis as will and vital impulse.[37] Agamben states that "what the Greeks meant with the distinction between poiesis and praxis was precisely that the essence of poiesis has nothing to do with the expression of a will".[38] This essence is found instead in the production of truth and in the subsequent opening of a work for man's existence and action.[39]

All living beings are in a form of life, but not all are a form-of-life. When form-of-life is constituted, it renders destitute and inoperative all singular forms of life. Form-of-life involves the revocation of all factical vocations, but it is not the thinking of a better or more authentic form of life. Likewise, inoperativity is not another form of work, but rather constitutively coincides with living a life.[40]

Agamben links poiesis to both thought and potential. Form-of-life is not defined by its relation to a praxis or a work but by a potential.[41] Agamben here connects the potential of politics to what he terms "multitude", which is connected to a "properly human potential", namely thought.[42] "Thought" is the unitary potential that constitutes multiple forms of life into form-of-life, as thought is always use of oneself.[43] Thought is not privileged over form-of-life, nor does it precede it. When thought thinks of the living being, it thinks of the potential that defines the subject and itself; when thought thinks itself, it thinks the potential that defines it.[44] In contrast to thought, will is premised on a different relationship to the living being. Will depends on the distinctions between means and end, which permit the will to command how the movement between them takes place.[45] Will precedes the living being, meaning it is capable of commanding when forms of life will appear. Rae states that "will" confuses its operations with a foundational status and takes itself to be that which chooses the form of life to be realised, when it is in fact neither universal nor foundational (because it depends upon a particular form of life and its potential).[46] As Agamben argues, a:

> [L]iving being, which seeks to define itself and give itself form through its own operation is … condemned to confuse its own life with its own operation, and vice versa.[47]

To affirm thought is to affirm a potential that is ignored by the privileging of will:

> [T]hought does not define one form of life among others in which life and social production are articulated: it is the unitary potential that constitutes the multiple forms of life into form-of-life.[48]

Agamben explains:

> There is a multitude because there is in singular human beings a potential (a possibility) to think, the existence of the *multitude* coincides with the generic actualisation of the potential to think, and, consequently, with politics.[49]

He explains that "[i]f there were only the multiple individual actualisations and their sum, there would not be a politics but only the numerical plurality of activities defined by the variety of particular goals".[50] The potential of thought is in relation with the singular use of a common potential.[51] As Agamben explained in *Means Without End*:

> I call *thought* the nexus that constitutes the forms of life in an inseparable context as forms-of-life. I do not mean by this the individual exercise of an organ or of a psychic faculty, but rather an experience, an *experimentum* that has as its object the potential character of life and of human intelligence. To think does not mean merely to be affected by this or that thing,

> by this or that content of enacted thought, but rather at once to be affected by one's own receptiveness and experience in each and every thing that is thought a pure power of thinking. … Only if I am not always already and solely enacted, but rather delivered to a possibility and a power, only if living and intending and apprehending themselves are at stake each time in what I live and intend and apprehend – only if, in other words, there is thought – only then can a form of life become, in its own factness and thingness, *form-of-life*, in which it is never possible to isolate something like naked life.[52]

Thought captures the non-specification that defines form-of-life.[53] Form-of-life has a double tension inside of it. It is a life inseparable from its form, and also separable from every thing and every context. It must live its own mode of being, as a monad, inseparable from its context because it is not in relation to it but is in *contact* with it (it is in a non-relational existence).[54] It is worth quoting Agamben's definition of "contact" in its entirety, especially given its connection to "thought":

> Just as thought at its greatest summit does not represent but "touches" the intelligible, in the same way, in the life of thought as form-of-life, *bios* and *zoè*, form and life are in contact, which is to say, the dwell in a non-relation. And it is in contact – that is, in a void of representation – and not in a relation that forms-of-life communicate. The "alone by oneself" that defines the structure of every singular form-of-life also defines its community with others. And it is this *thigein* [thought], this contact that the juridical order and politics seeks by all means to capture and represent in a relation. It will therefore be necessary to think politics as an intimacy unmediated by any articulation or representation: human beings, forms-of-life are in contact, but this is unrepresentable because it consists precisely in a representative void, that is, in the deactivation and inoperativity of every representation. To the ontology of non-relation and use there must correspond a non-representative politics.[55]

It is this contact or *thigein* (which Agamben also terms *touching*), when two entities are separated only by their void of representation, that the legal order and representative politics seek to capture and represent in the form of a relation which will always already have a negative ground. Form-of-life is without relation. This consists in the inoperativity of every representation; this must be signified by a non-representable politics.[56]

Thought contemplates a potential through rendering work inoperative. Contemplation and inoperativity are the metaphysical operators of anthropogenesis. They liberate human beings from every destiny and predetermined task. Politics names the dimension in which all works are deactivated and contemplated *as such* in order to liberate the inoperativity which remained imprisoned within them.[57] This is the greatest good which, according to Spinoza, a human being can hope for: "a joy born from this, that human beings contemplate themselves and their own potential for acting".[58] Contemplation is a paradigm of use. Life, which contemplates in the work its (own) potential of acting or making, is rendered inoperative in all its works and lives only in use-of-itself, lives only (its) liveability. Only through the contemplation of potential does something like an experience of an "own" and a "self" become possible.[59] Spinoza defined the essence of each thing as desire, the *conatus* to persevere in one's being. For Agamben our task is to insinuate a small resistance in this Spinozian idea. Each thing desires to persevere in its being, but it also resists this desire. This resistance is internal to desire, an inoperativity internal to the operation, but it alone confers on *conatus* its justice and its truth.[60]

So, what then is an alternative form of action which affirms form-of-life's potential? Rae sees this as achieved through affirming poiesis: "form of life is truly poetic [when], in its own work, [it] contemplates its own potential to do and not do and finds peace in it".[61] Poiesis is capable of this because "in it there has been preserved the experience of a relation to something that exceeds work and operation and yet remains inseparable from it".[62] For Rae:

> There is an intimate connection between thought, potential, and poiesis that ensures that thought-as-poiesis deactivates the instrumental logic of biopolitics while also unlocking the potential and alternatives that are necessary to transition to the coming politics.[63]

Hyper-hermeneutics

The key to form-of-life's ability to form the basis for a messianic politics relates to its *hyper-hermeneutic* construction. This is a neologism coined deliberately to reflect the position of how messianism can offer a new form of political intervention. It refers to both the grounding of Agamben's thought as well as Agamben's messianic move with whatever-being.

In order to appreciate the potentiality of hyper-hermeneutics, it is necessary to conduct a hermeneutical inquiry into Agamben's treatment of hermeneutics. Agamben sees bare life as created through the operation of the state of exception, which is tied to hermeneutics:

> Between the norm and its application there is no internal nexus that allows one to be derived immediately from the other … the impossible task of welding norm and reality together, and thereby constituting the normal sphere, is carried out in the form of the exception, that is to say, by presupposing their nexus.[64]

It is through the creation of an exception that legal norms gain their meaning. Only by delimiting when the law does not apply is it possible to denote when the law does apply. However, the exception is a practical nexus; when it is created cannot be presupposed. In short, the hermeneutic exercise of legal reasoning presupposes an indeterminate law. Every legal decision would be indeterminate, as it would never be sure or clear when and where an exception would be created. This conclusion can be reached as Agamben claims that potentially any legal action taken in the exception can gain legal force.[65] This conclusion would render all legal norms indeterminate. Any interpretation of a legal norm could be rendered legal, and any interpretation of a legal norm can lead to the creation of bare life.[66]

Despite taking this radical position with respect to the consequence of hermeneutics, Agamben's thought remains within the hermeneutic tradition.[67] In *What is an Apparatus?* Agamben notes, with respect to reading the works of Foucault, that:

> Whenever we interpret and develop the text of an author in this way, there comes a moment when we are aware of our inability to proceed any further without contravening the most elementary rules of hermeneutics.[68]

Hermeneutics is both responsible for the exception, and part of Agamben's thought. This double movement can be traced to Agamben's reading of Heidegger's hermeneutic circle. Agamben, through his reading of Heidegger, sees the hermeneutic circle as fundamentally negative. However, Agamben's response to this negativity, namely his messianism and the figure of whatever-being, is constructed hermeneutically. In this sense my approach is similar to Mathew Abbott's, who has stressed that the emphasis for change is on us; there is no hope of an outside intervention or event.[69] Abbott's reading leads him to see Agamben's happy life as akin to Heidegger's hermeneutic circle – namely, we must come to being in the right way.[70] In Agamben's terms, this life coincides completely with "the destitution of the social and biological conditions into which it finds itself thrown".[71] The task now is to attend to the fact that there will be no epochal event – once this is accepted, then we can think of what it means to be in common, exposed to the same world.[72]

I also want to emphasise that I read hyper-hermeneutics as having a form of universal applicability. I state this because in a 2012 interview Agamben mentioned that "European man" can approach "his truth" through a confrontation with the past. America offers a post-historical animality in their Way of Life and Japan offers snobbery through their tea ceremony devoid of any historical meaning. Europe, on the other hand, offers a culture that remains human and vital ever after the end of history, proceeding from its history to attain a "new life".[73] There remain questions over this Euro-centric approach. Notwithstanding this, I am reading the way forward as universal, as there is no indication in Agamben's thought that his prescriptions are only to be applied to Europe and Europeans.

Hyper-hermeneutics also conveys Agamben's response to the hermeneutic circle. Agamben perceives of several *aporias* with Heidegger's hermeneutic circle. To counter these *aporias*, Agamben proposes a *paradigmatic circle*, which aims to messianically render inoperative the *aporias* within hermeneutics.[74] This paradigmatic method aims to deactivate the hermeneutic circle. The term hyper in hyper-hermeneutics connotes Agamben's attempt to escape the hermeneutic circle. In order to do so, Agamben has to use non-hermeneutic means, namely the paradigm. It is these non-hermeneutic means that ultimately lay the foundation for a new form of political possibility.

For Agamben, the hermeneutic circle only acquires its true meaning from within this paradigmatic method. In order to appreciate the implications of this move it is necessary to turn back to Heidegger and question the exact importance of the hermeneutic circle within his philosophy. For Heidegger, the temporal structure of *Dasein*'s being-in-the-world is hermeneutic. *Dasein* interprets the world through its own understanding of the world. Understanding is an *existentiale*, a fundamental character of *Dasein*'s Being.[75] Understanding for Heidegger is tied up with *Dasein*'s own potentiality for being. In other words, understanding guides *Dasein* to know what it is capable of.[76] *Dasein* understands itself through projection, by being thrown before its own possibilities.[77] The projecting of *Dasein*'s understanding has its own possibility of developing itself, which Heidegger terms interpretation.[78]

It is through interpretation that understanding becomes itself, which allows *Dasein* to realise what its possibilities are. Interpretation allows *Dasein* to work out its own possibilities that are projected through understanding. To understand is to give the structure of something as something to a phenomenon. The "as" of this construction relates to the purpose of the something in question, which involves interpreting the phenomenon and making an assertion that characterises it.[79] The interpretation that leads to a thematic assertion about something *as* something is itself grounded in fore-having, fore-sight and fore-conception. These are known as the fore-structures of interpretation. The interpretation is grounded on things *Dasein* has in advance, sees in advance and grasps in advance respectively.[80]

In order to approach the hermeneutic circle in the right way, the hermeneutic circle must be understood as the structure of *Dasein*'s understanding of the world that *Dasein* has in advance of any interpretation. Heidegger writes of the hermeneutic circle:

> It is not to be reduced to the level of a vicious circle, or even of a circle which is merely tolerated. In the circle is hidden a positive possibility of the most primordial kind of knowing. To be sure, we genuinely take hold of this possibility only when, in our interpretation, we have understood that our first, last, and constant task is never to allow fore-having, fore-sight, and fore-conception to be presented to us by fancies and popular conceptions, but rather to make the scientific theme secure by working out these fore-structures in terms of the things themselves.[81]

It is vital to focus upon the fore-structures that make up the world into which *Dasein* is thrown. The reason for this is that the circle is the expression of the existential fore-structure of *Dasein* itself. By approaching the circle in the right way *Dasein*'s own possibilities for Being can be understood as being structured by the world into which *Dasein* is thrown. *Dasein* has a circular structure. Heidegger warns against resting any interpretation on popular conceptions without first questioning those conceptions themselves.[82]

It is this process of understanding fore-structures that forms the basis for Agamben's critique of the hermeneutic circle. Agamben does acknowledge Heidegger's explanation as an attempt to reconcile the difficulties of hermeneutics:

> Grounding this hermeneutical circle in *Being and Time* on pre-understanding as *Dasein*'s anticipatory existential structure, Martin Heidegger helped the human sciences out of this difficulty [caused by the hermeneutical circle] and indeed guaranteed the "more original" character of their knowledge.[83]

However, Agamben challenges the very idea that *Dasein* can come to the circle in the right way. Specifically, Agamben challenges the idea that these fore-structures can be worked out:

> [Heidegger's] guarantee was less reassuring than it at first appeared. If the activity of the interpreter is always already anticipated by a pre-understanding that is elusive, what does it mean "to come into [the circle] in the right way?"[84]

Agamben sees the pre-understanding of these fore-structures as elusive. As such, the hermeneutic circle appears defined by an ineffable foundation that can never be grasped – the hermeneutic circle repeats an empty foundationalism. The circle transmits this negativity that cannot be escaped from, an essence which will ultimately structure political possibilities. Agamben sees that any interpretative response to the hermeneutic circle is futile, as it is not possible to avoid its clutches:

> This can only mean – and the circle then seems to become even more "vicious" – that the inquirer must be able to recognise in phenomena the signature of a pre-understanding that depends on their own existential structure.[85]

An important and vital ambiguity arises in this statement. What does Agamben mean by "their"? It is unclear as to whether "their" refers to the existential structure of *Dasein* or the existential structure of the phenomena that form the fore-structures in question.

It is contended here that "their" refers to the existential structure of the phenomena in question. This implies that any pre-understanding of those fore-structures is impossible. The interpreter can never come to the circle in the right way as the interpreter will not have the pre-understanding of the world required to do so. This explains why Agamben feels it is necessary to move from hermeneutics to paradigms:

> The aporia is resolved if we understand that the hermeneutic circle is actually a paradigmatic circle. There is no duality between "single phenomenon" and "the whole" … the whole only results from the paradigmatic exposition of individual cases. And there is no circularity, as in Heidegger, between a "before" and an "after", between pre-understanding and interpretation. In the paradigm, intelligibility does not precede the phenomenon; it stands, so to speak, beside it.[86]

Agamben maintains that the "things themselves" (form-of-life) cannot be reached through the hermeneutic circle, or even through a pre-understanding. Rather, the paradigmatic circle allows for the phenomenon's intelligibility to be understood through the paradigm itself. A singular paradigm can allow for an understanding of a constellation of phenomena of which the paradigm stands as an example:

> The paradigmatic gesture moves not from the particular to the whole and from the whole to the particular but from the singular to the singular. The phenomenon, exposed in the medium of its knowability, shows the whole of which it is the paradigm. With regard to phenomena, this is not a presupposition (a "hypothesis"): as a "non-presupposed principle", it stands neither in the past nor in the present but in their exemplary constellation.[87]

It is this paradigmatic method that stands as being able to do the work of the hermeneutic circle. However, it does so not through any pre-understanding of the world, but rather it makes a phenomenon intelligible through the paradigm. It is this move that leads to the characterisation of Agamben's paradigmatic method as hyper-hermeneutic.

Therefore, there appears no need to undertake a detailed hermeneutic understanding of the world, or of the fore-structures of understanding. The paradigm does not need a fore, but rather will make those phenomena intelligible through its own operation. The paradigm, the singular gesture akin to an example, can therefore break the circle of oppression tied through hermeneutics to current forms of political belonging. Agamben's interpretation of Heidegger and the shift to paradigms has consequences for an understanding of the figure of form-of-life. Form-of-life cannot be based on the presupposition of the hermeneutic circle; rather, form-of-life must be understood paradigmatically.

The paradigm for Agamben is akin to an example. It stands neither clearly inside nor clearly outside of the group or set of phenomena that it identifies. A paradigm is the real particular case that is set apart from what it is meant to exemplify.[88] Agamben uses a number of different paradigms to represent form-of-life. These paradigmatic figures are varied. They include the nude body,[89] an adult pornographic actress who remains expressionless in her films[90] and the protesters in Tiananmen Square.[91]

All these figures stand as real particular cases, paradigmatic examples for singular being. Following Agamben's construction of the paradigmatic circle, each paradigmatic example shows the whole of which it is the paradigm. Therefore, these figures are not to be understood as examples that form the precursor to form-of-life. They *are* the evidence for the existence of an inoperative community. It is this paradigmatic gesture that stands as evidence for the hyper-hermeneutic nature of form-of-life. This move reflects Agamben's contention that there is no duality between the whole and the single phenomenon. As Paolo Bartoloni explains:

> Singularity is thus freed from the false dilemma that obliges knowledge to choose between the ineffability of the individual and the intelligibility of the universal.[92]

However, the paradigmatic figure of form-of-life is itself still reliant upon a hermeneutic interpretation and application in order to be understood. Although it is justified paradigmatically, form-of-life is still beholden to hermeneutics.

Agamben's thought treats hermeneutics as crucial to form-of-life, whose singularity refers directly to its taking-place and its concrete existence within the world. This concrete existence implies – by necessity – a hermeneutic influence. It is inconceivable that form-of-life's taking place is somehow separate from hermeneutics. To understand form-of-life's concrete existence, it is necessary to understand the world within which form-of-life exists. This hermeneutic existence is not based on a presupposition, but a truism that the taking-place of form-of-life must involve the world in which it exists. Moreover, this existence must be affected and conditioned by form-of-life's interpretation and pre-understanding of the world. Form-of-life's concrete existence is dependent upon its own understanding and interpretation of the phenomena in the world it interacts with, which must include other forms of life. Form-of-life's way of being is conditioned by the context of its existence in relation to the world and other beings it is in contact with. Hermeneutics is constituent of form-of-life's way of being.

Paradigmatic gestures and repetition

If Agamben's paradigm is to be understood as a singular example, then by definition a single act must be able to form the basis for rendering power's hold over life inoperative. Thus, if form-of-life is understood in this hyper-hermeneutic context the all-important moment for whatever-being becomes the singular paradigmatic gesture. This paradigmatic gesture becomes a messianic slight shift, a gesture which renders inoperative existing forms of political belonging. Hermeneutics can constitute form-of-life but requires a paradigmatic gesture to render inoperative the self-referential nature of the hermeneutic circle. Hermeneutics is freed unto a new use through a paradigmatic act.

The paradigmatic gesture is therefore crucial for the coming politics. What would such a paradigmatic gesture look like? Such an act would always be *subtle*, rather than decisive and revolutionary. Crucially, such an act cannot be prescribed. These paradigmatic acts are truly political, in the sense that singular beings are truly in-common, joined through their own experience of the limit of their finitude. It is this modest, and very human politics that the paradigmatic gesture unconceals.

A gesture does not produce or act on anything. Rather, in a gesture something is being endured or supported. It opens the sphere of *ēthos* as the more proper sphere of that which is human.[93] Agamben puts at the core of his philosophical journey the singular events that exceed the limits of subjectivities and promise the coming of another world out of the gestures in this one. There is the ethical necessity of maintaining oneself in relation (or contact) with one's own end.[94] Agamben writes: "Nothing, however, is as fragile and precarious as the sphere of pure means".[95] Agamben makes the point that gesture should be seen as a paradigm of "pure mediality".[96] This purity is not something which has a criterion in itself but is always subordinate to the relationship with something external.[97] A pure mediality is without end, and gesture is never a means to an end for the one who carries it out. Agamben states:

> To every human being a secret has been consigned, and the life of each one is the mystery that puts this arcane element … onstage, until it is ultimately displayed for what it is: a pure gesture, and as such – to the extent that it manages to remain a mystery and not inscribe itself in the apparatus of means and ends – unjudgable.[98]

Gesture is an activity which, in the manner in which it is carried out, at the same time stops itself, exposes itself and holds itself at a distance.[99] Agamben goes on:

> Gesture … is an activity or a potential that consists in deactivating human works and rendering them inoperative, and in this way, it opens them to a new, possible use. This holds for both the operations of the body and for those of the mind: gesture exposes and contemplates the sensation in sensation, the thought in thought, the art in art, the speech in speech, the action in action … Thus, inoperativity is not another action alongside and in addition to all other actions, not another work beyond all works: It is the space – provisional and at the same time non-temporal, localised and at the same time extra-territorial – that is opened when the apparatuses that link human actions in the connection of means and ends, of imputation and fault, of merit and demerit, are rendered inoperative. It is, in this sense, a politics of pure means.[100]

Agamben makes clear that form-of-life is something "that does not yet exist in its fullness" and can only be attested to in places that "necessarily appear unedifying".[101] What needs to be done is apply Benjamin's principle according to which the elements of the final state are hidden in the present, not in progressive tendencies but in insignificant and contemptible areas.[102] My first port of call are the writings of Søren Kierkegaard on repetition. *Repetition* is a pseudonymous text, written by a fictional narrator, which may not have reflected the views of Kierkegaard himself. My reading of the text could be framed as a reading of that fictional narrator rather than Kierkegaard – I am following Agamben's own reading of the text. Repetition has an existential repeatable singularity. Agamben has noted that it is not possible (with form-of-life) to distinguish what is unique from what is repetition.[103] To Kierkegaard we owe the insightful alignment between the exceptional and the existential, and the notion of exceptionality and repetition as kindred rather than opposed.[104] In *Repetition*, Kierkegaard makes the point that repetition is not recollection.[105] Recollection is the source of all knowledge, where learning is a recollection of what we once knew in a pre-existent state before our souls entered our bodies.[106] Recollection is the retrieval of an impression of a past actuality: someone who recollects is thinking about the past. Genuine repetition is recollected forwards.[107]

Kierkegaard's *Repetition* provides the tale of a narrator who moves back to Berlin to re-live the life he had there when younger. The narrator, Constantine Constantius, discovered that everything was the same on his return. However, Kierkegaard makes it clear that what Constantius experienced was not repetition but mere recollection. For Kierkegaard "the only repetition was the impossibility of a repetition".[108] Repetition is a movement of becoming, of coming into existence:

> Repetition means that a past actuality becomes actual once again: someone who repeats is renewing actuality. Recollection and repetition deal with the past in different ways: that which is recollected is complete within itself; it is contemplated as a finished totality, apprehended as an idea. On the other hand, if something is repeated it is re-enacted, actualized; it is not merely represented as an idea but recreated as a reality.[109]

Both recollection and repetition are movements of truth: the former moves towards a past eternity, and the latter moves towards a future eternity. This illuminates Constantine's remark that "repetition and recollection are the same movement, only in opposite directions".[110] Repetition is life that is lived in the moment itself. For Kierkegaard, the one that lives is the one that gives himself to the repetition of life.[111] Life is a succession of repetitions, but such repetitions create something new. Such a position raises the possibility that the very act of repetition (in my reading, through gestures) opens up to a new sphere of living, a sphere that for Kierkegaard must be embraced. The singular and the irreducible (gesture) are precisely what is repeatable.[112]

Kierkegaard's repetition, the repeatable singularity, is for me a model for Agamben's absolute immanence. It is true that Kierkegaard wrote that repetition is transcendence. Yet Agamben's immanent life sees Kierkegaard's repetition as a corollary. For Agamben the plane of transcendence extends no further than the plane of immanence, and it is in this sense that his engagement with Kierkegaard should be situated and the repeatable singularity represents absolute immanence.[113] Crucially, the political in Agamben is the existential in Kierkegaard:

> Politics is that which corresponds to the essential inoperability of humankind … There is politics because human beings are *argōs* – beings that cannot be defined by any proper operation – that is, beings … that no identity or vocation can possibly exhaust.[114]

For Agamben, the coming politics is going to be a "struggle between … whatever singularities and the state organisation".[115] Kierkegaard can be read as expressing himself in line with this:

> [T]he established order will not put up with consisting of something as loose as a collection of millions of individuals … The established order wants to be a totality that recognises nothing above itself but has every individual under it and judges every individual who subordinates himself to the established order.[116]

Kierkegaard traces the individual's "collision" with "the established order", pointing out that the established order would be upset by the fact that the individual wanted to live an immanent life - "that the single individual wanted to withdraw from his relation to the established order".[117]

In a way which evokes the operation of repetition, form-of-life is generated by the very act of living.[118] This ontology of this how presupposes a doing, a taking responsibility, a capacity for realising this how (this is the agential action Rae traces in thought-as-poiesis). The how is repetition, a repeatable singularity which is lived in the moment itself. For Agamben, this is where living and life coincide – but what are the limits of this living? To live life as a form indicates that one *must* realise and take responsibility for this condition. For Agamben, all identities are relational in the sense that every identity is a differential construct. Some people regard these differences as essential (for example, male and female, black and white, Jew and Gentile), while others (like St Paul) regard them as arbitrary constructs. The person who regards them as arbitrary constructs lives in "contact" with others, and focuses on how it lives its life, gesturally,[119] which involves ways of envisaging an immanent life on the threshold of its political and ethical intensification.[120] The person who regards these differences as ontic realities lives in relation with others, upholding these representational constructs as juridical.

Agamben opens up a new reading of Kierkegaard in a political context. The political is never an end in itself and can never be one except at the cost of the individual.[121] Agamben is arguing that existence precedes essence:

> Only if I am … delivered to a possibility and a power, only if living and intending and apprehending themselves are at stake each time in what I

> live and intend and apprehend … only then can a form of life become, in its own factness and thingness, *form-of-life*, in which it is never possible to isolate something like naked life.[122]

There is a corollary between Agamben's "living [which] is at stake each time in what I live and intend" and the view from *Repetition* that life is a series of repetitions, and such repetitions create something new. Form-of-life is a philosophical outlook. It is to say that one's identity is a constructed performance. This means that form-of-life is an embodied existential figure, subject to a continual process of repetition, a process that is always-already happening. In a similar vein to Kierkegaard (and explicitly referencing him), Agamben also sees repetition as bringing change:

> What is repetition? There are four great thinkers of repetition in modernity: Kierkegaard, Nietzsche, Heidegger, and Gilles Deleuze. All four have shown that repetition is not the return of the identical; it is not the same as such that returns. The force and the grace of repetition, the novelty it brings us, is the return as the possibility of what was, render it possible anew; it's almost a paradox. To repeat something is to make it possible anew.[123]

For Agamben, repetition restores possibility,[124] which is coterminous to potentiality.[125] Therefore we can say that in living our lives as inseparable from its form, a life which lets itself be, we do so through a series of repeatable singularities (gestures) which allow us to be capable of im-potentiality.

For both Agamben and Kierkegaard, the space of living is an act of radical self-determination in a world with others. Kierkegaard begins *The Sickness unto Death* by describing the idea that the human being is a self or has the possibility of becoming one:

> The self is a relation that relates itself to itself in the relation; the self is not the relation but is the relation's relating itself to itself. A human being is … a synthesis. A synthesis is a relation between two. Considered in this way, a human being is still not a self. In the relation between two, the relation is the third as a negative unity.[126]

The human being can be a self when the synthesis, the relation itself, relates itself to itself, or lets itself be. This can be connected to Agamben's potentiality – at a thing's realisation, there is nothing left that is able not-to-be. In both cases, the self is defined without being divided and separated through a decision. Kierkegaard's self (importantly not the human being) does not involve its being held in relation to anything other than itself. It is its own relation to itself, just like form-of-life.

The self in Kierkegaard is a life lived in the moment itself (the structure of repetition). This life is a version of contact between non-relational monads.

Becoming a self requires that an individual distance themselves from the world of others in the sense of defining themselves through a relation to another.[127] Instead, a self is a non-relational monad, which is held in relation to itself, who is nevertheless in contact with other monads. Here I am arguing that Kierkegaard can be read as opposing the sovereign division of life into citizen and bare life, which involves the production of individual subjects through the actualisation of their potentiality.

For Agamben and Kierkegaard a striving *to other* oneself or others makes no sense. Everybody should take care of themselves in order to become a true self that deserves the name. To secure one's true self no reference to others is necessary. The experience of *being othered* implies for Kierkegaard a dangerous distraction from the true relation of the self to itself – a corollary to Agamben's immanent form-of-life. For Kierkegaard, to be *othered* or to experience *othering* means to be threatened by an alteration that seems to make *something* or *someone* out of us. *Othering* produces an *othered self*, imagined as becoming someone or something other *which it is not* and *which it can never become* – a transcendent referent which the self is constantly defined in relation to. For Kierkegaard, if we have undergone an othering we should do our best to undo it and ultimately to rid ourselves of an otherness that threatens us with estrangement from our self.

The Sickness unto Death contends that once a self is formed, it does *not* stand outside the world, but is immersed in it, as an existential figure. True selfhood and true freedom must be an orientation toward oneself as a single individual.[128] Every self must turn toward itself and establish itself before reaching out to others. Existentially, there is no possibility of delegating the task of living one's own life. Therefore, the figure of the self lives through giving itself to the repetition of life. This opens up a new sphere of living in a movement of becoming. Each moment of becoming is a repetition; the self lives constantly anew, existing in its own history and own world it shares with others, avoiding the problem of othering.

What I must stress here, and this is a central argument of the book, is that form-of-life aims to form an ontology of life without relation to an Other, a non-relational ethics based on a monadic clinamen. This does produce a new basis for political existence and belonging. Yet form-of-life retains a crucial aporia when faced with liminal living figures. When Agamben's form-of-life is presented with liminal figures (in the case of this study I use the unborn human and the end of life adult patient), a life which is lived as a form becomes identifiable only through the exercise of a judgment; it is this judgment which Agamben sees as irrevocably connected to the law, and, in turn, Levinasian ethics. These liminal figures, which Agamben uses as examples of bare life, call into question the limits of a non-relational form of existence. In particular, it calls into question whether Agamben can escape the spectres of the law, and judgment, which he ties to Levinas and Levinasian relationality, and was so ready to critique. This argument is evident in this chapter's discussion of repetition above, and it is even more evident in the following discussion on use.

Gestures and destitute use

Agamben's focus is destituent potential, which he seeks to translate into a constituted political system. This would involve thinking:

> [A]n element that, while remaining heterogeneous to the system, had the capacity to render decisions destitute, suspend them, and render them inoperative.[129]

Only through an ontology and politics set free from every relation is it possible to think a "purely destituent potential".[130] This means remaining open to the possibility that the ontological difference is not, in fact, a relation. Agamben goes on:

> A new dimension for politics will be opened only when human beings – the beings who have *logos* to the same extent that they are possessed by it – have got to the bottom of this weakest potential that determines them and involves them in an errancy – history – that seems interminable. Only then – but this "then" is … always underway – will it be possible to think politics beyond every figure of relation.[131]

Where a relation is rendered destitute its elements are in contact, because the absence of every relation is exhibited between them.[132] The apparatuses are deactivated through an experience of potential, but a potential which exposes itself in its non-relation to the act, an impotential.[133] At the point of their deactivation, potential becomes a form-of-life as constitutively destituent.[134]

This gestural, destitute politics can be found in use. Use is a gesture. Use is also *the relation to an inappropriable.*[135] Use is a principle internal to potential which prevents it from being consumed in the act and drives it to turn once more to itself, to make itself a potential of potential, to be capable of its own potential (and own impotential).[136] Walter Benjamin, in "Notes toward a Work on the Category of Justice", establishes a close connection between the concept of justice and that of inappropriability.[137] For Benjamin, justice is not a virtue but a *state of the world*, an ethical category which corresponds to existence *as such*. Agamben translates Benjamin as follows:

> Justice does not appear to refer to the good will of the subject, but, instead, constitutes a state of the world [*einen Zustand der Welt*]. Justice designates the ethical category of the existent, virtue the ethical category of the demanded. Virtue can be demanded, justice in the final analysis can only be as a state of the world or as a state of God.[138]

Justice coincides with the condition of a good that cannot be appropriated. To make of the world a supreme good can only mean to experience it as absolutely inappropriable, to open it to use.[139]

Use is separate from *praxis* and work (in this sense it is a poiesis). Use is the field of tension whose poles are style and manner, appropriation and expropriation. Every use is a polar gesture: on the one hand, appropriation and habit; on the other, loss and expropriation.[140] Agamben notes:

> Etymologically, *ēthos* ('character') and *ethos* ('habit', 'way of life') are the same word (the reflexive pronoun *e* plus the suffix *-thos*), and thus both mean 'selfhood'. Selfhood, being-a-self, is expressed in a character or a habit.[141]

In turn, to inhabit means to be in a relation of use with something to the point of being able to lose and forget oneself in it, of constituting it as inappropriable. To inhabit with oneself, to inhabit-oneself, names the fundamental trait of human existence: the form of life of the human being is an "inhabiting life".[142]

With all this being said, it is striking that the lives Agamben refers to in order to bolster the figure of form-of-life are individuals with consciousness and not liminal figures in the sense of those beings on the fringes of biological existence (although it certainly could be claimed that these figures are *politically* liminal). I consider two here to support my argument – the slave and the monk. These figures are the "Ungovernable, which is the beginning and, at the same time, the vanishing point of every politics".[143]

The slave

Agamben's starting point in considering the use of the body is the slave in Aristotle's work:

> These human beings differ among themselves like the soul from the body or the human from the animal – as in the case of those whose work is the use of the body [*oson esti ergon he tou somatos chresis*], and this is the best [that can come] from them [*ap'auton beltiston*] – the lower sort are by nature slaves, for whom it is better to be commanded with this command, as said above.[144]

The slave remains a human being,[145] but is an "animate instrument" which can move itself on command.[146] By putting in use his own body, the slave is, for that very reason, used by the master, and in using the body of the slave, the master is in reality using his own body. The syntagma "use of the body" represents a point of indifference between one's own body and that of another.[147] In this sense use has a singular nature – every use or gesture is the use of self, and if I enter into a relation of use with something through a gesture, I must be affected by it, and constitute myself as one who makes use of it.[148] The self is nothing other than use-of-oneself.[149] Being is not thought of as substance (*ousia*), which could give rise to another hypostatic ontology, but use-of-oneself.[150] In making this argument, what Agamben omits is the position of children in ancient Greece and Rome, both as slaves themselves,[151] or being treated the same way as slaves by that society.[152] It appears implied that all of the references are to adult slaves.

Agamben then argues that mediating's one's own relation with nature through the relation with another human being (the master) helped define from the very beginning what is properly human. Slavery, it is argued, contains a memory of this original anthropogenetic operation. This leads to a curious claim (to say the least). Namely, that the perversion of this operation only begins when the reciprocal relation of use is appropriated and reified in juridical terms through the constitution of slavery as a social institution.[153]

Yet has there ever been a time in recorded history when slavery did *not* operate as a social institution? Agamben relies upon Aristotle here to make his argument, but Aristotle's writings were describing the very social institution of slavery as it existed in his time. Some of the earliest written records of the ancient world discuss slaves and slaveholding,[154] and slavery has been endorsed and encouraged by both states and major religions throughout history.[155] What is more, Aristotle wrote that slavery is both necessary and expedient, as some are marked out for submission from birth.[156] Given Agamben's critique of empty foundationalism, it is concerning to hear an appeal to a situation which may never have existed.

We are also told that the human being whose *ergon* is the use of the body is the slave.[157] As such he is *argos*, deprived of work.[158] The use of the body and absence of work of the slave evoke the paradigm of a human activity reducible neither to labour, nor to production, nor to praxis. The slave is a figure of bare life (or *haplos* Being), standing at the threshold that separates and joins *zoè* and *bios*. [159] Agamben claims that the slave represents the capture within law of a figure of human acting that remains for us to recognise.[160] But is this true?

What is omitted here is the biopolitical experimentation of slavery after ancient Greece and Rome, for example with the Atlantic slave trade, which undermines Agamben's claim that the slave's gestures can enable a form-of-life to be lived. By the eve of American independence Great Britain controlled the largest slave system in the New World.[161] Slaves who were thrown overboard and drowned were treated in English courts the same way as cargo for insurance purposes.[162] In addition, the plantation system in the United States of America manifested the figure of the state of exception. Achille Mbembé sees the slave condition as a triple loss – of a home, of the rights over their body, and of their political status. This triple loss is coterminous with being dominated and experiencing a social death. The slave is kept alive but in a "phantom-like world of horrors and intense cruelty and profanity".[163] Slaves were whipped to instil terror and randomly killed so that they lived in a form of death-in-life.[164] Even after the abolition of slavery in the USA, Jim Crow laws imposed harsh restrictions on the rights and freedoms of African Americans.[165]

Agamben states that the acts and gestures of the figure of the slave are *useful* but have been captured within legal apparatuses and reduced to the figure of bare life. If the apparatuses are deactivated, then the gestures of the slave will exist as he lives his life as a form. Again, this can be questioned. I will focus on three short points. First, in the United States, for example, slaves could sue for their freedom in court. These suits always proceeded from the legal fiction that the slave was already free, but if the court ruled for the slave token damages would be awarded to them as proof of their freedom.[166] Once their freedom had been won (as unlikely as this may have been) then the newly freed person could be said to be free to live a gestural existence (or certainly freer than they were prior to the judgment). Second, in the American context, Mbembé gives the example that the slave maintained an alternate perspective towards time, work and self, but not in terms of a memory of an original anthropogenetic operation. Rather, there is a history of slaves who were treated as mere instruments of production drawing upon any object, instrument, language or gesture and turn it into a stylised performance. This demonstrates the protean capability of the human bond through music and the body possessed by another through their very gestures.[167]

Finally, I turn to English law surrounding slavery in England. Slaves were socially and legally anomalous in Great Britain as there were no statutes sanctioning the institution.[168] The English constitution had been constructed by contrasting English legal liberties to those available in other jurisdictions in the Empire. There were at least two slavery regimes in the British Empire – one in England and another in the overseas colonies.[169] This led to England undertaking an imperial expansion whilst its dominions abroad developed arbitrary forms of government culminating in slavery.[170] There also existed several conflicting legal judgments – some held slavery was lawful in England,[171] others declared that "as soon as a negro comes into England, he becomes free: and one may be a villein in England, but not a slave".[172] Blacks in eighteenth-century England were caught in a "half-way stage" between colonial slavery and English domestic servitude, but through the ambiguities of their position they altered their status.[173] This is underscored by the uncertainty over the number of black slaves in Britain, with estimates being made without evidence.[174]

In 1772, the judgment of *Somerset v Stewart* was handed down by Lord Mansfield. In this case Lord Mansfield declared:

> So high an act of dominion must be recognized by the law of the country where it is used. The power of a master over his slave has been extremely different, in different countries. The state of slavery is of such a nature, that it is incapable of being introduced on any reasons, moral or political; but only positive law, which preserves its force long after the reasons, occasion, and time itself from whence it was created, is erased from memory: it's so odious, that nothing can be suffered to support it, but positive law.[175]

Somerset did not bring immediate freedom to all slaves in England. As late as the 1830s some black people were enslaved in Great Britain.[176] This is because the actual holding was narrow. Lord Mansfield held that a slave's master could not forcibly send the slave out of the realm, and habeas corpus was available to the slave to prevent their deportation.[177]

But what was decided was much less important than what was thought to be decided. Subsequent courts interpreted Lord Mansfield's judgment as meaning a black slave in England was free and no longer a slave.[178] It became, in the UK and United States, a "basic text of antislavery constitutionalism".[179] The judgment took on an existence of its own. It was believed that Lord Mansfield had held slavery inconsistent with the British constitution, and people acted on this assumption.[180] Slavery was in part ended in England through the escape of slaves living in England, with institutional elements such as the understanding of *Somerset*, English libertarianism and the rule of law providing a conducive climate to black resistance. The initiative of ending slavery came from individual members of the black community.[181] Perhaps this can stand close to an example of the freed gestures of the slave Agamben refers to.

The monk

Next, we can see the Franciscan monk. Agamben argues that "the most demanding legacy of monasticism" is its alternative way of conceiving of "human action" as the sphere of "form of life and life".[182] Cenobitic communities meticulously regulated every aspect of the monks' lives through monastic rules which were developed by the Church.[183] These monastic rules were norms, but aimed not to impose obligations but to declare and show to the monks the obligations they had agreed to when they made their monastic vow on their entry to the monastery.[184] Cenoby derives from *koinobion*, which is a life lived in common (*koinos bios*).[185] Their common life is defined as a life without "'private ownership of any possessions'" because "'everything they owned was held in common'".[186] How they dress is intricately linked to how they are supposed to conduct themselves. This link between dress and conduct puts forth, reveals, and exposes the "interior way of being", such that the attention paid to the "care of the body" is turned toward the *morum formula* "'example of a way of life'".[187] "To inhabit together" monks had "to share" a *habitus*, which was more than a style of dress or a place. The cenobites "attempt to make habit and form-of-life coincide in an absolute and total *habitus*".[188]

Compared to this regulated monastic existence, St Francis of Assisi and the Franciscan order attempted to integrate these monastic rules into a form of life itself, so that rule and life would become indistinguishable.[189] Francis's direction was that the monks should live not according to the "form of the Roman Church", the law, but the "form of the Holy Gospel".[190] Through this, the Franciscans were able to neutralise the law's hold over life.[191] The form of the Holy Gospel was not reducible to a normative code; rule and life became indistinguishable.[192] The rule to live by was the very life of Christ, whose life and devotion to God could not be separated:

> The form is not a norm imposed on life, but a living that in following the life of Christ gives itself and makes itself a form.[193]

Service to God and the life lead by the Franciscan monk is one and the same. To live this form-of-life the monks lived a communal life, according to the Holy Gospel. The monastic rules which were laid down by the Church did not govern the community, but the practice of living in common and the rules which were needed to sustain the common life were mutually reinforcing.[194] The law, *even in its nonrelation*, still retains a key role in the structuration of the common life. For the Franciscans, the law still existed, but it in no way applied to their lives, just as for the remnant, its existence is no longer determinatively ordered by the law. The forms-of-life which dwelt together all aimed to live by Christ.

As a result, we can see monasticism as standing as a life lived alongside all of the *dispositifs* which structure and create subjects. As the monks did not, however, define their existence through outside referents, the *dispositifs* which existed did not define them as subjects, and so had no control over them. They had rendered them inoperative. Agamben references Francis's own actions, which served as a summary and example for his followers. Francis refused to intervene in respect of those persons who had abandoned the Franciscan way of following the simple, poor life of Christ. Instead, Francis stated that if he were not able to correct those persons through preaching and example, he would not become a persecutor like the law.[195]

Such an example is telling. The monk orders his form-of-life not only through his own way of being (and acting through gestures) and interpreting the form of the Holy Gospel, but also through reference to the examples provided by other monks, living as they are as non-relational monads. This leads to a *collective* experience of a new relation to the law. The law may not judge the individual, nor persecute them. The regulation of the common life is done not through the law, but through individuals judging whether they are following the form of the Holy Gospel by relating their actions to others.

Crucially, whilst Agamben is clear to state that there is no place for an *application* of law to life in Franciscanism, this does not mean that the law has no role to play.[196] The rule, after all, mutually reinforces the life being led. The law does not order and define form-of-life, but law helps to order and reinforce the form of the life lived. The individual monks choose not to use the methods of the law, but they are aware of them and have used the law in a different, new manner. This is a gestural politics. The law no longer regulates life, but the common life of the monk is held in a negative nonrelation to the law: the existence of the law is necessary to differentiate the form-of-life the monks are practicing.

In this way, a life lived as its own form works on existing subjects to other them. Such a life defines its own way of living (the gestural use), to other itself, just as the Franciscan Order chose to. The monastic rules which were laid down by the Church did not govern the community, but the practice of living in common and the rules which were needed to sustain the common life were mutually reinforcing.[197] To oppose the Church would be to enter into its terrain and its terms. This would take the form of an antagonistic movement that would seek to vindicate itself and establish a new and "true Church". Oppositional power merely challenges the *dispositif* by establishing a new one, which challenges nothing because it is a constituent form of power. The Franciscans represent a destituent form of power. If their form of life is to remain pure, it must be formulated as completely indifferent (whatever, *qualunque*) to the liturgical *officium*.[198] The Franciscans sought to "*realize a human life and practice absolutely outside the determination of the law*".[199] For the Franciscans, the laws and rules still existed, and mutually reinforced the life being led, but the individual monks chose not to use the methods of the laws and rules. Instead, they were aware of them and used them in a different, new manner.[200] The common life of the monk is held in a negative nonrelation to the law and the rules (the *dispositif*): the existences of those *dispositifs* are necessary to differentiate the form-of-life the monks are practicing. They remain apart from this life, as there is nothing in this life which they can gain purchase on and control.

Here the Franciscans present an exemplar of form-of-life, but I wish to focus on a particular point implied by Agamben's argument. He states that use itself "could have been configured as a *tertium* with respect to law and life, potential and act", and thus it could have been used to define "the monks' vital practice itself, their form-of-life".[201] This presupposes an agent. It *must* presuppose an agent who acts through poiesis and gestures (as I have argued) to live their life as a form. This, much like Agamben's critique of *bios*, is a class of persons defined through an inclusive exclusion. If a living being is not able to act agentially, then the implication here is that they cannot live their life as a form, a mode of life. Buttressing this point, Agamben states that the Franciscan doctrine of use is a model where "life could be affirmed unreservedly as that existence which is situated outside of the law".[202] Someone must affirm. It is an agent who conceives of a form-of-life existing outside of the law, and who translates use into a form-of-life.[203] What this ultimately means is that Agamben's immanent politics contains an aporia which, I maintain, serves to undermine its ultimate goal. The last two chapters of this study turn to precisely this aporia.

Conclusion

In this chapter I have tried, as charitably as possible, to read Agamben to present a method for how the coming immanent politics can be put into effect. I have contended that human action and agency is central to the coming politics. In fact, the coming politics would not be able to be affected if immanent life was purely passive. Agamben uses the concepts of thought and poiesis to ground agential action. I have then, through my own hermeneutic study of Agamben and the early Heidegger, argued that form-of-life should be understood as being constructed hyper-hermeneutically. This neologism is coined for a construction of immanent life that retains a hermeneutic structure (via the hermeneutic circle) but is constructed through singular paradigmatic examples. These paradigms constitute a paradigmatic circle. I have argued that by stepping outside of the hermeneutic circle, Agamben's form-of-life can live non-relationally. What is more, I contend that these paradigms are gestural, ultimately revealing the possibility of new forms of living and being to us all. In seeking to support my arguments, I connected this gestural politics to Kierkegaard's concept of repetition. Not only did Kierkegaard strongly influence Agamben's development of the same concept, his work shows that repetitive gestures can create the subject and the world anew. This was then connected to Agamben's "use of oneself", a contemplative life that I argue is constituted through agential gestures. In this sense, form-of-life does allow us to imagine an immanent politics. However, it does contain an aporia, which should not be understated. It requires agential action in order for a life to be lived as a form. This has been shown through the examples of the slave and the monk. Yet this presupposes a being capable of acting. What form-of-life cannot account for, which I aim to show in the final two chapters, are biologically liminal figures of living. Ironically, given the strength of Agamben's earlier critique of Levinas, Levinasian ethics can answer the aporia that form-of-life cannot.

Notes

1 de la Durantaye (2009) 218–219.
2 Agamben (2009c) 27–28.
3 Heidegger (1962) 182–195.
4 Agamben (1999e) 174.
5 Agamben (2009c) 27.
6 Agamben (2016a) 214–219.
7 Agamben (2016a) 220–223, 233.
8 Agamben (2007b) 85.
9 Rae (2018) 978–996.
10 Laclau (2007) 11–22; Badiou (2009) 559.
11 de Boever (2015); Martel (2015) 125–138; Prozorov (2010) 1053–1073.
12 Connolly (2007) 22–23; Passavant (2007) 147–174.
13 Whyte (2013) 138.
14 Whyte (2013) 15–16.
15 Rae (2018) 979.
16 Bordeleau (2017) 490.
17 Agamben (1999c) 182.
18 Rae (2018) 979.
19 Rae (2018) 979–980.
20 Rae (2018) 980.
21 Agamben (2013a) 129.
22 Rae (2018) 980; Agamben (2016a) 213, 247.
23 Rae (2018) 980.
24 Rae (2018) 993.
25 Agamben (2016a) 273.
26 Agamben (2016a) 207–213.
27 Rae (2018) 981; Lagaay and Rauch (2020) 93–96.
28 Agamben (1999h) 68; Lagaay and Rauch (2020) 93–96.
29 Rae (2018) 988.
30 Agamben (1999h) 68.
31 Agamben (1999h) 68–69.
32 Agamben (1999h) 69.

33 Kotsko (2020) 22.
34 Agamben (1999h) 70.
35 Agamben (1999h) 70.
36 Rae (2018) 989.
37 Agamben (1999h) 71.
38 Agamben (1999h) 72.
39 Agamben (1999h) 72.
40 Agamben (2016a) 277.
41 Agamben (2016a) 247.
42 Agamben (2016a) 212.
43 Agamben (2016a) 213; Agamben (2000) 11.
44 Rae (2018) 991.
45 Rae (2018) 991.
46 Rae (2018) 990–991.
47 Agamben (2016a) 247.
48 Agamben (2016a) 213; see Rae (2018) 991.
49 Agamben (2016a) 212.
50 Agamben (2016a) 212.
51 Agamben (2016a) 213.
52 Agamben (2000) 9.
53 Rae (2018) 991.
54 Agamben (2016a) 232.
55 Agamben (2016a) 237.
56 Agamben (2016a) 237.
57 Agamben (2016a) 278.
58 Spinoza (1996) III, Proposition 53. In the English version this reads as: "When the mind regards itself and its own power of activity, it feels pleasure: and that pleasure is greater in proportion to the distinctness wherewith it conceives itself and its own power of activity".
59 Agamben (2016a) 63.
60 Agamben (2017b) 56.
61 Agamben (2016a) 247; Rae (2018) 991.
62 Agamben (2016a) 247; Rae (2018) 991.
63 Rae (2018) 992.
64 Agamben (2005c) 40.
65 Agamben (2005c) 23, 50.
66 Agamben (2005c) 51.
67 Agamben (2009d) 13.
68 Agamben (2009d) 13.
69 Abbott (2014) 11.
70 Heidegger (1962) 188–195.
71 Agamben (2014) 74.
72 Abbott (2014) 195.
73 Savà (1992).
74 Agamben (2009c) 27.
75 Heidegger (1962) 182.
76 Heidegger (1962) 184.
77 Heidegger (1962) 185.
78 Heidegger (1962) 188.
79 Heidegger (1962) 189.
80 Heidegger (1962) 190–191.
81 Heidegger (1962) 195.
82 Heidegger (1962) 195.
83 Agamben (2009c) 27.

84 Agamben (2009c) 27.
85 Agamben (2009c) 27.
86 Agamben (2009c) 27.
87 Agamben (2009c) 27–28.
88 Raulff and Agamben (2004) 618; de la Durantaye (2009) 218–219.
89 Agamben (2010) 91–103.
90 Agamben (2007c) 90–91.
91 Agamben (2007b) 85–87.
92 Bartoloni (2004) 11.
93 Agamben (2000) 57.
94 Bordeleau (2017) 483.
95 Agamben (2007c) 87.
96 Agamben (2018a) 80.
97 Agamben (2018a) 81.
98 Agamben (2018a) 83.
99 DeCaroli (2020) 271.
100 Agamben (2018a) 84–85.
101 Agamben (2016a) 227.
102 Agamben (2016a) 227.
103 Agamben (2018b) 57. For a more detailed discussion of the relationship between Agamben and Kierkegaard see Frost (2021).
104 Gould (2013) 93.
105 Kierkegaard (1983) 131.
106 Scott (1990) 74.
107 Kierkegaard (1983) 131.
108 Kierkegaard (1983) 170.
109 Carlisle (2005) 525.
110 Kierkegaard (1983) 131.
111 Kierkegaard (1983) 132, 133.
112 Gould (2013) 83–84.
113 Agamben (1999a) 226–228.
114 Agamben (2000) 141.
115 Agamben (2000) 88.
116 Kierkegaard (1991) 91.
117 Kierkegaard (1991) 93.
118 Agamben (2016a) 221.
119 Agamben (2016a) 231.
120 Bordeleau (2017) 482; Agamben (2018b) 115.
121 Heller-Roazen (1999) 17.
122 Agamben (2000) 9. The isolation referred to is the state of exception.
123 Agamben (2004a) 315–16.
124 Agamben (2004a) 316.
125 Agamben (2007b) 43.
126 Kierkegaard (1980) 15.
127 Kierkegaard (1995) 272.
128 Kierkegaard (2015) 236.
129 Agamben (2016a) 278–279.
130 Agamben (2016a) 268.
131 Agamben (2016a) 271–272.
132 Agamben (2016a) 273.
133 Agamben (2016a) 276.
134 Agamben (2016a) 277.
135 Agamben (2016a) 81.
136 Agamben (2016a) 93.

137 Benjamin (2011) 257–258.
138 Agamben (2016a) 81, quoting Benjamin (2011).
139 Agamben (2016a) 81.
140 Agamben (2016a) 87.
141 Agamben (2018b) 104.
142 Agamben (2016a) 88.
143 Agamben (2011) 65.
144 Aristotle (1984c) 1254b17–20.
145 Aristotle (1984c) 1254a16.
146 Agamben (2016a) 11; Aristotle (1984c) 1253b20–1254a1.
147 Agamben (2016a) 14.
148 Agamben (2016a) 30.
149 Agamben (2016a) 54.
150 Agamben (2016a) 56.
151 Laes (2008) 235–283.
152 Golden (1985) 91–104.
153 Agamben (2016a) 14.
154 Finkelman & Drescher (2017) 770.
155 Drescher (2009) 62–63.
156 Aristotle (1984c) 1254a18–23.
157 Agamben (2016a) 15.
158 Agamben (2016a) 17.
159 Agamben (2016a) 20.
160 Agamben (2016a) 23.
161 Drescher (1989) 85.
162 *Gregson v Gilbert* (1783) 3 Doug 232, 99 ER 629; Oldham (2007); Webster (2007).
163 Mbembé (2003) 21.
164 Douglass (1986) 51, 67–68.
165 Finkelman (1994) 354–365.
166 Finkelman (1994) 332.
167 Mbembé (2003) 22.
168 Drescher (1989) 87.
169 Bush (1997) 379–418. See also Bobb-Semple (2007) 660.
170 Hulsebosch (2006) 648.
171 *Butts v Penny* (1677) 2 Levinz 201; *Pearne v Lisle* (1749) Amb. 755, 27 ER 47, 48 (Lord Hardwicke); van Cleve (2006) 619–620.
172 *Smith v Browne & Cooper* (1701) 2 Salk 666, 91 ER 566 (Holt CJ); *Smith v Gould* (1706) 91 ER 567, 567 (Holt CJ); *Shanley v Harvey* (1762) 2 Eden 126, 28 ER 844.
173 Lorimer (1984).
174 Drescher (1989) 88.
175 *Somerset v Stewart* (1772) 98 ER 499, 510 (KB) (Lord Mansfield).
176 Finkelman (1994) 326; *The Slave, Grace* (1827) 2 Hagg. 94, 166 ER 179.
177 Wiecek (1974) 108.
178 *Williams v Brown* (1802) 3 Bos. & P. 69, 127 ER 39 (CCP); *Forbes v Cochrane & Cockburn* (1824) 2 Barn & Cres. 448, 107 ER 450 (KB).
179 Wiecek (1974) 141.
180 Wiecek (1974) 146.
181 Lorimer (1984).
182 Agamben (2013b) 61.
183 Agamben (2013b).47.
184 Agamben (2013b) 34.
185 Agamben (2013b) 6.

186 Agamben (2013b) 10.
187 Agamben (2013b) 14.
188 Agamben (2013b) 16.
189 Agamben (2013b) 72.
190 Agamben (2013b) 97.
191 Agamben (2013b) 111.
192 Agamben (2013b) 34, 47.
193 Agamben (2013b) 105.
194 Agamben (2013b) 92–94, 101.
195 Agamben (2013b) 101–102.
196 Agamben (2013b) 102.
197 Agamben (2013b) 92–94, 101; Agamben (1993) 4, 7.
198 Bird (2016) 145.
199 Agamben (2013b) 110.
200 Agamben (2013b) 102.
201 Agamben (2013b) 140–141.
202 Agamben (2013b) 144.
203 Agamben (2013b) 144.

6 The origins of form-of-life

Introduction

The final two chapters of this study involve testing the limits and construction of form-of-life. Essentially what is set out is a critique of Agamben's modal ontology, his form of living through (as I have argued it is best understood) a mode of destituent gestural use, and his immanent politics. Transcendence haunts Agamben's immanent thought. It is in his attempting to avoid slipping into transcendent relationality that his immanence fails to account for whole classes of beings. It is unarguable (in my view at least) that the figure of form-of-life provides a new way of understanding the actions of individuals who have been traditionally accepted as political actors, and also politically liminal figures who may be excluded or marginalised in the *polis* but who nevertheless constitute living beings with capacity to act as agents (even if it is unlikely that they can do so in practice in this biopolitical world).

What I argue is that Levinasian thought can account for the ethical existence of *biologically* liminal figures in a way Agamben's thought cannot, both through primary exegesis, and through secondary application by scholars. Agamben seeks to lay out an ethical life. To do so, form-of-life must be able to account for these liminal figures. Levinas gives us many more tools with which to approach (in terms of this chapter) the figure of the unborn.

This chapter considers the figure of a life that is not yet born, a figure around which debates regarding the start of existence revolve. The complexities of the debate over when life starts, and what value to place on the unborn, are not adequately accounted for in form-of-life. Agamben sees each living being as affected by a clinamen, a leaning towards others. Form-of-life is a monad, alone by oneself, but communicating with others, insofar as it represents them, as in a living mirror.[1] Form-of-life cannot adequately account for the figures of the embryo and foetus, and their role in the reproductive forms-of-lives of pregnant women. Ultimately, Agamben's failure to account for reproductive rights, and his esoteric treatment of intimacy and privacy in his thought leaves an ambiguity and difficulty in its application. This applies as much to the figure of the unborn (which gains scant direct attention) as well as the figure of the woman, who is cast as a privileged figure of ephemerality, unable to gain access

DOI: 10.4324/9781315191447-7

to the plane of immanence, yet instrumental in man's access to it. This ambiguity in Agamben's work is difficult to resolve. By drawing on Melinda Cooper's analysis, I argue that the most persuasive analysis of Agamben's work comes very close to the terrain of the Roman Catholic Church and support for the potential life of the unborn. In such a reading, the woman becomes a sovereign over the unborn, who is cast in a figure of a pseudo *homo sacer*.[2]

It is the case that Levinas's thought can be mobilized by both pro-choice and pro-life camps.[3] His thought can also be read as privileging masculinity over femininity. However, his transcendent thought provides a more coherent basis for considering the position of the unborn. I first draw upon Lisa Guenther's work on "the gift of the other", in which she constructs a defence of abortion rights using Levinasian thought and ethics. I then draw upon the work of Matthew Stone to show how the question of abortion can be considered on a practical level, based in relationality and judgment, by a legal system.[4] This dimension is lacking in Agamben's thought, given his eschewing of questions of law and extant political structures, and their equivalence to forms of biopolitical control. An ethical approach to questions of the start of life necessitates judgment. Without this, no such ethical existence or actions appear possible with respect to these biologically liminal lives.

Setting the stage

The status of the unborn – legal, moral, ethical – is a contingent and a contested matter. Legal and philosophical debates engage in incommensurable arguments over the status of the unborn. Abortion is the biopolitical example *par excellence* – "a medical procedure every aspect of which is heavily regulated".[5] The regulation of reproductive freedoms features heavily-politicised rhetoric and ideologically-inspired expressions of biopolitics.[6] Advocates of abortion rights have argued that the criminalization of abortion is tantamount to legal slavery.[7] For critics the reverse is true.[8]

The question of when life begins is at the crux of these debates. The potentiality argument (which evokes clearly Agamben's own writings on the topic) contends that a zygote has the potential to develop into an individual. Potential possession of a right entails therefore the actual possession of a right.[9] Yet our moral norms prohibit the intentional killing of other persons in all but the most exceptional circumstances. If a foetus *is* a person, abortion is in the same moral category of homicide.[10] As Peter Singer noted in 1994, "the traditional western ethic has collapsed" and we have entered "a period of transition in our attitudes about the sanctity of life".[11] John Rawls's conception of personhood also begs the question of when personhood begins. A person, Rawls asserted:

> [I]s someone who can be a citizen, that is, a normal and fully cooperating member of society over a complete life. We add the phrase "over a complete life" because society is viewed not only as closed … but as a more or less complete and self-sufficient scheme of cooperation, making room within itself for all the necessities and activities of life, from birth until death.[12]

The phrase "over a complete life" is crucial to the initial questions of who counts as a member of our community. When does our complete life begin? Personhood commences at birth as unborn children also have the capacity for a sense of justice and a conception of the good. The capacity does not have to be actualized. Rawls considered the question of abortion in relation to the political values of the due respect for human life, the orderly reproduction of political society over time, including the family in some form, and finally the equality of women as equal citizens. Rawls wrote:

> Now I believe any reasonable balance of these three values will give a woman a duly qualified right to decide whether or not to end her pregnancy during the first trimester. The reason for this is that at this early stage of pregnancy the political value of the equality of women is overriding, and this right is required to give it substance and force. Other political values, if tallied in, would not, I think, affect this conclusion.[13]

The difficulty for the pro-choice position is delineating some non-arbitrary criterion to distinguish the licit killing of a human being at one point on a developmental continuum from the illicit killing of the same being at some other point. This is, as we shall see, a difficulty that Agamben's form-of-life also shares, but it is by no means a conundrum which has affected his philosophy alone.

This distinction begs the question – if abortion is permissible, then why not infanticide? Michael Tooley broached the issue of infanticide in the pages of *Philosophy & Public Affairs*:

> One reason the question of the morality of infanticide is worth examining, is that it seems very difficult to formulate a completely satisfactory liberal position on abortion without coming to grips with infanticide.[14]

In Tooley's analytical framework a moral person is someone who "has a (serious) moral right to life".[15] The logical extension of abortion to infanticide was made by Peter Singer:

> [T]he fact that a being is a human being, in the sense of a member of the species *Homo sapiens*, is not relevant to the wrongness of killing it; instead, characteristics like rationality, autonomy, and self-awareness make a difference. Infants lack these characteristics. Killing them, therefore, cannot be equated with killing normal human beings, or any other self-aware beings.[16]

In 2012 Alberto Giubilini and Francesca Minerva published an article in the *Journal of Medical Ethics*, posing a similar philosophical question about the limits to abortion. Giubilini and Minerva contended that, first, new-borns and foetuses do not have the same moral status as actual persons. The fact that a foetus has the potential to become a person is not a reason for prohibiting abortion. Following this, they contend that when circumstances occur *after birth* such that they would have justified abortion, then *after-birth abortion* should be permissible. What this means is:

> [T]hat many non-human animals and mentally retarded human individuals are persons, but that all the individuals who are not in the condition of attributing any value to their own existence are not persons. Merely being human is not in itself a reason for ascribing someone a right to life. Indeed, many humans are not considered subject of a right to life: spare embryos where research on embryo stem cells is permitted, fetuses where abortion is permitted, criminals where capital punishment is legal.[17]

Giubilini and Minerva also argued that both foetuses and new-borns are potential persons because they can develop, thanks to their own biological mechanisms, those properties which will make them persons in the sense of "subjects of a moral right to life", when they can make aims and appreciate their own life.[18] If a potential person does not become an actual person then there is neither an actual nor a future person who can be harmed, which means that there is no harm at all. This means that the interests of actual people override the interests of merely potential ones. This does not mean that the interests of actual people always override *any* right of future generations, but the authors' focus is on the right to become a particular person.[19]

The reply to the defender of infanticide is simply that "infants do not become persons when they start thinking they are persons. Thinking is just one stage of personal development, made possible by the capacity to do so".[20] As Dyer explains:

> A coherent defense of abortion requires at least an initial distinction between (and thus fixed definition of) human beings and human persons. But to distinguish human persons from human non-persons is simply to offer a different variation of the same tautology: Persons are those human beings who have moral rights because they have attribute Y, and non-persons are those human beings who do not have moral rights because they lack attribute Y. The relevant attribute, however, is simply posited by people with power.[21]

This essentially points out that the distinction of what is, and what is not, a human being is dependent upon a sovereign decision. An adult exercises the decision over whether another prenatal human being is a person and should have their life protected or ended. As Agamben has said, what is life is ultimately a political decision. It is this decisionism that, I think, explains in part Agamben's reticence to engage with this question in any detail.

Form-of-life and the unborn

My starting point for engaging Agamben's work with these debates, and lines of thinking, is to sketch out the limits of a modal form-of-life. As has been mentioned previously, life is a political, not a biological question.[22] There is no neutral ground with respect to the question of who counts as a full person or human being in our political order (and all the judgments as to when life starts or when it is permissible to carry out abortions are just that – judgments which exist on the plane of the law). Who therefore counts as a member of our political and moral community?

Form-of-life presupposes a capacity for doing and living, but this capacity does not engage with some crucial questions and issues. This can be illustrated by way of Agamben's writings on intimacy, which are at no time connected to questions of reproductive rights, or indeed any decision to reproduce or not. We read that forms-of-life communicate by contact, in a void of representation that is also a care for the inappropriable – a care for opacity. This contact participates in an ontology of nonrelation and use from which derives, in the final instance, a politics of intimacy in which life is inappropriable and inseparable from its form – a life that actively preserves its sense of nonknowledge and the generative limits of its own mystery.[23] This dimension of life is precarious. The politics of intimacy is expressive and performatively shaped as a preamble to a life to come,[24] and more completely explained in the following quotes:

> We can call "intimacy" use-of-oneself as relation with an inappropriable. Whether it is a matter of bodily life in all its aspects ... or of the special presence-absence to ourselves that we live in moments of solitude, that of which we have an experience in intimacy is our being held in relation with an inappropriable zone of non-consciousness. ...
>
> [I]t is necessary to remember that intimacy can preserve its political meaning only on condition that it remains inappropriable. *What is common is never a property but only the inappropriable.* The sharing of this inappropriable is love. ...
>
> "Alone by oneself" is an expression of intimacy. We are together and very close, but between us there is not an articulation of a relation that unites us. We are united to one another in the form of our being alone. ... For this reason, lovers show themselves nude to one another: I show myself to you as when I am alone with myself; what we share is only our esoterism, our inappropriable zone of non-knowledge. This inappropriable is the unthinkable; it is what our culture must always exclude and presuppose in order to make it the negative foundation of politics.[25]

Intimacy therefore appears to presage living one's life as a form. United in the form of being alone is a pithy descriptor of this intimate relation between the living being and an inappropriable. The reference to lovers is also deliberate. Love is closely connected to intimacy, as love is living:

> [I]n intimacy with a stranger, not in order to draw him closer, or to make him known, but rather to keep him strange, remote: unapparent – so unapparent that his name contains him entirely. And, even in discomfort, to be nothing else, day after day, than the ever open place.[26]

These comments on intimacy reinforce my presumption that form-of-life as a modal existence presupposes *an ability to live one's life in a manner of contemplative use.* Such a life necessitates actions or behaviour – a form of action that the unborn or the new-born cannot replicate given their stage of development. We are also told that form-of-life represents other forms of life, as a living mirror. Yet this living mirror does not encompass the figures of the embryo and foetus *from their perspective.* It is perfectly possible to imagine a parent, or a sibling, or indeed any being with the capacity to do so to represent the figure of the unborn in themselves. But it is unclear when Agamben sees life as starting, and what the mother's relation to the unborn child comprises. There are indications that form-of-life would not apply to the unborn child. Form-of-life is not able to recognize itself or be recognized, as the contact between monads is situated beyond every possible recognition.[27] Agamben accepts that it is not possible to think of existence and a community beyond all relation, but the relationality that exists for form-of-life is of a different kind than that produced by apparatuses such as the law.[28] If the other is not able to represent itself as a living mirror in another, or if it is not possible to live a life as a how, then that other cannot be said to live its life as a form.

Agamben does speak of the fate of unbaptised babies but instead of making a political point about their status or worth, rather makes the point that those children would find their souls in Purgatory. They become an example for the operation of form-of-life. These souls would be subject to God's forgetfulness, but because they do not know God has forgotten them, so instead of being punished they are in a state of "natural felicity".[29] Those souls in purgatory are not indicative of the unborn, but are a philosophical argument contending that we need to reach that self-same state of grace, through the very how of form-of-life. Even with this reference there remains an uncertainty over the status of unborn life. The uncertainty is, I contend, due to Agamben's failure to engage with any form of explicit reproductive politics.

Most striking is the connection made by Agamben between intimacy and privacy (as the term is understood today). In intimacy we experience our being held in relation with an inappropriable zone of non-consciousness.[30] It is in this sphere of non-awareness that modernity subsumes into the notion of privacy. In privacy the individual is defined by means of their faculty to regulate the access to their intimacy. Intimacy becomes an apparatus by which, through regulating access to the self, the individual constitutes himself as the presupposition and proprietor of his own privacy. As such, privacy comes to replace the use of bodies. Use-of-oneself is transformed into a "jealous possession" which has a political significance.[31]

It is not possible to read this without thinking of the role privacy has held in debates over abortion in common law legal systems. In the United States, the constitutional right to abortion is presaged on a right to privacy.[32] A similar analysis has been taken in Nigeria,[33] and India.[34] The UK Supreme Court has found that a right to abortion can be supported by the Article 8 ECHR right to privacy,[35] and issues relating to bodily autonomy and confidentiality in treatment are closely intertwined with access to reproductive healthcare.[36]

Yet there is no engagement with questions of reproduction. All we have from Agamben is ambiguous at best. To connect his writings on privacy to his earlier work – we know that the sovereign subject is first sovereign over their body. If intimacy (or the use-of-oneself as an inappropriable) becomes the fundamental biopolitical substance, then it is true to state that each individual has the right to share their liking of the other's inappropriable.[37] We also read that potentiality is that through which Being founds itself sovereignly, giving itself to itself.[38] So in this sense the question of liking the other's inappropriable – because it is a question of sovereignty – is also a question of potentiality. But this has implications. We know that the negation of potentiality is described as evil, as it is a decision to remain in a deficit of existence, and regards potentiality as a fault that must be repressed.[39] This statement must be applied to Agamben's description that the attempt to appropriate the inappropriable to oneself, by right or force, to transform it into privacy, is to constitute it as an *Arcanum* of sovereignty, and to fall into a *dispositif*. The attempt to appropriate the inappropriable is the equivalent of trying to actualise potentiality. This is a sovereign decision, turning potentiality into privacy, reducing the living being into a subject. This is the way to read Agamben's statement that the relation with the inappropriable can be violently appropriated by "lords of intimacy".[40]

This lack of focus on questions of reproduction means that Agamben's work does not easily fit within either a pro-choice or pro-life position. A pro-choice position would make the foetus the object of a sovereign decision which determines whether it has value or not. The decision can claim that this potential life has no essence which requires protecting or saving. Contrarily, the pro-life position would oppose reproductive choices which would terminate a pregnancy. However, this would (by any measure) severely curtail women's reproductive choice. Furthermore, pro-life positions project onto the unborn an image of an essence and a life to be protected – a sovereign decision has been made to assign a value to the potential life of the unborn even before it can live its life as a how. Under Agamben's schema, both pro-life and pro-choice positions repeat the division of life which is the fundamental activity of sovereign power. Pro-choice politics allow for the sovereign decision over the unborn; pro-life politics have already decided that the unborn are lives that are worth protecting.

Women

In my reading, this ambiguity over the start of life must be connected to another area of Agamben's thought which is lacking – his treatment of women. When Agamben does consider the thresholds between human and inhuman, he tends to stress a consideration of a "new living dead man, a new sacred man",[41] and not the production of the threshold "prelife" or "prior to human life".[42] This formulation is problematic in that it presupposes the existence of a human in order for the human/inhuman distinction to operate. More importantly, whilst questioning the human, with a few exceptions such as Karen Quinlan, women's bodies are noticeably absent from Agamben's writings.[43]

This has been described by Colby Dickinson as deliberate. Theories of gender and sexuality severely limit our ability to embrace those forms of life lived beyond the borders within which we are typically inscribed.[44] For Dickinson, the messianic vocation in Agamben's work has a relevance for a vast re-envisioning of the nature of the human body as a sexual body.[45] Agamben does not provide a detailed history of sexuality but attempts to see the body presented beyond its ostensive functions.[46] This glorious body:

> [I]s not another body, more agile and more beautiful, more luminous and more spiritual: it is the same body, within the act where idleness freed from enchainment and open to a new common usage is possible.[47]

He beholds bodies as beings not preinscribed with a fixed list of stated characteristics and given over neither to the dictates of common sense nor to stereotypical pronouncements on our gendered being.[48]

For Penelope Deutscher this analysis misunderstands:

> [T]he peculiar form of biopolitics covering women's reproductivity, the interest in termination, and the conflicting and agitated interests in what is termed "life", "rights-bearing life", or life requiring responses identified as "protection", which have taken extreme and on occasion murderous forms.[49]

What of the body of the woman? Agamben does mention "the woman" as one of many social-juridical entities that supersede "the Marxian scission between man and citizen":

> The Marxian scission between man and citizen is thus superseded by the division between naked life (ultimate and opaque bearer of sovereignty) and the multifarious forms of life abstractly recodified as social-juridical entities (the voter, the worker, the journalist, the student, but also the HIV-positive, the transvestite, the porno star, the elderly, the parent, the woman) that all rest on naked life.[50]

Yet here the "woman" is a mere outcome of sovereignty's operation on naked life. I cannot read this passage without connecting it to Agamben's description of the operation of the *dispositif.* To recap, Agamben proposes a division between, on the one hand, living beings, and on the other, *dispositifs* in which living beings are incessantly captured:

> To recapitulate, we have then two great classes: living beings (or substances) and dispositives, and between these two, as a third class, subjects. I call a subject that which results from the relation and, so to speak, from the relentless fight between living beings and dispositives.[51]

The other connection I want to make is to the fact that form-of-life cannot be based on the mutual sharing of properties or form a politics of social movements.[52] There must be a shared non-identity, "beyond personal identity".[53]

These passages read together appear to place the "woman" as a subject that is produced by *dispositifs*, and therefore a figure in opposition to form-of-life. To speak of form-of-life as being beyond personal identity and able to be in a community which shares nothing more than their singularities precludes a feminist interpretation of Agamben's thought. Offering such a feminist reading could, on Agamben's terms, collapse potentiality into actuality, introduce a presupposition and qualification to life and would reproduce the divisions Agamben seeks to avoid. No gradation of the divisions of life are provided; it is the division itself which is an issue – there are not better or worse divisions. As such form-of-life is a particularly *male* form of life. To bring the challenge of sexual difference to Agamben's project is to look for the moments where such questions are broached, and to re-read the text through this prism and refract it accordingly.[54] It is such a reading which is attempted here.

The reference to "naked life" in the English translation of *Means Without Ends* is a direct transliteration of the Italian *nuda vita*, which in other translations has been rendered as "bare life". Agamben makes clear that:

> Life – in its state of exception that has now become the norm – is the naked life that in every context separated the forms of life and their cohering into a form-of-life.[55]

Deutscher argues that it is "surely fair" to name the woman's reproductive body as that which Agamben would prefer not to mention in these considerations of life. A woman whose status as potentially reducible to naked life is associated with her reducibility to reproductive life.[56] Women who bear a redoubled and additional status by virtue of their potential or actual, symbolic and historical relation to reproductivity are reducible to bare life.[57] This is the paradox of figuring the woman as a threatening and competing sovereign power over the foetus that is falsely figured as *homo sacer*: to do so is to reduce the woman to a barer, reproductive life exposed to the state's hegemonic intervention as it overrides the woman who is erroneously figured as a "competing sovereign" exposing life. As she is figured as that which exposes another life, she is herself gripped, exposed and reduced to barer life.[58]

Building on this critique, Ewa Ziarek sees Agamben as strangely *including*, while failing to follow, the implications of the race, ethnic, and historical diversity of his own examples:

> Although Agamben's heterogeneous examples of bare life—for instance, the father-son relation in antiquity, Nazi euthanasia programs for the mentally ill, the destruction of the Romany, ethnic rape camps in the former Yugoslavia, Karen Quinlan's comatose body, and especially the most important case of the *Muselmann* — are always diversified along racial, gender, and ethnic and

> historical lines, his conceptual analysis does not follow the implications of such heterogeneity.[59]

Catherine Mills has made clear that there is also a "gender-blindness" throughout Agamben's work.[60] An example of this can be found in the essay "The Idea of Communism", where Agamben focuses on pornography:

> In pornography, the utopia of a classless society displays itself through gross caricatures of those traits that distinguish classes and their transfiguration in the social act.[61]

He goes on:

> If we look for the truth content of pornography, it immediately displays is artless and insipid claim to happiness.[62]

In explaining this "happiness", Agamben invokes the figure of a woman:

> To demonstrate that the potential for happiness is present in every least moment of daily life wherever there is human society: this is the eternal political justification for pornography. But its truth content, which sets it at the opposite pole from the naked bodies which crowd *fin de siècle* monumental art, is that pornography does not elevate the everyday world to the everlasting heaven of pleasure, but rather shows the unremediably episodic character of every pleasure – the inner aimlessness of every universal. This is why it is only in representing the pleasure of the woman inscribed solely in her face, that pornography achieves its intention.[63]

In Mills's view, there is a long tradition of casting women as the privileged figures of ephemerality, unable to gain access to the universal (yet nevertheless instrumental in man's access to it). This is a tradition Agamben is a part of. He has referred to the "two essential figures of femininity" being "woman (or mother) and girl (or virgin)",[64] and referred to feminine figures as being the threshold between animal and man (and god).[65] What is more, he does not offer an analysis of gender as part of his figurations of sexual fulfilment and happiness.[66] Mills asks:

> What would it be to address questions of gender and by extension other forms of difference such as sexuality, race and class, within the conceptual framework that motivates Agamben's theory of political liberation? Indeed, can such questions be asked within that framework?[67]

In *Profanations*, Agamben revisits pornography. This time he describes it as an "apparatus" which seeks to neutralise the profanatory potential of human erotic behaviour.[68] Pornography can be put to a good use. But again, Agamben turns to the image of a woman's face to illustrate this. This reference to the face does not provide the basis for engaging in an ethical relation, as in Levinas. The face does not command in the sense of responsibility. But it does command in a different way. One porn star, Chloë des Lysses, remains absolutely impassive and indifferent.[69] Her impassive face:

> [B]reaks every connection between lived experience and the expressive sphere; it no longer expresses anything but shows itself as a place without a hint of expression, as a pure means.[70]

The face shows what an immanent politics could be like. It is not an ethical imperative but an exemplar showing us that things could be different. Pornography as an apparatus seeks to capture the human capacity to let erotic behaviours idle, to profane them, by detaching them from their immediate ends. Yet these behaviours can open themselves to a new possible use, which concerns a new collective use of sexuality: "The solitary and desperate consumption of the pornographic image thus replaces the promise of a new use".[71] But again the woman's body is framed as a means to an end, an animate instrument allowing use-of-oneself to be grasped. The parallels to Agamben's writings on slavery and the body of the slave are clear.[72] Just as the slave put in use his own body, showing human activity not reducible to labour, production or praxis, so the woman's body in pornography cannot be appropriated as a means to an end. The connections alluded to earlier in the chapter between slavery and abortion are also striking – this is part of a long philosophical tradition of positing women's close relation to the physiological or biological. Agamben continues this tradition in his attempt to articulate a philosophy of infancy. It places Agamben closer to a pro-life platform, and one where the woman is subordinated below the potential life of the embryo and foetus.

Infancy and potential life

Infancy is understood as a wordless, mute condition that precedes speech; infancy coexists with language and is expropriated by it in the constitution of the subject.[73] Mills explains it best – infancy is the experience from which the human subject emerges.[74] Man constitutes himself as a speaking subject by falling away from the originary, transcendental experience of infancy, a sort of experience prior to linguistic appropriation but related to language.[75] Crucially, infancy is a beginning which constitutes the subject of experience and language, but this state does not refer to a biologically or developmentally inclined conception of subject formation.[76] Infancy, for Agamben:

> [C]oexists in its origins with language – indeed, is itself constituted through the appropriation of it by language in each instance to produce the individual as subject.[77]

In writing about infancy Agamben equates the life of the child to the life of the woman:

> The child … *adheres so closely to its physiological life that it becomes indiscernible from it*. … Similar in this respect to a woman's life, the life of the child is ungraspable, not because it transcends toward an other world, but because it adheres to this world and to its body in a way that adults find intolerable.[78]

He then, in *The Idea of Prose*, goes further, reading the life of a child as a cipher for form-of-life.[79] This should not be misunderstood. This claim does not mean that children necessarily live their lives as a form. Rather the idea of a child as a cipher is important. To live one's life like a child is what Agamben sees as setting the stage for the politics to come as the child is a figure that has not yet been trapped in *oikonomic* apparatuses like language. It is as if Agamben is channelling the words of Jesus in the Gospel of Matthew:

> Truly I tell you, unless you change and become like little children, you will never enter the kingdom of heaven. Therefore, whoever takes the lowly position of this child is the greatest in the kingdom of heaven. And whoever welcomes one such child in my name welcomes me.[80]

And in turn, Agamben would seem to disagree with Paul's approach:

> When I was a child, I talked like a child, I thought like a child, I reasoned like a child. When I became a man, I put the ways of childhood behind me.[81]

Melinda Cooper notes that bare life corresponds to the unborn, a life lived in pure *potentia* but nonetheless subject to the most violent of political *actions* in the sovereign power to kill.[82] How can we explain Agamben's silence on this question of the unborn, and his positioning of the woman as a subject? One explanation is found by Deutscher, who makes clear that the examples of bare life Agamben has considered are examples which one could identify as having been human and then being stripped of that status – for example the PVS patient, the refugee, and the *Muselmann*.[83] Foetal life, as it is not situated at the threshold of depoliticization of previously politicised life, does not fit Agamben's series of figures of bare life. Rather, the foetus represents the "zone of contested and intensified political stakes" surrounding the threshold between prelife and nascent, human, rights-bearing life. Deutscher continues:

> Thus the ambiguous politicised life least separable from some women's bodies happens to be a formation least appropriate for Agamben's analysis. An emergent foetus usually is not considered to have had a political, legal, or linguistic status subsequently suspended. Rather, its original ambiguity is in contention when it comes to the anxieties of biopolitics. This may be one reason foetal life, despite being one of the major modes of biopolitics, makes only the faintest of appearances in Agamben's work, remaining an ambiguous threshold of life in which he has been least interested.[84]

Agamben's ambiguity over questions of the unborn can best be resolved by reading Agamben in a pro-life manner. Cooper draws attention to Agamben's reading of Aristotle's theory of life in *De Anima*. Agamben notes that: "It is important to observe that Aristotle does not at all define what life is", but rather "merely divides it up in isolating the nutritive function and then orders it into a series of distinct and correlated faculties (nutrition, sensation, thought)".[85] Cooper explains that Aristotle's natural philosophy is a theory of attribution in which a generic term – life – is defined first by its minimal substance (plant life, the faculty of nutrition) and progressively complicated by the predication of a series of hierarchical faculties leading from the plant to the animal to the human soul.[86]

Agamben's philosophy works in the reverse order to Aristotle's. He wants to dwell upon the irreducible substance that underlies all forms of life; the substance without which no organised form of life would be possible. This is where Aristotle locates the absolutely minimal, nutritive or vegetative life of the plant. Agamben reminds us that this minimal vegetative life must also be understood in temporal terms, as the first stage in the generation of human life, foetal life being the human equivalent of the plant within a classification of nature.[87]

Despite relying on this underlying framework for his thought, Agamben remains mute on the figure of potential life and does not develop the connection between the foetus and vegetative life. This is curious at first glance, especially considering that Michel Foucault, whose work Agamben is so influenced by, did not shy away from discussing issues of reproductive rights and abortion. Foucault's work opened itself up to an interrogation of the intersection between an eventual notion of "reproductive rights" and the constitution of reproductivity as a biopolitical substance, inflecting state-based and other attempts to suppress abortion and the concurrent resistance to those attempts.[88] Power's operation, such as its investment in the body, becomes a focus for resistance. Foucault reads instances of state or medical panic at demands for free abortion in these terms.[89]

Agamben's muteness on the question of potential life is an entirely logical expression of his politics of witnessing. In *Remnants* he makes clear that the true witness can only ever be mute:

> What cannot be stated, what cannot be archived is the language in which the author succeeds in bearing witness to his incapacity to speak. In this language, a language that survives the subjects who spoke it coincides with a speaker who remains beyond it.[90]

The speaker "who remains beyond it" is the unborn. The true testimonial is one that bears witness to the "silent voice",[91] "the "infant" in the etymological sense, a being who cannot speak",[92] who remains in "a position even lower than that of children".[93]

Whereas the child appears as the cipher for form-of-life, Cooper has cogently argued that there is a consistency across Agamben's work: the "unborn" appears unequivocally as the "tragic hero" of an age in which onto-theology is assumed to be irremediably in decline.[94] Cooper distinguishes between the born and the unborn. The child is a cipher, the unborn an exemplar. In *Language and Death*, the last volume where Agamben explicitly mentions the unborn, he argues that:

> Only ... not being born ... can overcome language and permit man to free himself from the guilt that is built up in the link ... between life and language. But since this is precisely impossible, since man is *born* (he has a birth and a nature), the best thing for him is to return as soon as possible whence he came, to ascend beyond his birth through the silent experience of death.[95]

In *Language and Death*, Agamben ends the text with invoking the unborn as a new homeland that functions as the foundational value of the politics to come:

> The geography and politics of this land, to which man was no brought by any birth and in which he no longer seems mortal, go beyond the limits that we proposed in this seminar. And yet the experience of language expressed here can no longer have the form of a voyage that, separating itself from the proper habitual dwelling place and crossing the marvel of being and the terror of nothingness, returns there where it originally was; rather, here language ... returns to that which never was and to that which it never left.[96]

This is the last text in which Agamben mentions the unborn; in later texts, the unborn disappears entirely from the written page.[97]

For Cooper, Agamben's thought places him "irresistibly" on the terrain of Roman Catholic debates about the unborn's status, although this is not admitted by Agamben. His history and diagnosis of modern state violence is consistent with that of the Catholic Church. He adheres to the standard themes of late twentieth-century Catholic doctrine – the evocation of Auschwitz and state eugenics coupled with a denunciation of biomedicine, medical vegetative states, legal brain death and euthanasia. Agamben only differs in his political and ethical response to the presumed violence of the modern state, which consists in a radical refusal of all politics of rights, dignity or legal personhood, calling for "an ethics of a form of life which begins where dignity ends".[98]

Agamben's writings on potentiality and potential life are clearly applicable to abortion debates. He renders the language of pure potentiality into the Christian idiom of the *gift of life*, asking what it would mean to conceive of life as the potential not-to-actualise:

> Contrary to the traditional idea of potentiality that is annulled in actuality, here we are confronted with a potentiality that conserves itself and saves in actuality. Here potentiality, so to speak, survives actuality and, in this way, *gives itself to itself.*[99]

And it is the impossible task of rendering into language the voice of the unborn that leads Agamben to his solution of a theology in suspended animation,[100] the experience of a silent scream:

> Philosophy, in its search for another voice and another death, is presented, precisely, as both a return to and surpassing of tragic knowledge; it seeks to grant a voice to the silent experience of the tragic hero and to constitute this voice as a foundation for man's most proper dimension.[101]

Here Agamben comes very close to Catholic doctrine. In *Remnants of Auschwitz* Agamben notes that:

> [J]ust as in the fetus organic life begins before that of animal life, so in getting old and dying it survives its animal death.[102]

This reading emphasises the potential and fragile life of the unborn, and the implication is that it deserves protection. In attempting to avoid falling into the perceived trap of sovereign decisionism over which lives are worth living and which are not, Agamben avoids the question of reproduction yet his work still implies that the unborn has a more prominent role in Agamben's thought than the body of the woman. It also takes pre-eminence over the woman's body. The woman is reduced to *homo sacer*. Either her body becomes a home for a potential life which needs protection, or she exercises sovereign power to end a potential life. This clearly has major implications for how Agamben can be read. His thought is much less useful for thinking about reproductive politics than – I contend – Levinas's thought.

Levinas on sexual and ethical difference

Levinas's thought can be mobilised by both pro-life and pro-choice camps. I have in previous chapters explored details of Levinas's thought and their relation to Agamben's philosophy. The point in turning to Levinas here is to argue that his transcendent ethics provides a much more coherent basis for considering the existence of the unborn – his thought does not contain the aporias in relation to the start of life which exist in Agamben's. Levinas's thought can show the complexities of the debates around the start of life in a way form-of-life cannot.

This is not to suggest that Levinasian ethics are unproblematic. Levinas's own comments indicate a troubled approach to femininity in contrast to masculinity. Derrida claimed that Levinas persistently subordinated sexual difference to ethical difference:

> E.L's work seems to me to have always rendered secondary, derivative, and subordinate, alterity as sexual difference, the trait of sexual difference, to the alterity of a sexually non-marked Other.[103]

Derrida argues that by trying to maintain ethical difference in a position of indifference or neutrality about sexual difference, Levinas is effectively privileging the masculine, engaging in a mastery of sexual difference and, hence, subordinating the feminine.

What then is the relation between maternity, embodiment and sexual difference? In a 1987 interview, Joel Doutreleau and Pierre Zallo posed the following question:

> The I as ethical subject is responsible to everyone for everything; his responsibility is infinite. Doesn't that mean that the situation that the situation is intolerable for the subject, and for the other whom I risk terrorising by my ethical voluntarism? So isn't there an impotence of ethics in its will to do good?[104]

Levinas responded:

> I don't know if this situation is intolerable. It is not what you would call agreeable, surely; it is not pleasant, but it is the good. What is very important – and I can maintain this without being a saint myself, and I don't present myself as a saint – is to be able to say that the man who is truly a man, in the European sense of the word … is the man who understands holiness as the ultimate value, as an unassailable value.[105]

Humanity – the "truly European man" understands holiness and sainthood as the ultimate value. Lisa Guenther asks whether the reference to European manhood an unfortunate remark, or does it reveal an inability or unwillingness of his ethics to respond to the *difference* of Others as well as their alterity?[106]

Levinas also invoked the value of sainthood in a 1985 interview without explicitly connecting it to European culture:

> I have never claimed to describe human reality in its immediate appearance, but what human deprivation itself cannot obliterate: the human vocation to saintliness; I can say that man cannot question the supreme value of saintliness.[107]

As human beings, we are called to saintliness, as though the very definition of the human were to be the sort of creature who is commanded to exceed the limitation of its own finite abilities.[108] If the human were unfailingly saintly there would be no need for an ethics of responsibility.[109]

In the next section, I draw upon Guenther's work on the gift of the other in which she constructs a defence of abortion rights using Levinas's thought and responds to this charge of subordinating sexual difference to ethical difference. This is a pro-choice reading but does support my argument that Levinas's thought can provide a more coherent theoretical basis for considering the position of the unborn. For Guenther, even if Levinas emphasised the masculinity of the self who is called to saintliness, his account of ethical substitution implies a certain feminisation of the human, an alteration of virility in response to the Other. This risks identifying femininity too closely with saintliness, confirming the patriarchal ideal of a woman who thinks nothing of herself and gives selflessly to the Other.[110] But there is nothing particularly feminist about the theme of maternal responsibility. In *Otherwise than Being*, Levinas compares ethical responsibility to a maternal body that bears the Other without integrating him or her into the same. To be responsible is to substitute oneself for the Other in the sense of bearing responsibility for the Other's own responsibility, and even for the persecution that she may inflict on me.[111]

The next challenge Levinas's thought needs to answer is how ethical imperatives can be translated into a form of institutional justice. Barbara Hudson argued that there is a dichotomy that runs through any consideration of Levinasian ethics which is as if Levinas claimed:

> [W]e must have justice, then what would a justice of alterity be like, how would it operate? One clear principle that is central is that there must be a 'deep' equality: if responsibility to the Other is not dependent on reciprocity, desert, or any special characteristics, then all have equal claims. There can be no question of rights being sacrificed because of irresponsible behaviour, or because of being assessed as dangerous or risky. Acceptance of this radical justice of alterity, basing justice on an ethics of responsibility to Otherness is, Levinas's writing suggests, the only safeguard against oppression of the different; it is the only defence against the Holocaust.[112]

Hudson has issued a seemingly impossible challenge; Levinas's ethics cannot be accommodated in institutional justice. Alterity must defy systemic application as all processes must inevitably betray the otherness of the Other. The Other will not be normalised. Levinas extols and endorses Western philosophical conceptions of justice and is not seeking to subvert traditional ideas of justice.[113] Yet institutional justice is essential if we are to have any meaningful and constructive social interaction and the consequences of failing to uphold it are obvious.[114]

To show how Levinasian ethics can both account for reproductive politics and translate this account into institutional justice I draw upon the work of Matthew Stone. In this construction I show how the contested nature of abortion and the start of life can be considered ethically through the law. This practical dimension is absent from Agamben's work. Institutional justice is not pro-choice or pro-life. Levinas's philosophy does not provide "a rule of algorithm by which to test and evaluate specific claims".[115] My aim here is to demonstrate that Levinas's recourse to relationality, law and judgment are integral to his institutional justice, and such concepts, eschewed by Agamben, actually help provide a more coherent understanding of these biologically liminal lives.

Lisa Guenther on the "gift of the Other"

My starting point for how Levinas's work can address the complexities of this debate is with Lisa Guenther's *Gift of the Other*. Guenther makes an extended reading of Levinas's work to understand how maternity is thought in his work. Her work draws on hospitality in *Totality and Infinity* and maternity in *Otherwise than Being*. I am given this capacity to welcome Others in hospitality by a feminine Other who has always already opened the space of welcome within the home. The command to welcome the Other is a command to be feminised by the Other. Responsibility for the Other obligates me to bear her "like a maternal body".[116]

To become like a maternal body for someone is to become responsible for her *as if* she were my child.[117] The way beyond the oppression of women's reproductive rights involves a reinterpretation of maternity as an ethical situation.[118] To give birth is to bring an Other into the world: a distinct self with her own future, her own embodied existence, and even her own capacity to reproduce.[119] A woman's body is the starting point for a world, forming the material basis for her experience of things and my interaction with Others.[120] The feminine Other both *gives* me a home and allows me to *make a gift* of my home to the stranger. The feminine Other provides a quiet place where this responsibility might emerge in the face-to-face encounter with an (implicitly masculine) stranger.[121] Ultimately responsibility for the Other requires that I become *like* the feminine Other in giving hospitality to an Other.[122] The feminine welcome is the ethical gesture par excellence because it is a truly generous gift: a gift that was never mine to give, and does not claim to give me anything in return.[123]

Paternity and maternity

In *Totality and Infinity*, parenthood is understood almost exclusively as the transcendent relation of a father to his son. For Levinas, giving birth is paternity. Guenther argues that paternity cannot coherently be restricted to fathers and sons.[124] The alterity of the child engenders in the parent an alteration of the self to one who welcomes an Other.[125] The child is *both* me and not-me, both a stranger and myself.[126] In giving birth to a child who is both familiar and strange, the self becomes like a stranger to itself, a guest in its own home. The child brings a future that is discontinuous with the past and the present. Levinas calls this future of the child an "absolute future";[127] it opens an infinity of generations beyond the limited future of projects represented by the phrase "I can" (one can here draw a distinction to Agamben's clear emphasis on potentiality and the possibilities of the saying "I can").[128] The identity of the father recommences in the son, marking a certain *rebirth* of the self in giving birth to an Other.[129] The radical promise of the child not only brings hope for the future, but also hope for the past: hope that the significance of the past might be altered in forgiveness. Forgiveness redoubles my responsibility; I am responsible not only for my own existence and actions but first and foremost for the time of the Other.[130] Guenther argues that the problem with forgiveness in *Totality and Infinity* concerns a certain reciprocity in the relation between father and son. The father gives birth to the son, engendering in him desire and responsibility, but the son gives time to the father by forgiving him and releasing him from the burden of his own past.[131] As long as birth is understood solely in terms of the father and the son it risks lapsing into a circular exchange that compromises the radical gift of birth.[132]

Levinas's language is offensive. He calls the feminine "infantile",[133] "a bit silly",[134] an "amorphous non-I",[135] a "virgin" who remains "forever violable and inviolable".[136] She is almost not even human, resembling "an irresponsible animality which does not speak true words".[137] He goes on:

> The frailty of the feminine invites pity for what, in a sense, is not yet, disrespect for what exhibits itself in immodesty and is not discovered despite the exhibition, that is, profaned.[138]

Guenther adapts Levinas here, arguing that to resist this masculine privilege, the gift of time must be extended toward mothers and daughters. Maternity signals for Levinas a protective relation that is different from paternity.[139]

It is in *Otherwise than Being* that Levinas focuses upon the maternal body, stating that everyone is called on to bear the Other "like a maternal body".[140] Before I can confirm my own identity through self-awareness, I am exposed to the Other.[141] In pregnancy, a woman is exposed to an Other whom she has never seen but with whom she is in the closest proximity. In pregnancy, the temporality and identity of the woman is altered. The pregnant woman bears an Other who is birth in her womb and not present as an existent; she responds to an Other who has not yet spoken or appeared. To give birth is to grant the Other a time in which she will have found asylum or refuge, as in the gestation of the child in the body of a woman.[142] Ethical maternity is the figure of "bearing par excellence".[143] The Other escapes me yet is inescapably close but not together with me in my time.[144] For Levinas, this proximity between self and Other signifies as "passive to the point of becoming inspiration, that is, precisely alterity-in-the-same".[145] The passivity leads me to being inspired by the Other, transformed into a self who is *for-the-Other* to the point where my own identity is expressed as a relation to the Other: "alterity-in-the-same". My ability to respond to the Other comes as *the gift of the Other*.[146]

Guenther asks how this infinite alterity of the Other relates to the cultural, racial and sexual differences which flesh out our ethical and political encounters.[147] Motherhood is not always a patient, generous, compassionate practice of ethical substitution. Woman and men who raise children have moments of impatience, fatigue, distraction, selfishness; these moments confirm the difficulty of ethical life and the vulnerability of human creatures who are both limited and responsible for Others who push their limits.[148] To utilise Levinas's thought to defend issues of reproductive choice, Levinas's thought requires a politics of justice to critique what Guenther sees as the "unshared social burden" which is "heaped" on certain groups of people: anyone whose contribution to collective life goes unnoticed or unreciprocated.[149] There is a long history of women being coerced, directly and indirectly, into producing children; we must find different ways of thinking about women and birth.

A Levinasian defence of reproductive choice

Guenther seeks to reconcile a demand for reproductive choice with Levinas's work. Levinasian ethics may not sit easily with pro-choice politics – Levinas commented on the nobility of women dying in childbirth: "I think that the heart of the heart, the deepest point of the feminine, is dying in giving life, in bringing life into the world".[150] Without a feminist politics of reproductive choice, a maternal ethics of embodiment for the Other threatens to confirm the traditional view of women and mothers as humbled, self-sacrificing supports for other people. Guenther contends that we need to ground women's reproductive freedom not on the assumption of an autonomous subject who owns her body and therefore has a right to choose but rather on the ethical sensibility of an always-already embodied self whose very exposure to the Other calls for justice and equality, and *therefore* for women's right to choose.[151] The possibility of a certain *ethical* responsibility for the prenatal Other does not preclude the vital necessity of women's *political* right to safe and accessible abortions.

Justice is the transformation of present practices considering a future that will not quite arrive in the present moment.[152] Levinas distinguishes between justice and any particular legal or political system:

> This means concretely or empirically that justice is not a legality regulating human masses, from which a technique of social equilibrium is drawn, harmonising antagonistic forces. That would be a justification of the State delivered over to its own necessities. Justice is impossible without the one that renders it finding himself in proximity.[153]

Guenther argues that there are resources in Levinas for a feminist defence of reproductive choice. If the ethical asymmetry of my responsibility for Others is to be rigorously distinguished from the asymmetry of injustice, then a defence of social and political symmetry or equality is necessary.[154] It is for the sake of the *other* Other – the third party – that such an approach to politics that defends against violence becomes necessary. Justice is a rational discourse through which rights and responsibilities can be balanced and negotiated.[155] The demand for justice recalls the importance of defending the self against violence and protecting it from a reduction to this or that objective identity.[156]

Reproductive justice involves a defence of women's individual selfhood against the reduction to a fixed social or biological role as well as a defence of women's access to the resources and support required to make an informed decision about their pregnancy.[157] Ethics requires politics but politics is only justified – oriented toward justice – by remaining open to ethical critique. That which the proximity of the Other made impossible – namely, the understanding of an Other in terms of an intelligible theme that grants me certain reasonable rights and duties – this very impossibility returns, with the advent of the third party, as the necessity of justice.[158] Justice requires me to compare the incomparable, to calculate my resources and balance my commitments. This act of compassion and calculation is only *just* insofar as it remembers the ethical proximity to the Other and attends to the third party.[159]

Guenther lays out her understanding of a politics of reproduction. It is politically important to defend the singularity of individual women against a reduction in advance to the status of a she whose future is already determined by her capacity to reproduce. An ethics of maternal bearing requires a political recognition of mothers as singular and irreplaceable.[160] This politics acknowledges that a foetus may make a claim on a woman, calling her to respond in the best way possible under the circumstances. To understand ethics as the process of becoming like a maternal body for the Other is to propose a vision of maternity as the gift of time and incarnation, a gift that carries over the imperative to give to an Other.[161] The ethical situation of birth *should not* be translated into a command to carry every pregnancy to term. Birth suggests an interpretation of existence that turns on the fortunate *dispossession* of being given to Others.[162] While I may die alone, I am never born alone; already, I am bound to at least one Other before I can grasp hold of myself. The unchosen contingency and passivity of birth discloses a limit of human existence that orients me toward Others without whom I could not be who I am. This passivity refers to the affective exposure of oneself to the Other, a profound sense of not controlling one's existence from the ground up. To be born is to be received into the world as someone utterly new, but it is nevertheless to be received *by an Other*.

Guenther thus ably demonstrates how it is possible to utilise Levinasian ethics and philosophy to construct a critical reproductive politics. Ultimately, Levinas gives us more tools (for want of a better word) for conceptualising start of life decisions than Agamben. Agamben would surely agree that the individual woman is a singular being, but would not accede to Guenther's acceptance of a transcendent relationality that means that the human is exposed to the Other, and maternity can be conceived as a gift. The foetus makes a claim on the woman for *her* to respond in the best possible way – this avoids discussions of potentiality and potential life, as well as modal ontology. Finally, Guenther's call for reproductive justice presupposes a decision-maker – the woman. Whilst this is, for her, a question of ethics, it is for Agamben (as stated before) a pseudo *homo sacer*.

Judgment and institutional justice

I want to extend this analysis of Levinas and the unborn from the philosophical to the institutional. Levinas's philosophy lends itself more easily to conceptualising issues of reproductive rights on an institutional (or legal) level. This does not presuppose a pro-choice or pro-life approach.

My starting place is the observation that Guenther avoids the central ethical question of limits and when we must set them.[163] When claiming a Levinasian interpretation of reproduction we need to address the question of whether the foetus has a face. The face reveals the Other in an epiphany through which the I affirms its subjectivity and engages in an ethical relation. This involves an:

> [I]nfinite ethical requirement … that meets me, dissimulated by its appearance, and the appearance of the other as an individual and as an object.[164]

The face does not need to be revealed through a face: "a hand or curve of the shoulder … can express the face".[165] The key question to ask is whether the foetus has a face, and therefore an ethical status. For Levinas, language is not a prerequisite for a face to be recognised (again this can be placed in contrast to Agamben's construction of form-of-life and its ability to live its life as a form).[166] He also suggested that a dog has a face, and that the dog's face has a "child-like character".[167] This certainly implies that the foetus *could* have a face. But the issue remains ambiguous on some level.

Perhaps this conclusion is as far as we can pull Levinasian ethics before we make a value judgment of our own. The experience of pregnancy is an engagement with an other that is not yet an other human. But the demand of the Other is not absolute, as that would be a form of injustice.[168] There are limits to our understanding in ethics, and we need to be informed by medical and scientific knowledge. The word foetus is not unequivocal. The difference of a few months in relation to a foetus captures a huge amount of biological development.[169] How then can this be translated into the institution of law?

Drucilla Cornell sees law as "embedded in ontology, in a shared social reality".[170] The root of just law is a pre-legal asymmetrical debt to the Other. Although the rationality of the law undermines the infinite demand of the ethical, it is only the aspiration to the ethical that can give us reason.[171] The "obligatory character of law depends upon its ethical content".[172] But as Stone has contended, moving from the ethical to the legal is an irreducible problem within the Levinasian framework.[173] Ethics aspires to be embodied in the state. Ethics need laws and political structures to be expressed in the social, yet such apparatuses will always necessarily fail ethics by reducing the signification of transcendence to totality.[174]

Central to this institutionalization of ethics is an unavoidable judgment. In fact, to even speak of justice being effected through the institution of the law, a judgment is necessary. The law is a human institution involving human actors. To avoid questions of judgment, as Agamben attempts to, means that the institution of the law may never be able to reach just decisions. Conversely, using Levinas, we can construct an institution of the law that is able to reach just decisions, even on disputed questions such as the status of the unborn.

To understand institutional justice, we turn back to the third, which was considered above in Guenther's work. Ethics determines the subject, but upon its emergence the subject finds itself in a world surrounded by others and faced with dilemmas. The third disrupts the ethical relation, demanding attention and distancing the subject from the other.[175] It also demands comparing, ranking, and deciding between incommensurable demands by assimilating them within a coherent framework.[176] Likewise, the demands of justice call for "the political structure of society under the rule of law" and an institutional framework to reflect a "perfect reciprocity of political laws that are essentially egalitarian or held to be so".[177]

This framework can be found in the liberal state. This is another marked difference between Agamben and Levinas. Agamben seeks a messianic completion of politics and talks about form-of-life being attested to in unedifying places and in insignificant and contemptible ideas.[178] Conversely, Levinasian institutional justice can be conceptualised within the modern state, a position which is much easier to both grasp and picture. Levinas frequently wrote in favour of the liberal state and found liberal ideas enduring.[179] Levinas was cynical about political frameworks in general: "Politics left to itself bears a tyranny within itself".[180] But Levinas's is an "inverted liberalism" in which the individual is prioritised "not for the sake of the individual, but rather for the other".[181] He talked of the way in which there must be "an element of violence in the state".[182] If left unchecked, this means state power tends toward totalitarianism. Even democratic regimes have an inherent violence: this is the consequence of politics addressing itself to the multiplicity.[183]

The liberal state has the potential for a workable but tense co-presence of ethics and politics.[184] This is a "state capable of extending beyond the state" in meeting the demands of the face of the other, committed to "the rights of man".[185] It must always be restless, never static in the pursuit of justice.[186] This state provides a platform for the extraterritorial demands of justice to be met, which would come from the work of its people.[187] A liberal state allows its people to criticise authority and incorporate a concern for fellow citizens into government via the democratic process. In relation to the role of the state, Levinas describes the challenge of how:

> The liberal state is a state which holds justice as the absolutely desirable end and hence as a perfection.[188]

Justice is not the last word – within justice, we seek a better justice. That is the liberal state. When the verdict of justice is pronounced, there remains for the unique I that I am the possibility of finding something more to soften the verdict. The truly democratic state is never democratic enough.[189]

We know that justice must attend itself to the third party. The political or legal responsibility felt in the presence of the third must be understood very differently to the ethical responsibility provoked by the other: where the latter is singular and infinite, the former is both measures and capable of universalization amongst all people within a representable principle.[190] As Stone explains, justice undermines the radical ethical relation yet is necessary if law seeks to articulate our responsibilities to each other, however imperfectly. In a sense, responsibility demands justice.[191] Justice requires the reduction of the other to the same, traversing the chasm between the proximity of the other and the totality of law and politics. The work of justice is a betrayal of the other and its anarchic call,[192] but it also cements a social bond.[193] Through the presence of the third and the exigency of justice, the I is not just an ethical subject but also an other for all the other others, and is accounted for in the structures of law and politics that arise out of justice's demands.[194]

The gap between these two orders, ethics on the one hand and the ontological realm of the juridical and political on the other is described as a *hiatus*.[195] Stone asks how the subject can know what justice entails if the preceding order of ethics escapes its ontological graspability. How does the subject survive this passage, unconditionally bonded to the other in one (ethical) moment, and required to justify its (legal) judgment the next?[196] Levinas does not provide us with a direct answer to these questions. The problem of passage will continue to (de)limit the direct application of this ethical philosophy to questions of law.[197]

Legal adjudication and justice

Legal adjudication demands that a decision must pass through the aporetic passage from singular ethical duties to general, intelligible principles. Justice is never just enough and will always erase the signification of the other in the very gesture that seeks to transpose the ethical into the legal.[198] Stone argues that justice for Levinas takes on an adjudicative form. Law can arise out of the demands of justice, and justice is achieved through qualities we naturally associate with law in modern Western society: the mediation of disputes, the comparing and ranking of the priority of parties' demands, a concern for equality and equity between parties, and so on.[199] Despite its radicalized understanding of alterity, it contorts and reimagines elements of a distinctly liberal jurisprudence, one which is constituted in the superimposition of formal equality and reciprocity over the radical singularity of ethics.[200]

Levinas's concept of the third presents us with a limited account of law, which is how law can be constituted in response to, but not reducible to, ethics. Law is not always an expression of justice. Subjectivity is born out of a constitutive ethical debt to others, but there is no guarantee that this always filters into our institutions and our shared ontology.[201] The Levinasian outlook requires the judge to adopt a more radical position, to the extent that they are cast in the role of the rebel.[202] Their job requires them to apply the law in all its generality, but due to an exceptional process of ethical exposure, interpretation and judgment, justice may still demand the rupture of the prevailing legal framework in a gesture of fidelity to the other, effacing existing law in a commitment to justice. Why would we trust the judiciary to effectuate the ethical rupture of law's synchrony? For Cornell, the answer may address a commitment to the very integrity of law and its contended origin in the ethical encounter. If we entertain the claim that adjudication requires the effacement of law in a moment of rebellion, we might ask ourselves how anarchic an institution the judiciary can be expected to be.[203]

In relation to this question, Cornell focuses on Levinas's inclination toward the transcendent other as crucial to reason,[204] and as vigilance against the "bad infinity" of a dispassionate rationality that assumes it has no exterior.[205] Cornell situates these themes within the domain of the judge. The judge is not above the parties in a dispute but is an engaged *part* of the triangular relationship in which the unconditionality of ethics is turned over to the question of justice.[206] The judgment seeks to do justice to ethical demands.[207] To put it another way:

> The time of justice differs from the time of interpretation. ... It addresses the Other here and now in each here and now, and answers or denies the call.[208]

The role of the judge incorporates the unique, interpersonal relation, where the judge "is always involved and implicated, called upon to respond to the ethical relationship when he judges".[209] For justice to be ethical, to be faithful to the ethical encounter with the Other, it must be immediate in its response to her and resist the temptation to assemble facts and to attempt to know all.[210]

Cornell traces this capacity for doing justice to ethical demands in *Roe v Wade*.[211] The act of judgment is more complex than retroactively justified creativity and evinces a type of responsibility that is absent from a mechanical application of existing precedents. To offer the promise of meaningful transformation, justice must come from the other.[212] The responsibility inherent in judgment must aspire to justice. The work of memory in judging, in which precedents and codes are interpreted, cannot be divorced form the responsibility for justice's futurity:

> [W]hen the judge remembers the past she does so through the "ought to be" implicit in the not yet of the never has been.[213]

Justice is not limited to precedent, as justice is always addressed to a future that is other. For Cornell this is a justice that is directly implicated in judges' interpretations of past cases and established sources of law. In *Roe*, Justice Blackmun confessed that the question of when life begins was not one the Justices could answer:

> We need not resolve the difficult question of when life begins. When those trained in the respective disciplines of medicine, philosophy, and theology are unable to arrive at any consensus, the judiciary, at this point in the development of man's knowledge, is not in a position to speculate as to the answer.[214]

Cornell argues that the responsibility and integrity of judicial office must be affected by the ethical demand of the Other. Justice Blackmun was able to decide whether and when a foetus becomes a *legal* person through imaginatively recollecting a legal norm in the right to privacy. For Cornell, his decision was an activism that is *inevitable* in judgment and decision, but an activism exercised in accordance with responsibility and the call to justice.[215]

Yet I do not want to give the impression that a pro-choice interpretation of Levinas is all that is possible. What I want to stress is the way in which ethics can be institutionalised and decided through the law. The duty of the judge in this situation, as in all cases, arises out of the presence of the third and the necessary relationship between both the singular ethical relationship with an other and the duty to limit or extend responsibility in the form of general principle or rule. A Levinasian justice of adjudication involves ethical demands being placed upon the judge, but it is a type of procedural justice. It demands the weighing and comparing of competing ethical demands, of the priority of others, and the necessity of weaving the ethical call of the other into the ontology of law.[216]

How then can we judge the judge? How do we know if she has weaved the ethical call of the other into the ontology of law? Levinas occasionally invites us to interpret a relation between his ethics and broad normative ideas. For example: "Irrefusable responsibility nonetheless never assumed in complete freedom, is *good*".[217] Goodness involves "taking up a position in being such that the other counts more than myself".[218] The good is a description of the structure of ethical subjectivity: "no one is Good voluntarily".[219] Levinasian ethics show how we come to be bound to others – legal norms tend to hold people accountable. They do not provide a formula for making good choices – only that the other can bind us into a situation in which a choice must be made.[220]

In a 1986 interview, Levinas was asked how people can act unethically. He replied that in the *conatus essendi*, which is the effort to exist, existence is the supreme law. The appearance of the face emerges as a limitation of the *conatus essendi*. It is not a rational limit. Interpreting it necessitates thinking it in moral terms, in ethical terms. It is in the human being that a rupture is produced with being's own law, with the law of being.[221] Our responsibility towards the other is what pulls us away from our commitment to securing our own lives, whilst the capacity to be absolutely unethical is given its justification precisely by this instinct to be primarily-for-ourselves. In short – when we act unethically it is because we prioritise ourselves above the other.[222]

This brings us back to a judgment. But I want to make two important distinctions here with Agamben's thought. First, Agamben's thinking of potential does, as I have argued, bring him very close to a strident defence of unborn lives. This is due both to his failure to engage with questions of reproductive ethics and politics, and in the fact that the non-relational figure of form-of-life does not easily apply to biologically liminal figures. In contrast, Levinasian ethics, based as they are in relationality, provide us with many more resources for engaging with contested debates over when life starts, and the rights a mother may have vis-à-vis the foetus. Lisa Guenther's work illustrates this.

Secondly, and importantly, Levinasian ethics can be translated into institutional justice in the liberal states in which we currently live. The centrality of *oikonomic* apparatuses in Agamben's thought forecloses any such interpretation of the institution of law, without us first embracing a messianic politics. As such, Agamben's coming politics remains ephemeral in a way that Levinasian ethics do not.

Conclusion

This has been the first of two chapters seeking to test the construction of form-of-life. What I have attempted to show is that form-of-life, in its attempt to eschew all forms of transcendent thought, cannot account for the figure of the unborn human being. Moreover, Levinasian ethics, which are transcendent and represent the form of philosophy Agamben is trying to critique, provides us with resources that enable us to comprehend the potential human in a way Agamben's thought cannot. I have further argued that Agamben's thought contains an ambiguity (at best) in his treatment of reproductive ethics and politics. The most persuasive analysis of Agamben's writings comes very close to the terrain of the Roman Catholic Church and support for the potential life of the unborn. In such a reading, the woman becomes a sovereign over the unborn, who is cast in a figure of a pseudo *homo sacer*. To support my contention about Levinas's thought, I first drew upon Lisa Guenther's work to show how Levinasian philosophy can be utilised to critically engage with questions of abortion. I then engaged with Matthew Stone's work to show how Levinas's work lends itself to a form of institutional justice, grounded in relationality and judgment. In the next and final chapter, I turn to end of life decision-making to further test Agamben's philosophy, and again to argue that Levinas offers us more to work with in his ethics.

Notes

1 Agamben (2016a) 232, 238.
2 I first set out many of the arguments developed here in relation to Agamben and abortion in Frost (2020).
3 Guenther (2006b) 144.
4 Stone (2016).
5 Parry (2005) 872.
6 Perry (2006) 553–560.
7 Dworkin (1993) 103.
8 George (1999) 193.
9 Boonan (2012) 48.
10 Greasley (2017) 13.
11 Singer (1995) 1.
12 Rawls (2005) 18.
13 Rawls (2005) 243–244 n.32.
14 Tooley (1972) 37–38.
15 Tooley (1972) 38.

16 Singer (2011) 160–161.
17 Giubilini and Minerva (2013) 262.
18 Giubilini and Minerva (2013) 262.
19 Giubilini and Minerva (2013) 263.
20 Kavanaugh (2001) 67.
21 Buckley Dyer (2013) 176.
22 Agamben (1998) 64.
23 Bordeleau (2017) 490.
24 Bordeleau (2017) 488.
25 Agamben (2016a) 91, 93, 237–238.
26 Agamben (1995) 61.
27 Agamben (2016a) 248.
28 Agamben (2010) 46.
29 Agamben (1995) 78.
30 Agamben (2016a) 91.
31 Agamben (2016a) 92.
32 *Planned Parenthood v Casey*, 505 U.S. 833 (1992); *Roe v Wade*, 410 U.S. 113 (1973); Goldenberg (1973) 336–357.
33 Anozie (2020) 483–510.
34 Magill (2020) 160–194.
35 *The Northern Ireland Human Rights Commission Judicial Review* [2018] UKSC 27, [2018] All ER (D) 28.
36 Mokrosinka (2018) 117–143; McHale and Jones (2012) 31–34; Hewson (2001) 10–14; *Gillick v West Norfolk and Wisbech Area Health Authority* [1986] AC 112 (HL).
37 Agamben (2016a) 92–93.
38 Agamben (1998) 46.
39 Agamben (2007b) 44.
40 Agamben (2016a) 93.
41 Agamben (1998) 131.
42 Agamben (2002) 135.
43 Deutscher (2008) 59.
44 Dickinson (2015c) 167.
45 Dickinson (2015c) 175.
46 Dickinson (2015c) 179.
47 Agamben (2010) 103.
48 Agamben (2007b) 48.
49 Deutscher (2008) 60.
50 Agamben (2000) 6–7.
51 Agamben (2009d) 19.
52 Agamben (2007b) 86.
53 Agamben (2010) 54; Agamben (1995) 82.
54 Deutscher (2017) 137.
55 Agamben (2000) 6.
56 Deutscher (2008) 67.
57 Deutscher (2017) 127.
58 Deutscher (2008) 67.
59 Ziarek (2008) 93.
60 Mills (2008b) 114.
61 Agamben (1995) 73.
62 Agamben (1995) 73–74.
63 Agamben (1995) 74.
64 Agamben and Ferrando (2014) 3.
65 Agamben and Ferrando (2014) 44.

66 Cavarero (1992) 32–47.
67 Mills (2008b) 115.
68 Agamben (2007c) 88–89.
69 Agamben (2007c) 90–91.
70 Agamben (2007c) 91.
71 Agamben (2007c) 91.
72 Agamben (2016a) 14.
73 Mills (2008a) 16, 21.
74 Mills (2008a) 22.
75 Agamben (2007a) 55.
76 Agamben (2007a) 4.
77 Agamben (2007a) 55.
78 Agamben (2001) 122.
79 Agamben (1995) 95–98.
80 Matthew 18:3–5.
81 1 Corinthians 13:11.
82 Cooper (2009) 142.
83 Deutscher (2008) 57–58.
84 Deutscher (2008) 58.
85 Agamben (1999a) 231.
86 Cooper (2009) 144.
87 Agamben (1999a) 231.
88 Deutscher (2008) 55–56.
89 Foucault (1980a) 56.
90 Agamben (2002) 162.
91 Agamben (2002) 129.
92 Agamben (2002) 121.
93 Agamben (2002) 113.
94 Agamben (2006) 96.
95 Agamben (2006) 90.
96 Agamben (2006) 97.
97 Cooper (2009) 154.
98 Agamben (2002) 69.
99 Agamben (1999c) 184.
100 Cooper (2009) 155–156.
101 Agamben (2006) 90.
102 Agamben (2002) 152.
103 Derrida (1991) 40.
104 Levinas (1998a) 203.
105 Levinas (1998a) 203.
106 Guenther (2006a) 121.
107 Levinas (1999) 180.
108 Guenther (2006a) 121.
109 Guenther (2006a) 128.
110 Guenther (2006a) 121–122.
111 Guenther (2006a) 119; Levinas (2008) 75.
112 Hudson (2003) 196–197.
113 Loumansky (2006) 148.
114 Loumansky (2006) 148–149.
115 Perpich (2008) 126.
116 Levinas (2008) 67.
117 Guenther (2006b) 7.
118 Guenther (2006b) 18.
119 Guenther (2006b) 27.

120 Guenther (2006b) 17.
121 Guenther (2006b) 58.
122 Guenther (2006b) 61.
123 Guenther (2006b) 64.
124 Guenther (2006b) 76.
125 Guenther (2006b) 77.
126 Levinas (1969) 267.
127 Levinas (1969) 268.
128 Guenther (2006b) 79.
129 Levinas (1969) 268.
130 Levinas (1969) 282; Guenther (2006b) 82.
131 Levinas (1969) 283.
132 Guenther (2006b) 84.
133 Levinas (1969) 259.
134 Levinas (1969) 263.
135 Levinas (1969) 259.
136 Levinas (1969) 258.
137 Levinas (1969) 263.
138 Levinas (1969) 262.
139 Levinas (1969) 278.
140 Levinas (2008) 67.
141 Guenther (2006b) 98.
142 Guenther (2006b) 101–102.
143 Levinas (2008) 75.
144 Guenther (2006b) 104.
145 Levinas (2008) 67 (translation altered).
146 Guenther (2006b) 104–105.
147 Guenther (2006b) 131.
148 Guenther (2006b) 137–138.
149 Guenther (2006b) 140.
150 Levinas (2001a) 9.
151 Guenther (2006b) 142–143.
152 Guenther (2006b) 147; Levinas (1969) 245.
153 Levinas (2008) 159.
154 Guenther (2006b) 148.
155 Levinas (1985) 90.
156 Guenther (2006b) 149.
157 Guenther (2006b) 149–150.
158 Guenther (2006b) 152–153.
159 Levinas (2008) 157.
160 Guenther (2006b) 154.
161 Guenther (2006b) 155.
162 Guenther (2006b) 163.
163 Evans (2017) 58.
164 Levinas (1998a) 177.
165 Levinas (1969) 262.
166 Levinas (1988a) 169.
167 Levinas (1988a) 172.
168 Evans (2017) 60.
169 Evans (2017) 58–59.
170 Cornell (1992) 107.
171 Cornell (1988) 1626.
172 Crowe (2006) 432.
173 Stone (2016) 57.

174 Stone (2016) 58.
175 Levinas (2008) 157.
176 Levinas (1998a) 88–89.
177 Levinas (1999) 143.
178 Agamben (2016a) 227.
179 Stone (2016) 112.
180 Levinas (1969) 300.
181 Alford (2004) 162.
182 Levinas (1988c) 167.
183 Stone (2016) 114.
184 Levinas (1993) 123.
185 Levinas (1998a) 174–175.
186 Levinas (1988a) 175.
187 Levinas (1988c) 181.
188 Levinas (1988a) 177.
189 Levinas (1988a) 175.
190 Simmons (1999) 96.
191 Levinas (2008) 45.
192 Levinas (2008) 158.
193 Stone (2016) 59.
194 Stone (2016) 59–60.
195 Critchley (1999) 275.
196 Wolcher (2003) 114.
197 Stone (2016) 61.
198 Levinas (1988a) 175.
199 Levinas (1998a) 89.
200 Stone (2016) 61.
201 Stone (2016) 63.
202 Stone (2016) 113.
203 Stone (2016) 86.
204 Levinas (1969) 219; Levinas (2008) 167.
205 Levinas (1998b) 8.
206 Gibbs (2006) 402.
207 Stone (2016) 83.
208 Douzinas and Warrington (1994) 238.
209 Douzinas and Warrington (1994) 184.
210 Douzinas and Warrington (1994) 240.
211 *Roe v Wade*, 410 U.S. 113 (1973).
212 Cornell (1992) 137.
213 Cornell (1992) 152–153.
214 *Roe*, 410 U.S. at 159 (Blackmun J).
215 Cornell (1992) 150.
216 Stone (2016) 85.
217 Levinas (2003a) 53.
218 Levinas (1969) 247.
219 Levinas (2008) 11.
220 Stone (2016) 71.
221 Levinas (1988a) 175.
222 Stone (2016) 148.

7 The limits of form-of-life

Introduction

The final chapter of this book turns to the other limit of form-of-life: death. The previous chapter considered the unborn as a liminal figure at the start of life. This chapter turns to a liminal figure at the end of life; the biologically liminal figures of the patient in a vegetative state and end of life decision-making for a patient lacking capacity. The figure of the patient in a vegetative state is chosen deliberately, because it is an example Agamben uses to illustrate the political, rather than biological, nature of life.[1] The figure of the patient in a vegetative state has generated commentaries from Levinasian scholars.[2] Agamben does not write on the question of patients lacking capacity generally, but I focus on this here as it mirrors the position of the patient in a vegetative state in that they do not have any opportunity to make decisions as to their future medical treatment.

It could be argued that any individual at the end of their life would be a more natural selection, given that the previous chapter was dealing with figures at the very start of their lives. However, there is a crucial difference. Persons at the end of their lives can be, and very often are, fully cognisant of their circumstances and often able to make decisions about their treatment options. These figures could be argued to be paradigmatic of form-of-life, living the end of their lives as a 'how'. In contrast, the figure of the patient in a vegetative state, much like the patient lacking capacity at the end of their life, illustrate the aporias in form-of-life. Agamben's eschewing of relationality and judgment leaves form-of-life unable to account for these liminal biological figures. In addition, Agamben aligns medicine and medical decisions with the creation of *homo sacer*, precluding the possibility for an ethical medical encounter between the incapable patient and their doctors.

This chapter draws upon medical and legal literature surrounding patients in a vegetative state and patients lacking capacity and their treatment, including sources from English law. The examples of patients I draw upon are adults. This choice is deliberate. The question of children's rights in terms of consenting to medical treatment is a live one. Yet as was argued in the previous chapter, Agamben's writings on children place them in a lower position than

DOI: 10.4324/9781315191447-8

adults. Form-of-life as constructed reflects the position of adults *with* capacity. This is why I have chosen to focus on adults *without* capacity. These sources illustrate the difficulties involved in being able to apply or transpose Agamben's form-of-life and its uses to these figures. The very figure of these patients presupposes a medical judgment surrounding diagnosis and decisions surrounding when, and how, to remove or cease treatment, as well as an underlying legal framework which structures the actions of medical professionals. Levinasian ethics can account for these decisions in an ethical way that form-of-life cannot. In this way form-of-life discloses its limits.

The end of life

That everyone must die is a fact that many of us spend our lives ignoring due to its implications; end-of-life care in most health services focuses upon minimising pain and discomfort for the individual. Generally speaking, it is permissible, at least in some cases, to withhold medical treatment and allow a patient to die, but it is never permissible to take any direct action designed to kill the patient. Despite this, however, there remains an indeterminacy surrounding those types of medical judgments at the end of life. As Justice Antonin Scalia made clear in the United States Supreme Court in *Cruzan v Director, Missouri Department of Health*:

> [T]he point at which life becomes 'worthless', and the point at which the means necessary to preserve it become 'extraordinary' or 'inappropriate', are neither set forth in the Constitution nor know to the nine justices of this court any better than they are known to nine people picked at random from the Kansas City telephone directory …[3]

Agamben is correct, albeit blunt, to state that what is at stake in these situations is the definition of a life that may be killed without the commission of a homicide.[4] The legal risks inherent in end of life decision-making are clear:

> [A] murder prosecution is a poor way to design an ethical and moral code for doctors who are faced with decisions concerning the use of costly and extraordinary 'life support' equipment.[5]

Until relatively recently in human history, medicine had not advanced to the stage whereby people could be kept alive artificially. Mitchell Dean has observed that:

> The capacity to manipulate our mere biological life, rather than simply to govern aspects of forms of life, implies a bio-politics that contests how and when we use these technologies and for what purposes. It also implies a redrawing of the relations between life and death, and a new 'thanato-politics', a new politics of death.[6]

From this, two points can be made. First, human beings' increasing ability to manipulate their biological functions has consequences for traditional notions of health and illness, and life and death. Technological developments in medicine and the life sciences have had the effect of transforming social and cultural perceptions of what it means to be alive.[7] Secondly, those developments are also sources of conflict. The enhanced capacity to sustain human life and to manipulate its fundamental components results in questions concerning, and disputes over, the extent to which medical practice ought to deploy those capabilities in particular cases.[8]

I turn to English law to demonstrate this conflict and ambiguity, which I argue cannot be resolved adequately by Agamben's thought. In the UK case of *Bland*, the House of Lords made clear that the state of death itself had changed:

> Until recently … A man was dead if he stopped breathing and his heart stopped beating. There was no artificial means of sustaining these indications of life for more than a short while. Death in the traditional sense was beyond human control … Recent developments in medical science have fundamentally affected these previous certainties. In medicine, the cessation of breathing or of heartbeat is no longer death. By the use of a ventilator, lungs which in the unaided course of nature would have stopped breathing can be made to breathe, thereby sustaining the heartbeat. Those … who would previously have died through inability to swallow food can be kept alive by artificial feeding. This has led the medical profession to redefine death in terms of brain stem death, i.e., the death of that part of the brain without which the body cannot function at all without assistance. In some cases it is now apparently possible, with the use of the ventilator, to sustain a beating heart even though the brain stem, and therefore in medical terms the patient, is dead; "the ventilated corpse".[9]

Brain stem death became the new criterion for death. Agamben's critique is not that brain-death (in his terms) is an adequate way to determine death. Rather he makes the broader point that death as a concept now has "the greatest indeterminacy".[10]

For my purposes here I am considering a specific aspect of end of life decision making, to test the limits of the construction of form-of-life. This will not consider euthanasia or assisted dying as Agamben has explicitly avoided taking a position on such issues in his writings.[11] My focus is the claim that a life that does not deserve to be lived is the "fundamental biopolitical structure of modernity", corresponding to the life of *homo sacer*.[12] It is this critique that sees medicine as fallen prey to management and manipulated consensus-making (as opposed to seeking a diagnostic consensus).[13] The change in the state of death has led doctors and courts to assume a managerial role in relation to the lives and deaths of incapable patients. Every society sets its limits beyond which life ceases to be politically relevant.[14] This limit, which has moved inside every human life, is clearly visible in end of life decision making made for incapable patients.[15]

These points cannot apply to fully capable individuals. We read that an ethical life would involve the expectations and legitimate desires of the individual,[16] as living one's life as a form is a possibility for a singular being who has agency, with the ability to make decisions as to how to live their life. Such a being exists in contact with others, living its life as one of non-relation and use. Use prevents potential from being consumed and drives it to turn once more to itself, to allow a being to be capable of its own potential and *impotential*.[17] The clear implication from this is that form-of-life is able to make decisions as to which medical treatment to assent to or refuse to, even if in the latter example it would lead to harm to themselves or lead to their death.

This construction of form-of-life and its agency is reflected in fundamental principles of medical law. A fully competent adult who is able to voluntarily consent to treatment they understand also has the right to refuse medical treatment. This was famously stated by Cardozo J in an American case: "Every human being of adult years and sound mind has a right to determine what shall be done with his own body".[18] This refusal must be respected even if it leads to the patient's death.[19] Lord Donaldson MR made this clear:

> An adult patient who … suffers from no mental incapacity has an absolute right to choose whether to consent to medical treatment, to refuse it or to choose one rather than another of the treatments being offered … This right of choice is not limited to decisions which others might regard as sensible. It exists notwithstanding that the reasons for making the choice are rational, irrational, unknown or even non-existent.[20]

A patient with capacity can also express their wishes on refusing potential future treatments through an advance decision or a living will.[21] This is a statement, made when the patient is competent, setting out what they want or do not want if they become incapacitated, which (if valid) must be respected by doctors.[22] A patient can even refuse life-sustaining treatment in advance.[23]

This chapter's focus is, however, on the patient who lacks capacity at the end of their life, and the patient in a vegetative state. What is notable in relation to these patients is we cannot escape another person making a decision over whether they should continue living, and how they should die. If the individual cannot speak for themselves, and if they have not made clear their wishes in advance, then someone else must decide for them. Whether and how this decision-making can be done ethically is not adequately accounted for in form-of-life, and it is partly due, I think, to Agamben's view of the role of medicine in modern society.

Agamben on medicine, the incapable patient and the end of life

Perhaps the best way to introduce Agamben's critique of the role of modern medicine in society is to view his writings on the COVID-19 pandemic which started in late 2019. Agamben's response to the pandemic has accused the media and authorities of spreading a state of panic, using the virus to govern through a state of exception and maximising the virus's virulence and severity:

> [I]t is almost as if with terrorism exhausted as a cause for exceptional measures, the invention of an epidemic offered the ideal pretext for scaling them up beyond any limitation.[24]

We are told that social distancing "will become the model for politics that awaits us", and that "there have been more serious epidemics in the past, but no one ever thought of declaring a state of emergency like today, one that forbids us even to move".[25] What is more, we are governed through a "health terror",[26] and informed that the pandemic was "already present".[27] Emphasis is placed on the overreaction of the state and the opportunity for biopolitical modes of control to tighten their grip on living beings, with all peoples in an enduring war with themselves because the enemy is potentially within us all,[28] in a form of civil war.[29] The living being is transformed into a subject gripped by the medical apparatus.

Yet Agamben's views on medicine itself (which in his schema should be treated as a *dispositif* in the same manner that law is), rather than just his reaction to COVID-19, are far from mainstream. Agamben equates medicine (and more broadly science) to a religion of our time, akin to how capitalism should be viewed as a religion.[30] Medicine as a religion treats every part of the life of human being as a place of an uninterrupted cultic celebration – the enemy of disease is always present and must be fought unceasingly. Medicine is articulated through a dualist opposition between the malign god of disease whose agents are bacteria and viruses, and a beneficent god of recovery, whose agents are medicines and therapy.[31] This leads to a clarion call against the religion of medicine and the restrictions imposed on our lives to deal with COVID-19:

> [C]learly the thought of those who continue to seek the truth and reject the dominant lie will be, as is already happening before our eyes, excluded and accused of spreading fake news (news, not ideas, because news is more important than reality!) … All this has already happened and will continue to happen, but those who testify to the truth will not stop doing so, because no one can bear witness for the witness.[32]

I think that these writings provide an invaluable background to understanding Agamben's other writings on medicine and medical judgments, and what hints he has given about the complexities of end of life decision-making. What Agamben forecloses and cannot conceive of, in my reading, is whether there can be an ethical encounter between the doctor and the incapable patient, due to his negative view of medicine. *That* patient is not able to live their life as a form, and as a result they become the object of managerial decision-making that treats them as bare life. There is no other option available.

The incapable patient

In relation to patients who lack capacity, life and death are certainly political concepts which acquire a meaning through a decision or judgment. This is a judgment as to what a particular society or legal system finds acceptable as life or death. This judgment or *krisis* has an originally medical meaning.[33] In the medical tradition the *krisis* is inseparable from the connection to a determinate moment of time, in particular the decisive days in which the doctor judged whether the sick person will survive.[34] In Agamben's terms this leads to a plethora of medical and legal decisions operating on the living being,[35] and the hospital room delimiting a space of exception in which a purely bare life, entirely controlled by man and his technology, appears for the first time.[36]

This contention can be evidenced through an excursus into capacity in English law. In England, all adults are presumed to have capacity, but this can be rebutted evidentially.[37] If a patient lacks capacity, then they can be treated without their consent in their "best interests".[38] This can (and often does) involve the removal of treatment, even if it is life-sustaining. In addition, treatment intended to relieve pain and discomfort is not unlawful even if it has the incidental consequence of shortening the patient's life.[39] Central to this determination is a decision, or judgment, made by a medical professional. Capacity is determined through a two-stage test in English law. The first stage is to ask if the patient is suffering from 'an impairment of, or a disturbance in the functioning of, the mind or brain' which can be temporary or permanent.[40] This is known as the diagnostic threshold, which is determined by a medical professional's clinical judgment. The second stage asks whether the patient can make a decision for themselves. A person is unable to make a decision if they are unable to meet one of four criteria, again decided by medical professionals (and, if contested, by the courts, showing the oscillations which exist between legal and medical decisions over life and death) – that they are unable to understand the information relevant to the decision (in broad and general terms);[41] that they are unable to retain that information; that they cannot use or weigh that information as part of their decision-making process; or that they cannot communicate their decision by any means.[42]

There is evidence of indeterminacy and of the crucial role medical judgment can play in such treatments. If an individual has borderline capacity, the courts retain an inherent jurisdiction which can be invoked to protect vulnerable but capacitous adults.[43] One study focused on the decision-making capacity of acutely ill hospital patients and found that nearly half lacked capacity. Despite this, doctors overlooked their incapacity as they treated their acquiescing to treatment as a valid consent.[44]

On its face, none of this calls into question the thesis that the incapable patient at the end of their life is a potential *homo sacer*, and that the doctors (and the courts) exercise a sovereign power over which lives are worth living. However, I wish to develop this line of thought. English law states that the patient's best interests are supposed to be judged subjectively, taking into account clinical needs, and the patient's emotional and welfare interests, with treatment only interpreted to be futile is *the patient being treated* would consider it to be futile.[45] Where the patient's views are unknown, the question turns to whether the treatment in question is overly burdensome.[46] The law does encourage doctors, lawyers and judges to see the issue of end of life treatment through the eyes of the patient in question, before they make their decision. In Levinasian terms, they must try and see the issue through the eyes of the Other. But it is worth reiterating here that whilst the other person's face is an opening and threshold to that person for Agamben,[47] it involves the subject experiencing an exteriority, having "an *outside* happen to me".[48] This allows the subject a chance to understand themselves and *their own* being exposed.[49] The incapable patient, in this reading, becomes an unwitting agent for the decision-maker, be they doctor, lawyer or judge. Much like the woman, the patient who can no longer decide for themselves is a privileged figure of ephemerality, allowing the decision-maker to gain access to the plane of immanence, whilst remaining unable to gain access themselves.[50] This may imply that the doctor can act ethically through being exposed to the face of the patient, and through making an ethical decision (based on living their own life as a form) as to whether treatment should continue or not. But this indicates that much like a pregnant woman who becomes sovereign over the unborn who is cast as a pseudo *homo sacer*, the decision-maker becomes sovereign over the incapable patient. This can be further illustrated in relation to the patient in a vegetative state.

Disorders of consciousness and the question of judgment

For Agamben the "overcoma" is a stage of life beyond the cessation of all vital functions – it is the full fruit of new life support technology: artificial respiration, maintenance of cardiac circulation through intravenous perfusion of adrenaline, technologies of body temperature control, and so on.[51] The patient in such a condition appears as a divided life, both dead and alive. Medically speaking, the overcoma conflates a number of different prolonged disorders of consciousness (PDOC) which lead to further complications regarding end of life decision-making. PDOCs persist for more than four weeks following sudden onset profound acquired brain injury, and may also occur in the final stages of dementia or other chronic progressive neurodegenerative disorders.

Perhaps more importantly for my argument here, PDOCs are quite distinct from brain stem death. Brain stem death implies the loss of all brainstem functions, as confirmed by the absence of brainstem reflexes (pupillary, corneal, oculovestibular and cough) and spontaneous respiratory effort in response to rising carbon dioxide levels. Patients with brainstem death can be maintained for short periods on artificial ventilation, to allow clinical and best interests decision-making, or support organ donation, but will cease to maintain physiological function within a relatively short period after withdrawal of treatment.[52] In contrast, many patients in PDOCs can breathe on their own. In

Homo Sacer Agamben draws on the example of Karen Quinlan, who was kept alive for years by means of artificial respiration and nutrition. After her artificial respiration was withdrawn, Karen began to breathe naturally and survived in a state of artificial nutrition until 1985. For Agamben, her body had entered a zone of indetermination in which the words life and death had lost their meaning.[53] Her life became pure *zoè*, and her body became a legal being as much as it was a biological being.[54]

The exact legal status of Karen Quinlan's life was indeterminate. This does reflect the indeterminate medical and legal states patients in PDOC can be in. Patients can be in comas (a state of unarousable unresponsiveness which they cannot be awakened from),[55] vegetative states (VS) or minimally conscious states (MCS).[56] These are fluid categorisations:

> Following severe brain injury, many patients progress through stages of coma, VS and MCS as they emerge into a state of full awareness. Some will remain in a vegetative or minimally conscious state for the rest of their lives.[57]

Like Karen Quinlan, patients in a VS or MCS may require a tracheostomy, but typically maintain their own cardiac output and respiration, and so may survive for months or years without cardiorespiratory support, as long as they are provided nutrition and hydration.[58]

Again illustrating the way in which these patients are not in the same position as those with brain stem death, VS and MCS patients also may show degrees of consciousness. Consciousness is an ambiguous term, encompassing both wakefulness and awareness, where wakefulness involves motor arousal and awareness is the ability to have an experience of any kind.[59] VS patients can have their eyes open spontaneously for periods of the day, giving the impression of a sleep-wake cycle. MCS patients can demonstrate a range of conscious behaviours from visual pursuit to language processing or communication.[60] An MCS patient exists in a state where altered consciousness with minimal but clearly discernible behavioural evidence of self or environmental awareness is demonstrated.[61]

My focus here will be turned to VS patients, as they are the focus of Agamben's reference to Karen Quinlan. A VS patient may exhibit a range of spontaneous movements (like crying or smiling) or reflex responses (like biting their tongue or grasping). However, there is no awareness of self or environment, the patient cannot interact with others, they cannot undertake sustained purposeful or voluntary behaviours, and lack language, comprehension or meaningful expression.[62] In this sense Agamben is right to state that they appear to be in a liminal state between life and death. Still alive, yet no longer who they were, and with (usually and sadly) a very poor prognosis. Patients with non-traumatic injuries have a shorter window for recovery and greater long-term severity of disability than patients with traumatic injury.[63] For patients in VS, the large majority of those who regain consciousness have done so by 12 months for traumatic brain injury, and by three months for non-traumatic injury.[64] There are isolated reports of recovery of consistent consciousness even after many years,[65] but these are a rarity, and those who recover remain profoundly disabled. It may be obvious to state, but important – an individual in a vegetative state is not able to live their lives as a form, for as long as they are in such a state. It is not possible to live and intend and apprehend and deliver oneself to a potentiality.[66]

The question of judgment is central to the patient in a vegetative state and how their life will end. First there is the diagnosis, which is a medical judgment. This diagnosis requires the cause of the condition to be established as far as possible, reversible causes to be excluded, and for trained assessors to examine the patient over a period of time using validated tests, alongside conventional clinic assessments.[67] After diagnosis, and if the vegetative state persists, the question arises as to whether treatment (which is primarily artificial nutrition and hydration, or ANH) should be withdrawn and the patient allowed to die. In English law, the best interests test would be applied by medical professionals when seeking to withdraw ANH, meaning that a medical judgment and decision would determine whether an individual would continue to live, or would die. Whilst primarily a medical judgment, these have been underpinned by legal decisions. English courts have taken the position that if a diagnosis of a vegetative state is correct, keeping a person alive will not be in their best interests:

> In essence medical treatment is of no benefit to a person in a PVS [a persistent vegetative state] because they are not sensient and have no prospect of recovery. Thus, whether or not the withdrawal of life-sustaining treatment measures is in [the patient's] best interests will depend upon whether or not his diagnosis of PVS is correct. If it is correct, in other words if he has no awareness of self or environment and no prospect of recovery, then the provision of any treatment is futile and cannot be in his best interests.[68]

Furthermore if invasive medical care is not in the best interests of the patient, then the doctor cannot lawfully continue the care; as a result a doctor who withdraws life sustaining care in such circumstances cannot be in breach of any duty to maintain the patient's life and cannot be guilty of murder by omission.[69] In this sense Agamben is right that a patient in a vegetative state can be killed without the commission of a homicide,[70] and a law that seeks to decide on life is embodied in a life that coincides with death.[71] The patient lacks a voice in this decision.[72] The UK Supreme Court has gone as far as to hold that there is no legal requirement that an application must always be made to the court before ANH can be withdrawn in respect of a patient in a vegetative state.[73] As long as medical professionals agree that removing ANH is in the patient's best interests then there is no need to seek legal approval through the court. A court declaration would only be appropriate where the way forward for treating a patient is not clear, or where there is a difference in medical opinion or a lack of agreement to a proposed course of action.[74]

As before, Agamben's analysis invites us to consider the patient in a vegetative state as a *homo sacer*, with the courts and doctors exercising a sovereign power to decide when the patient's life is no longer worth living. Being-in-common is not available to the incapacitated patient as they cannot grasp the simultaneity of visages that constitute their face.[75] Yet the medical professionals and the judges are once again privileged actors able to access the ethical life through taking their own face's communicability upon themselves, and existing in contact with an other like the patient. The crucial dimension missing from this analysis is to question whether, if at all, an *ethical* decision can be made by doctors and judges in relation to the incapable patient. Agamben simply does not provide us with the resources or philosophical avenues to answer this question adequately. Form-of-life encounters its limit in the face of the adult patient without capacity, who can only be conceived as a potential victim, waiting to be killed by a sovereign decision.

Levinas and the end of life

What I have found striking (even more than when comparing how the thought of Agamben and Levinas could be applied to the unborn) is the way in which Levinas's thought can provide a ready theoretical and philosophical basis for *ethical* end of life decision-making. It is an inversion of the limitations of Agamben's form-of-life and his writings on *homo sacer*. My aim here is not just to focus on Levinas's texts directly, but to illustrate how scholars have focused on biologically liminal figures such as the patient in a vegetative state to explore how Levinas's thought can help construct an ethics of suffering or an ethics of compassion.[76]

Suffering and ethics

The authentic medical situation is that in which is immediately acted with the appearance of a suffering fellow-man in need of help.[77] Our experience of suffering provides the basis for ethical action and relations. Surprisingly little has been written about suffering in relation to truth, ethics, subjectivity and the significance of compassion in Levinas.[78] Yet there are still lines of thought to follow.

The descriptions of suffering in Levinas's early texts are generally presented from the perspective of the suffering self.[79] It is through our experiencing or witnessing suffering that leads to compassion, responsibility and ultimately ethics and justice. Someone who expresses himself in his nudity by the face is appealing to me, placing himself under my responsibility. I have to respond to them.[80] Suffering (which for my argument here would involve the witnessing of the experiences of patients lacking capacity at the end of their lives or in a vegetative state) can therefore lead to ethical judgments (both legal and ethical) being made in relation to these suffering beings. Ethics and justice owe their existence to the vast sea of suffering occurring in the world.[81]

Levinas's account of suffering reveals our relationship to something that does not come from ourselves; suffering is excessive and the concrete manifestation of what is not able to be integrated.[82] Suffering is useless in that it is for nothing.[83] All suffering is evil beyond meaningfulness and redemption (although it could be contended Levinas here is ignoring pain's utility as an alarm signal for danger or harm to ourselves).[84] To suffer is to undergo an impact that is *too* much; it is passivity. Levinas spoke of suffering as an impasse.[85] Physical suffering in its most extreme form effaces subjectivity and all subjective attitudes as it involves the irremissibility of being and the absence of all refuge.[86] And hence, it must be said:

> Suffering is … not a matter of a passivity which would degrade man by striking a blow against his freedom. Pain would limit such freedom to the point of compromising self-consciousness, permitting man the identity of the thing only in the passivity of the submission. The evil which rends the humanity of the suffering person, overwhelms his humanity otherwise than non-freedom overwhelms it: violently and cruelly, more irremissibly than the negation which dominates or paralyzes the act in non-freedom … The evil of pain, the harm itself, is the explosion and most profound articulation of absurdity.[87]

Significant suffering corrodes all the structures of meaning that we project into the world; it overwhelms all virility – or the effort to be masters of our own fate – until finally one is reduced to a state resembling helpless infancy:

> Where suffering attains its purity, where there is no longer anything between us and it, the supreme responsibility of this extreme assumption turns into supreme irresponsibility, into infancy. Sobbing is this, and precisely through this it announces death. To die is to return to this state of irresponsibility, to be the infantile shaking of sobbing.[88]

This is not the same as infancy in the sense Agamben gives it. It is not an originary experience of language as such, nor a precursor to an ethical life, but a reduction of the self to a child-like state where they cannot be responsible. In turn, suffering announces death.[89] Suffering and death bring an end to every effort to be.[90]

We can ask: can suffering ever be meaningful? Suffering that is witnessed in the face of the other is a scandal; the witness is prompted to reach out to the sufferer. The suffering of the other cannot be made meaningful from my perspective, but my own suffering can have meaning if I suffer for the other and thereby respond to her suffering:

> In this perspective a radical difference develops between *suffering in the other*, which for *me* is unpardonable and solicits me and calls me, and suffering *in me*, my own adventure of suffering, whose constitutional or congenital uselessness can take on a meaning, the only meaning to which

> suffering is susceptible, in becoming a suffering for the suffering – be it inexorable – of someone else.[91]

More than suffering, the death of the other puts me in question, signifying the impossibility of abandoning the other to his aloneness. Death's meaning begins in the inter-human relation.[92] The other individuates me in my responsibility for them. The death of the other affects me in my identity as a responsible me.[93] The relation with the other's death is an ex-ceptional relation (in the same meaning as Agamben gives to the exceptional – to set outside of the series).[94] The death of the other affects me more than my own death.[95] Suffering (and death) can therefore be seen as a precursor to ethical existence. Subjectivity is a suffering for the Other, a "passivity of wounds" and a "haemorrhage" that bleeds my own comfort for the sake of the Other.[96] The suffering of others initiates subjectivity in the call to responsibility (and compassion) which is given in the face of the Other, revealing a transcendental framework for ethical responsibility and caring:

> The epiphany of the Absolutely Other is a face by which the Other challenges and commands me through his nakedness, through his destitution. He challenges me from his humility and his height ... The absolutely Other is the human Other ... And the putting into question of the same by the Other is a summons to respond ... Hence, to be I signifies not being able to escape responsibility.[97]

Subjectivity is an assignation: "I exist through the other and for the other".[98] Unconditional hospitality and succour of the suffering other are offered as one of two possible options when confronted with this scandalous shameful realisation. First, the realisation of non-interchangeability and *alterity*; second, the embarrassment that comes with the realisation that, simply by occupying a place under the sun *I/we displace another* or rob them of a possible refuge. Indifference is not an option.[99] The *face-to-face* connotes a *pre-reflective* phase of human proximity. The face signifies pure irreducible alterity and demands to be cared for as if they were absolutely unique and also higher Other. Alterity brings a future that resurrects the present, rupturing the suffocation of being, the enchainment to the self that is suffering. This appears in what Levinas terms the "infinitely mysterious" event of compassion.[100]

Levinas writes that compassion is the nexus of human subjectivity, but this seems to contradict the insistence on the primacy of responsibility. In *Otherwise than Being* Levinas occasionally characterises pity and compassion as events of a psychological order.[101] Levinasian responsibility is the suffering of a burden, a compassionate suffering for the suffering Other outside the psychological. In the same text, however, Levinas employs "pity" and "compassion" to characterise the weight of responsibility that precedes autonomy, a being-for-the-other constituted by a suffering for the Other.[102] Levinasian compassion is a wounding, a sensibility that is not the affectivity of sympathetic feelings but the affectivity to the moral command of the Other.[103] This ambiguity reflects Levinas's concern to distinguish the ethical subjectivity of responsibility from the moral sentiments of sympathy and compassion, while simultaneously characterising responsibility and substitution as a suffering for the Other.

Compassion bears witness. This witnessing requires no unique experience or special capacity. The compassionate witness does not seek to recuperate the witnessed Other into a representation or a concept; it breaks forth as testimony, as pure saying, "*me voici*".[104] This is in contrast to Agamben who, in the Christian and post-Christian imagination, argues that compassion signifies as an instance *anarchic economy* that is always already assumed as justified. Compassion is used through a providential economy to justify the ad hoc suspension of the rigour of domestic and international law. Diamantides reads Agamben's thesis as suggesting that – for the West – what Levinas calls compassion's "ethical anarchy" is instrumentalised at the expense of both the rule of law and of democracy and in favour of biopolitics and anomic management.[105] For my reading, the compassionate exposure to the Other is an openness to responsibility: "in saying suffering signifies in the form of *giving*".[106] And this is ethics:

> [E]thics is the breakup of the originary unity of transcendental apperception … Witnessed, and not thematised, in the sign given to the other, the infinite signifies out of responsibility for the other, out of the one-for-the-other, a subject supporting everything, subject to everything, that is, suffering for everyone.[107]

It is only in suffering that I have access to the Other:

> Only a being whose solitude has reached a crispation through suffering, and in relation with death, takes its place on a ground where the relationship with the other becomes possible.[108]

Ethics is the sacrifice of my own nourishment for the other.[109] It is the painful loss of my own satisfaction: it is "an offering oneself that is a suffering".[110] The opening and exposure to the Other *is* the generosity of ethics.

But what if the Other is an incapable patient? Here Levinas makes the connection between the suffering of the individual who does not fully appreciate their suffering (who experience pure pain) and the responsibility of the Self, in particular the medical professional who may be treating those patients. The "essential facts of pure pain" are evoked by considering the "pain-illnesses" of:

> [B]eings who are psychically deprived, backward, handicapped, in their relational life and in their relationships to the Other, relationships where suffering, without losing anything of its savage malignancy, no longer covers up the totality of the mental and comes across novel lights within new horizons. These horizons none the less remain closed to the mentally deficient, except that in their 'pure pain' they are projected into them to expose them *to me*, raising the fundamental ethical problem of the medication which is my duty.[111]

Encountering the incapable Other who is suffering and in pain makes an ethical demand on me. As stated above, this stage is reflected in my attempt to see how a medical professional can live their lives as a form whilst being in contact with these patients. But, crucially, Levinas goes further. Medicine is not a religion, or a cult, nor does it produce subjects out of living beings. Rather, it can "nourish persons and … lighten their sufferings".[112] The incapable patient may be suffering, but a beyond appears through my witnessing their pain:

> Is not the evil of suffering … also the un-assumable, whence the possibility of a half opening that a moan, a cry, a groan or a sign slips through – the original call for aid, for curative help, help from the other me whose alterity, whose exteriority promises salvation? … For pure suffering, which is intrinsically senseless and condemned to itself with no way out, a beyond appears in the form of the inter-human.[113]

The "inter-human" perspective is the Self-Other relation, and it means that their suffering is meaningful to me, even as it is useless for the Other.[114] In the inter-human there lies a primordial responsibility of one being for another. I am responsible for the other person without pausing to see if they can or will reciprocate, in order to help them gratuitously.[115] Levinas expands on this point:

> [T]he suffering of suffering, the suffering for the useless suffering of the other person, the just suffering in me for the unjustifiable suffering of the Other, opens upon suffering the ethical perspective of the inter-human. In this perspective a radical difference develops between *suffering in the Other*, which for *me* is unpardonable and solicits me and calls me, and suffering *in me*, my own adventure of suffering, whose constitutional or congenital uselessness can take on a meaning, the only meaning to which suffering is susceptible, in becoming a suffering for the suffering – be it inexorable – of someone else.[116]

To think suffering in an inter-human perspective can subsist, but can also be lost, in a political order where the law establishes mutual obligations between citizens.[117] Through the law and justice (however imperfectly) we can conceive of this ethical relation of suffering. In this manner, Levinas's thought does provide us with the necessary tools to conceive of decision-making over incapable patients ethically, not just in terms of the sovereign power over a *homo sacer*.

People always seem to *crave* a better world, and in their craving they persistently yearn for relief from the world they have. Because of this, suffering remains the ever-renewed raw material of ethics and justice.[118] Justice is not ethics, but it is nonetheless *explained* in terms of the ethical relation.[119] The ethical I must deny and efface its very essence in order to metamorphose into the agent of justice. The passage from ethics to justice goes from an intimate relation without reciprocity to a structured relation in which reciprocity – conceived as the formal equality of all citizens – characterises the I's new attitude and comportment towards others:

> My search for justice presupposes just such a new relation, in which all the excess of generosity that I must have toward the other is subordinated to a question of justice.[120]

Ethics does most definitely *lead* to justice in Levinas's thought. Given this, I turn to how this ethical decision can be constructed over these incapable patients using Levinas's thought. This is needed not least because on the one hand health care workers have a primary obligation towards their patient in giving proper human care, but that individualized care has to be measured, weighed and traded against the needs of all potential patients waiting for health care.[121]

Levinas, judgment and the incapable patient

Levinas wrote that legal and political judgments are "born of charity".[122] This presupposes an irreducible, and inescapable, existential human vocation for asymmetrical openness to and hospitality for the vulnerable other, of which compassion is a key aspect. Levinas's philosophy emphasises that "the other's facing me, makes me responsible for them, and this responsibility has no limits",[123] then judges, lawyers and doctors who face the incapable Other on a regular basis must account for the call of the Other's face in their decisions and actions. Compassion is both the irreducibly anarchic condition of the possibility of sociality and a source of embarrassment that causes us (in this case the courts who adjudicate and the doctors who treat) to *try* to deal with others dispassionately by recourse to general principles of legal or social justice. Yet such dispassionate sobriety is always lacking as we care for some more than others. Therefore, compassion is the reason for and the limit of theories of justice.[124]

I follow Diamantides in his arguments here to show how the law can (try to) account for the incapable patient, and in his contention that to appreciate Levinas's complex thesis, one must set aside key assumptions that legal and political institutions were created by man in order to put an end, or at least to give meaning or a useful structure, to suffering or violence. Levinas's ethical ontology of society entails bearing the burden of reflecting on this experience of the other's suffering, comparing sufferings and attributing causes, and justifying to third parties why this instance of suffering mattered to me whilst another was neglected.[125] For Simon Critchley and Robert Bernasconi:

> Levinas does not at all want to reject the order of political rationality, and its consequent claims to legitimacy and justice. Rather, Levinas wants to criticize the belief that *only* political rationality can answer political problems. He wants to indicate how the order of the state rests upon the

> irreducible ethical responsibility of the face-to-face relation ... Levinas' thinking does not result in apoliticism or an ethical quietism ... Rather, ethics leads back to politics, to the demand for a just polity. Indeed, I would go further and claim that ethics is for the sake of politics, that is for the sake of a more just society.[126]

"Justice" is a notion that makes us think of the relation between ethics and law. Diamantides, in language evoking Agamben's own work in *The Use of Bodies*, states that to make a claim about the "justice" of a judgment implies a *contact* between ethics and law and either to affirm that this contact has, or has not, led to a contraction or fusion.[127] This contact, however, implies a relation between ethics and law, not a non-relation as Agamben would have it. Judgment in this Levinasian reading involves a relation between the individual making the judgment and the individual being judged. Justice:

> [C]alls for judgment and comparison, a comparison of what is in principle incomparable, for every being is unique; every other is unique. In that necessity of being concerned with justice that idea of equity appears, on which the idea of objectivity is based. At a certain moment, there is a necessity for a "weighing", a comparison, a pondering, and in this sense philosophy would be the appearance of wisdom from the depths of that initial charity [of ethics], the wisdom of love.[128]

As part of this justice, Levinas's thought calls for the necessity of judgment:

> I must judge, where before I was to assume responsibilities. Here is the birth of the theoretical; here the concern for justice is born, which is the basis of the theoretical. But it is always starting out from the Face, from the responsibility for the other that justice appears, which calls for judgement and comparison, a comparison of what is in principle incomparable, for every being is unique; every other is unique.[129]

Drucilla Cornell has argued that there is an "unavoidable character" to judicial inventiveness, which needs to be put to "good use". The judge should heed their ethical responsibility before the singular individual of the particular case if they *act* so as to "imaginatively recollect" the relation of this other with law. Through this imaginative recollection the judge puts the individual in a negative relation to law and conceives and imagines her beyond the "traditional exclusions of established law".[130]

Cornell is a reader of Levinas. But in equating ethical responsibility with judicial activism, she overlooks the emphasis Levinas puts on the *passively patient* dimension of ethical responsibility. Legal or political justice must proceed *from* the individuated, daily human experience of a pre-reflexive, obsessive, hyperbolic, extra-legal and extra-political *anarchic* ethical obligation to open up to and alleviate another's suffering.[131] Levinas described the relation of ethics to law/politics as an interminable existential drama with ethical consequences. The wider implication is that, instead of assuming that the law has its basis on individual rights, freedom, and autonomy, we can see it as based on the individual's un-chosen obligations, where their autonomy and freedom are questioned.[132] Iain Wilkinson has contended that the relation of compassion to law is a *perennially controversial* one. Law and compassion remain locked together in a way that invites a constant management of controversy.[133]

How can this help the law face the incapable patient? Patients in a vegetative state represent an exemplar of this problematic. Such patients exist in a liminal space between being alive and being dead, necessitating law's treatment of them as subjects of law, yet lacking any of the faculties that would give them that construction of subjectivity content. By failing to accord with the essence of being expressed by law, the patient signifies as otherwise-than-being but still calls upon the law for some form of recognition.[134] These are exceptional ethical demands, and in this sense the law will always fall short of achieving those demands. To think of oneself as a judge and of a judgment as legal is to be caught in an active, though never conclusive, strife:

> First, it is to view and comprehend the unique judged *as if* she were an *object* of judgement rather than a source of responsibility. Second, it is to view and understand the ethically bound judgement *as if* it was a mechanical *function* within law's closed system. The two instants of *as if* are synchronic aspects of judicial activity which essentially boil down to the work of visual and conceptual metaphor. This work coincides with the judge's evasion of his/her personal ethical responsibility. This coincidence *is* the apophantic possibility of judgement. However, this work is always never enough, always inconclusive and thus always susceptible to the ethical responsibility from which it flees.[135]

Medical law more generally represents a site of ethical provocation within a legal framework, but also represents the realities of law's limitations in responding to the Levinasian injunction, and moreover the inadequacy of a Levinasian jurisprudence being reduced to some general imperative to adopt mere superficially ethical processes of adjudication. Being affected by the suffering of the other person is one of the most Levinasian of experiences, issued from an indeclinable sense of singular responsibility that constitutes us as subjects.[136]

Judges do take the time to visit conscious patients in disputed cases in order to ascertain whether that patient does lack capacity. Encountering the face of the patient and being affected by their suffering can make a crucial difference to the judge's decision, and allow the judge to do justice to the Other. In relation to a patient who refused consent to an operation to amputate his foot, in the knowledge that this would lead to his death, Peter Jackson J visited him in hospital and this made a profound difference to his judgment:

> Mr B has had a hard life. Through no fault of his own, he has suffered in his mental health for half a century. He is a sociable man who has experienced

> repeated losses so that he has become isolated. He has no next of kin. No one has ever visited him in hospital and no one ever will. Yet he is a proud man who sees no reason to prefer the views of others to his own. His religious beliefs are deeply meaningful to him and do not deserve to be described as delusions: they are his faith and they are an intrinsic part of who he is. I would not define Mr B by reference to his mental illness or his religious beliefs. Rather, his core quality is his *"fierce independence"*, and it is this that is now, as he sees it, under attack …
>
> I am quite sure that it would not be in Mr B's best interests to take away his little remaining independence and dignity in order to replace it with a future for which he understandably has no appetite and which could only be achieved after a traumatic and uncertain struggle that he and no one else would have to endure. There is a difference between fighting on someone's behalf and just fighting them. Enforcing treatment in this case would surely be the latter.[137]

Seeing the face of the patient can also show the decision-maker that the patient is more than their description in court papers, and it also can show that their characterisation before the court has been mistaken:

> I took the view that it would be right if I were to meet CD face to face and I did so at the mental hospital on the first day of the hearing. It was an enlightening experience and one which I would recommend to any judge hearing a similar case. Mr Justice Jackson met Mr B and it is obvious from his judgment that the encounter was critically valuable. The reason it was enlightening for me was that the person I met was different in many respects to the person described in the papers. CD was engaging and polite. She was articulate. She was amusing. She listened carefully to questions and answered them equally carefully. True, there were comments that suggested powerful delusional forces; and Dr FH explained that she was heavily medicated. But even so, the person I met was a world away from the violent sociopath described in the papers.[138]

It is true that these decisions involved patients who had, at the very least, limited capacity, and were not in vegetative states, for example. But a wider point can be made. Encountering the face of the Other provides what Alphonso Lingis refers to as "depth-perception":

> By a depth-perception of the other, I mean the perception that views the colored and palpable surfaces of the other as surfaces of a physiological and biological depth; sees these surfaces shifting, tensing, and relaxing and divines, beneath them, glandular functionings, circulatory currents, a specific metabolism … Perception perceives through the surface turned to us, into the depth of the organism and into the depth of the world.[139]

The face is the entire being and not just its visage. The ethical demand of the face is a demand not to be killed, and is the very basis of ethical freedom.[140] The "Other is the sole being I can wish to kill",[141] but the Other's face "that imposes itself does not limit but promotes my freedom, by arousing my goodness".[142] How does goodness and this injunction not to kill relate to the incapable patient?

Michael Dahnke makes clear that "though 'don't kill' is a basic, epiphanous obligation", in the real word of difficult ethical problems, it might sometimes need to be overridden.[143] Levinas recognises that close to death the subject loses its ego:

> What is important about the approach of death is that at a certain moment we are no longer *able to be able* ... It is exactly thus that the subject loses its very mastery as a subject.[144]

Levinasian ethics provides a framework for a patient-centred autonomy ethic even for the patient lacking capacity. Seeing the face of the Other means that doctors and judges have to intimately understand the life and condition of the patient as a person. This is not the same as occupying the place of the Other which would exile him and doom him to a miserable condition.[145] In an incapable patient, decisions must be taken with a full appreciation of the patient.[146] This is consistent with Levinas's statement that the face:

> [C]ommands me to not remain indifferent to this death, to not let the Other die alone, that is, to answer for the life of the other person, at the risk of becoming an accomplice in that person's death.[147]

The medical professional and the law must answer for the life of the other person. Not letting the Other die alone means accepting that they *will die* or *are dying*. Providing pain relief or removing treatment which is not providing a benefit can therefore be read as taking clinical decisions with respect to the Other's face and not being indifferent to his death. An indifference to the death of the Other could therefore involve letting the Other suffer in the time before their death, or to sustain treatment which was of no positive effect.

It is certainly the case that law has struggled with this command. For Diamantides, the House of Lords judgment in *Bland* treatment of vegetative patients reveals how their judgment elided the full radicality of this ethical demand being placed before them, instead choosing to construct the patient as if living, as if an abstract legal subject.[148] *Bland* involved a legal subject whose status as living is uncertain. The courts denied Bland's mortality, reducing it to judicial memory and dealing with his life-as-closure through its representation as a judicially instituted living person who is a subject of interests. The judicial effort to maintain or "keep alive" the best interests test depends on the visual metaphor of the vegetating patient as somehow "still alive".[149]

Given the mystery of death, we are in a relationship that does not come from ourselves.[150] The expression of the Other's mortality cannot be properly conceived or pictured, though it remains a source of responsibility for the survivor (the medical professional or the lawyer or judge) who encountered the face of the dying.[151] But what we can do is allow ourselves to confront that mortality, which is:

> [A]n unlimited responsibility ... with which one is never done, which does not cease with the neighbor's utmost extremity – despite the merciless and realistic formula of the physician who "condemns" a patient – even if the responsibility amounts to nothing more than responding "here I am", in the impotent confrontation with the Other's death.[152]

The medical professional, to act ethically, is not in a job to provide diagnoses, whether of terminal illnesses or otherwise. They, and law, must confront the Other's death, however impotently. Levinasian ethics provides us with ways of approaching the conundrum of the treatment of incapable patients that Agambenian form-of-life, and his critique of transcendent relationality simply cannot.

Conclusion

This chapter has tested the limits of form-of-life in relation to incapable patients. I chose the incapable patient at the end of their life and the patient in a vegetative state to show how Agamben's thought can only provide a critique for thinking about these individuals. They are conceived as potential victims of the exercise of sovereign and managerial decisions over when and how to end their lives. This, coupled with Agamben's reductive and negative conception of medicine and its potential to ensnare living beings as medical subjects, means that his thought simply does not have the tools or resources available to conceive of how the law and medical professionals can make ethical or just decisions in relation to these patients. Once more, I turned towards Levinasian ethics to show how these figures can be *ethically* considered by the disciplines of medicine and the law, however imperfectly. Levinasian ethics therefore discloses the limits of form-of-life, and how it cannot account for biologically liminal figures.

Notes

1 Agamben (1998) 164.
2 Diamantides (2000) 13.
3 *Cruzan v Director, Missouri Department of Health* (1990) 110 S.Ct. 2841, 2859 (Scalia J)
4 Agamben (1998) 165.
5 *Barber v Superior Court of State of California* (1983) 195 Cal. Rptr. 484, 486 (Compton J).
6 Dean (2004) 16.
7 Veitch (2006) 139–140.
8 Veitch (2006) 140.

9 *Airedale NHS Trust v Bland* [1993] AC 789, 878 (HL) (Lord Browne-Wilkinson).
10 Agamben (1998) 162.
11 Agamben (1998) 139.
12 Agamben (1998) 137.
13 Diamantides (2017) 208.
14 Agamben (1998) 139.
15 Agamben (1998) 139–140.
16 Agamben (1998) 142.
17 Agamben (2016a) 93.
18 *Schloendorff v New York Hospital*, 105 NE 92, 93 (NY 1914) (Cardozo J).
19 *In re B (Consent to Treatment – Capacity)* [2002] 1 FLR 1090 (CA).
20 *Re T (Adult: Refusal of Treatment)* [1993] Fam 95, 102 (Lord Donaldson MR) (CA).
21 Mental Capacity Act 2005, s.24.
22 *Malette v Shulman* (1990) 72 O.R. (2d) 417 (Ontario Court of Appeal).
23 Mental Capacity Act 2005, ss.25(5)-(6).
24 Agamben (2020c).
25 Agamben (2020b).
26 Agamben (2020a).
27 Agamben (2020f).
28 Agamben (2020d).
29 Agamben (2015b) 17.
30 Agamben (2019) 66–77.
31 Agamben (2020d).
32 Agamben (2020d).
33 Agamben (2015a) 13; Agamben (2015b) 52.
34 Agamben (2015a) 58.
35 Agamben (1998) 163.
36 Agamben (1998) 164.
37 Mental Capacity Act 2005, s.1(2).
38 *In re F (Mental Patient: Sterilisation)* [1990] 2 AC 1 (HL), Mental Capacity Act 2005, s.4(2).
39 *Airedale NHS Trust v Bland* [1993] AC 789, 867D (Lord Goff), 892 (Lord Mustill); *R (Pretty) v Director of Public Prosecutions* [2002] 1 AC 800, 831H-832A (Lord Steyn).
40 Mental Capacity Act 2005, s.2.
41 *Heart of England NHS Foundation Trust v JB* [2014] EWHC 342 (COP).
42 Mental Capacity Act 2005, s.3(1).
43 *Re G (An Adult)* [2004] EWHC 2222 (Fam); *Re SA (Vulnerable Adult with Capacity: Marriage)* [2006] 1 FLR 867; *Re SK* [2005] 2 FLR 230.
44 Raymont et al (2004) 1421–1427.
45 *B v D* [2017] EWCOP 15; *Aintree University Hospitals Foundation Trust v James* [2013] UKSC 67, [2014] 1 All ER 573.
46 *Abertawe Bro Morgannwg University Local Health Board v RY* [2017] EWCOP 2.
47 Agamben (2000) 91.
48 Agamben (2000) 100.
49 Agamben (2000) 92.
50 Mills (2008b) 115.
51 Agamben (1998) 160.
52 Royal College of Physicians (RCP) (2020) 24.
53 Agamben (1998) 164.
54 Agamben (1998) 186.
55 RCP (2020) 27.

56 RCP (2020) 20. Different jurisdictions use different terminologies for the different disorders of consciousness. I am following the RCP's guidelines here. See Laureys et al (2010) 68.
57 RCP (2020) 21.
58 RCP (2020) 24.
59 RCP (2020) 23.
60 RCP (2020) 30.
61 Giacino and Kalmar (2005) 166–167; *M v Mrs N (By her litigation friend, the Official Solicitor)* [2015] EWCOP 76 [20] (Hayden J).
62 RCP (2020) 28–29; *M v Mrs N*, [19] (Hayden J).
63 Giacino and Kalmar (2005) 36–51.
64 Luaute, Maucort-Boulch et al (2010) 246–252.
65 Wijdicks (2006) 1155–1158.
66 Agamben (2000) 9.
67 RCP (2020) 26. There are three common validated tests used by the UK Court of Protection – the JFK Coma Recovery Scale – Revised (CRS-R), the Wessex Head Injury Matrix (WHIM), and the Sensory Modality Assessment and Rehabilitation Technique (SMART) – see RCP (2020) 48.
68 *A Primary Care Trust v CW* [2010] EWHC 3448 (COP) [70] (Ryder J).
69 *Bland*, 883–884 (Lord Browne-Wilkinson).
70 Agamben (1998) 165.
71 Agamben (1998) 186.
72 *An NHS Trust and others v Y (by his litigation friend, the Official Solicitor) and another* [2018] UKSC 46, [2018] 3 WLR 751, [118] (Lady Black).
73 *An NHS Trust v Y* [93] (Lady Black).
74 *An NHS Trust v Y* [125] (Lady Black).
75 Agamben (2000) 99.
76 White (2012) 112; Diamantides (1995) 209.
77 Tiermersma (1987) 132.
78 For scholarship that addresses one or more aspects of Levinas's approach to suffering, see Pitkin (2001) 231–46; Keenan (1999) 82–88.
79 Edelglass (2006) 46.
80 Levinas (2000) 12.
81 Wolcher (2003) 98.
82 White (2012) 112.
83 Levinas (1988b) 157–158.
84 Kang (1997) 487.
85 Levinas (1998a) 91–101.
86 White (2012) 113–114.
87 Levinas (1988b) 157.
88 Levinas (1987) 72.
89 Levinas (1987) 69.
90 Levinas (2008) 129.
91 Levinas (1988b) 159.
92 Levinas (1998a) 130.
93 Levinas (2000) 12.
94 Levinas (2000) 16.
95 Levinas (2000) 105.
96 Levinas (2008) 74.
97 Levinas (1996d) 17.
98 Levinas (2008) 114.
99 Diamantides (2017) 199.
100 Levinas (1978) 93.
101 Levinas (2008) 125, 128, 146.

102 Edelglass (2006) 47–48; Levinas (2008) 166, 195n12, 196n21.
103 Edelglass (2006) 48.
104 Edelglass (2006) 49–50.
105 Diamantides (2017) 198.
106 Levinas (2008) 50.
107 Levinas (2008) 148.
108 Levinas (1987) 76.
109 Levinas (2008) 74.
110 Levinas (2008) 54.
111 Levinas (1988b) 158.
112 Levinas (1988b) 159.
113 Levinas (1988c) 165–166.
114 Levinas (1988b) 164.
115 Levinas (1988b) 165.
116 Levinas (1988b) 159.
117 Levinas (1988b) 164–165.
118 Wolcher (2003) 98.
119 Wolcher (2003) 106.
120 Levinas (1999) 102.
121 Nortvedt (2003) 31.
122 Levinas (1988c) 165–166.
123 Peperzak (1993) 22.
124 Diamantides (2017) 198.
125 Diamantides (2017) 201.
126 Critchley and Bernasconi (2002) 24–25.
127 Diamantides (1995) 209.
128 Levinas (1998a) 104.
129 Levinas (1998a) 104.
130 Cornell (1992) chs 4 & 5, 146–154.
131 Diamantides (2017) 201.
132 Diamantides (2017) 203.
133 Wilkinson (2017) 212–224.
134 Diamantides (2000) 38.
135 Diamantides (1995) 211.
136 Levinas (1993) 115.
137 *Wye Valley NHS Trust v B* [2015] EWCOP 60, [43], [45] (Peter Jackson J).
138 *A Hospital NHS Trust v CD* [2015] EWCOP 15, [31] (Mostyn J).
139 Lingis (1994) 23.
140 Levinas (1969) 77.
141 Levinas (1969) 198.
142 Levinas (1969) 200.
143 Dahnke (2012) 412.
144 Levinas (1987) 74.
145 Levinas (1987) 110.
146 Bierlein (2007) 76–77.
147 Levinas (1987) 109.
148 Diamantides (2000) 40.
149 Diamantides (1995) 216.
150 Levinas (1987) 69–70.
151 Diamantides (1995) 226.
152 Levinas (1987) 110.

Abandoning a continued project

I have stayed away from labelling this chapter a conclusion, and from trying to reach conclusions in this work. This is because I do not believe that I have presented, nor have I set out to present, a conclusive account of form-of-life. I am not sure such a conclusive account is able to be written. A conclusion presupposes a closure or an end, and this is the antithesis of this study's arguments. I accept Agamben's own comments about his *Homo Sacer* study that it "cannot be concluded but only abandoned (and perhaps continued by others)".[1]

Form-of-life

I have sought to investigate the role of agency in Agamben's thought, and the figure of form-of-life. Form-of-life is an immanent life not defined through forms of presupposition, a being of potential lived through a messianic politics. Each of these elements has been subject to an idiosyncratic excursus in Agamben's corpus and must be understood in a way oriented to immanent philosophy. Broadly speaking Agamben's immanence stands outside of representational dualistic thought. He rejects transcendent *relationality*, and any line of thought that defines a concept, being or idea through its being held in relation to an ungraspable ground or origin. As a result, we read about potentiality not in terms of its relationship to actuality, or being considered as unactualized potential, but as pure potential, thought of in terms of what it means to say something or someone has the potentiality-not-to do something. Messianism in Agamben, which he primarily traces through the Pauline Epistles, does not seek to transcend the world in which we live, or posit a new, better world that we much strive towards, but instead it seeks to deactivate apparatuses of control (like the law), allowing the world as we live in now to be experienced anew. Form-of-life can therefore be understood as an ethical form of living which allows us to grasp our world without recourse to presupposition, be they gods, a transcendent Justice or Right, or a transcendent relation to the Other.

In this study I have been concerned with two main issues. The first has been to situate form-of-life within Agamben's broader set of philosophical ideas, and to show what form-of-life is *not*. This has meant I have needed to explain Agamben's critique of Western philosophy and politics, showing how this critique leads

DOI: 10.4324/9781315191447-9

Agamben to posit an immanent philosophy as the only way out of the current biopolitical nihilism in which we live. The second has been to (quite deliberately), explore the potential of form-of-life, and to ask in as practical and concrete a way as possible, what it would mean to live one's life as a form. I have done this whilst striving to avoid essentialist or programmatic accounts of immanent politics. The exploration of these issues predates this book, and can be traced back to my doctoral studies, a decade and a half ago. It was during this period that I started to explore the potential connections which may exist between the thought and work of Agamben and Levinas. This book is the result of those investigations, thoughts and connections I have made and been making in my research. It is why Levinas has such a prominent role in a book about Agamben (perhaps counter-intuitively). Ultimately, I have sought to show how Levinas has (in the most part) been a silent partner to Agamben's philosophical investigations.

The problems of transcendent relationality

Ethics must be immanent for Agamben. This is the only genuine manner through which to approach another living being. If life itself is defined through a presupposition, then that will always already provide a negative basis for that life. This is how and why the first chapter focused on this ever divided life. Agamben presented this as the division between *bios* and *zoè*, political life and natural life, the division that denies us access to life as such. We can only experience this through a political system. This thought presupposes a transcendent relationality. Holding immanence in relation to transcendence provides a negative transcendent origin for immanence. Moreover, the presuppositional structure *always* leads to the subjection and dominion of one part over the other and the production of a remainder – bare life, or *homo sacer*. The division of life is perpetuated through the state of exception, a zone of indeterminacy which holds opposing terms in relation to one another, valorising one term (such as *bios*) on the condition that the inferior term (*zoè*) be abandoned and produced not as pure and independent *zoè* but as bare life.

The second chapter introduced the apparatus, a decisive term for Agamben, which refers to a multitude of things (like law, medicine, technology) which have one thing in common – they all act on living beings to produce subjects. Apparatuses of control divide life, allowing it to be defined through a transcendent sphere and captured by processes of sovereignty, biopolitics and management. Apparatuses of control cannot be transcended, or rethought, only deactivated. To avoid life being divided and defined through a negative transcendent relationality, Agamben posits his form-of-life.

I have argued that form-of-life should be read as a critique of the relational ethics of Emmanuel Levinas. Levinas's thought is unashamedly transcendent, focusing on the relationship between the individual and the Other. This relationship defines us. This transcendence does not trap subjects in apparatuses, but rather allows us to live an ethical life. It is precisely this element of Levinas's thought that Agamben uses as a foil. Is it possible to construct an ethical existence which needs the presupposition of a transcendent defining ground? Agamben thinks not. In fact, the extant critical comments that Agamben has made towards Levinasian ethics are, in my interpretation, necessary for Agamben's own project. They allow a critical distance to be generated to place clear blue water between form-of-life and Levinas's relation with the Other.

Can an immanent existence be ethical? Levinas felt only transcendence allowed for an ethical life to be lived.[2] Agamben's argument is that Levinas perpetuates a negative foundation of the self by defining the I with reference to an ungraspable Other. Agamben goes so far as to label Levinas's ethics as essentially negative in nature. This criticism is not tangential to Agamben's aim to theorise the *ethos* of the politics to come, but rather represents his attempt to think an ethics (and law) distinct from those of Levinas. For Agamben, law is an apparatus that dominates the subject and creates bare life. Agamben reads Levinas's subject as defined negatively through holding itself in relation to a negative foundation. Agamben opposes an ethics of responsibility, meaning that his non-relational ethics must eschew all forms of judgment and relationality.

As I have sought to demonstrate, Agamben's project is no small task, made more difficult because Levinasian ethics provides us with many resources for thinking about an ethical existence that involves the law and existing legal systems. Levinas's thought enables us to prioritise competing ethical or political or legal demands precisely because it is based in relationality. How then can Agamben offer an alternative?

Hyper-hermeneutics

The middle three chapters of this book considered both Agamben's critique of transcendent relationality, and how form-of-life, as a messianic figure of potentiality, can help us think in terms of a modal ontology, and living as a mode of potential. This is the alternative to Levinasian relationality, and relational thought more broadly. By focusing on potentiality Agamben exhorts us to find the answers we need in the world we live in. By a non-relational existence Agamben infers that any form of life which defines itself through its relation to another will inevitably lead to the creation of the remainder of bare life. Life must instead be thought of beyond this form of relationality. To put it another way:

> We differ from other animals in that we are initiated into our lives. Which is to say, we must first lose ourselves in the human so as to rediscover ourselves as alive, and vice-versa.[3]

In the third chapter I argued that Agamben provides an uncharitable account of Levinasian alterity and the ethics of relation, by connecting the law and judgment to the creation of bare life, and the works of Agamben and Levinas are much closer in reality than Agamben would at first admit. The move to distance his work from Levinas was needed by Agamben in order to open up a sphere for non-relational living.

In the fourth chapter I explored the details of this form-of-life, and also showed how Agamben's messianic thought is distinguishable from the messianism in Levinas. We are told that this non-relational life is based on non-responsibility, contact, and a monadic clinamen (a form of being-in-common) with others. It is an opening to the potentialities of life, a mode of living, lived in contact with others. In distinction to Levinas's relation to the Other, I have argued that a non-relational form-of-life should be understood as exhibiting its own negative relation to its other. Form-of-life is a monad, alone by oneself, but communicating with others, insofar as it represents them, as in a living mirror. This being-with the other is not positive in the sense that the other does not directly define the living being. But it is also true that conceptualising form-of-life is difficult due to the central role transcendent relationality has in our world today. We need to be attuned to the ethical imperative to form a community based on one's singular encounter with other singular beings.

In the fifth chapter I sought to develop this ethical imperative, arguing that form-of-life lives (in my terms) a hyper-hermeneutical existence. Form-of-life retains a hermeneutic structure to its existence, but this existence does not take place in the hermeneutic circle. Rather, form-of-life is constructed through singular paradigmatic examples. This means that the singular being does not live its life as a form through engaging in the modes of understanding and interpretation (hermeneutics) that already exist in the world, such as forms of legal subjecthood or political identities. Rather, the living being lives its life as a "how" through singular, paradigmatic gestures. In doing so, it constructs a paradigmatic circle, which exists non-relationally, deactivating hermeneutic apparatuses of control. These very gestures show how a form-of-life does not require a revolutionary movement, but, akin to Kierkegaard's formulation, these repeat gestures will create the world anew, as a being uses itself in a style of living. This does create new possibilities for imagining resistance, ethical dwelling and non-relational politics. That cannot be denied and for me is the main strength of Agamben's thought.

But here I make a point that is, I think, vital for judging the applicability or efficacy or utility of form-of-life for legal, political and philosophical thought. Even though form-of-life presupposes nothing but itself, I have argued that this itself is a living being that is a fully capable, conscious, existent. Form-of-life presupposes a being that is able to be a form-of-life. Given the way in which Agamben has constructed form-of-life, it is not possible to live one's life as a form or style of living if you are incapable, or lack the ability to grasp immanent existence. This is a key aporia.

This is why I have argued that form-of-life is a flawed attempt to present an alternative to an ethics of alterity. The aporias of form-of-life can be best evidenced by turning to what I have termed biologically liminal figures. Form-of-life cannot account for figures who are not capable or conscious existents, beings who cannot live their lives as a form. In these situations, Agamben's immanent philosophy runs aground, and it transpires that transcendent relationality (and in particular Levinasian ethics) is able to *ethically* account for these beings in a way Agamben cannot.

Liminal lives

The final two substantive chapters critically consider the biological liminal living figures, engaging with debates about the start and end of life, looking specifically at the unborn and at questions of reproductive rights as well as the patient in a vegetative state and the incapable patient nearing the end of their life. These are all figures of bare life in Agamben's work. What is more, they illustrate how transcendent relationality still haunts Agamben's immanent thought. Levinasian ethics can account for the ethical existence of these figures.

The debates over abortion, when life starts and how politically to account for reproductive rights are complex, but Agamben's work does not engage with these in his works. His failure to account for reproductive rights leaves an ambiguity in how form-of-life applies to the pregnant woman. Given his writings on the sovereign decision, it is difficult to see how a woman *does not* cause the unborn to become *homo sacer* through a decision to seek an abortion. This not only provides a one-dimensional perspective, but the lack of focus on the ethics of pregnancy and autonomy also illustrates another point about Agamben – namely that the figure of the woman in his work is often cast as a privileged figure of ephemerality, unable to access the plane of immanence but instrumental in man's access to it. I then demonstrate how the most persuasive analysis of Agamben's thought on reproductive rights comes very close to the position of the Roman Catholic Church and a defence of the potential life of the unborn. Whilst Levinasian thought can be read as privileging masculinity over femininity, his transcendent ethics can be utilised to provide for an ethics of pregnancy and reproductive rights that are far more developed than anything Agamben's modal ontology can offer, including how those ethics can be considered practically by a legal system. This is a dimension especially lacking in Agamben given his eschewing of questions of law and extant political structures, and their equivalence to forms of biopolitical control. Ultimately, any ethics of reproduction require judgment – a judgment as to the rights (ethical and legal) a woman has over her own body, a judgment as to the rights an unborn human can expect (again ethical and legal) and judgments legally as to situations where those rights are contested.

The book's final chapter considers aspects of the end of life. Specifically, I have focused on the adult patient at the end of their life who lacks capacity and the adult patient in a vegetative state. Patients who have capacity can easily fit into a paradigmatic figure of form-of-life, whereas the figures I chose clearly cannot live their lives as a form in the same way. Once again Agamben's eschewing of relationality and judgment, and his view of medicine as an apparatus of control, precludes the possibility in his thought for there to be an ethical encounter between those patients and the medical and legal professionals who decide on their future treatment. Agamben's thought can characterise the end-of-life decision-making as a sovereign or managerial exercise of power over a helpless individual cast as *homo sacer*. I turn again to Levinas, arguing that he can ethically account for end-of-life decisions in a way form-of-life cannot. Levinasian thought does not provide easy answers, or indeed any answers, but it does provide a framework with which to try and find answers, and this framework is grounded in transcendent relationality. Agamben's attempt to think a new form of politics is left flawed and incomplete, and form-of-life runs aground against the limits of biologically liminal lives.

What next?

It is with this conclusion that I have abandoned this work. I leave this study genuinely believing that Agamben's thought can offer us new ways to approach philosophy, law and politics. His coming politics presents us with avenues of resistance for politically liminal figures, and presents those of us already accepted as active political actors with ways to disarm the biopolitical apparatuses of control that dominate today's modern world. But his thought remains a double-edged sword.

By rejecting politics of social movements, and identities as not being form-of-life, Agamben makes it very difficult to conceive of applications of his work to questions of (for example) race and gender. Not every aspect of biopolitics impacts every life equally. I am uncertain as to whether a feminist reading of Agamben is possible, or whether Agamben's work can be applied to critical race theory, but I am of the view that this is the next stage for testing the limits of Agamben's work. In order for it to be of real use to scholars, critical theorists and activists, it must speak to the woman who is being coerced or forced by others or the laws of the country in which she lives to continue with a pregnancy. It must be able to provide options to those persons in the black community who face police misconduct, violence and brutality, which is all too everyday an occurrence in the United States and the United Kingdom. It must offer something to the sex workers who are criminalised for what they do, and who face violence, threats and danger in trying to do their jobs. It must actually treat women as political actors with agency, not just as means to an end, allowing men to live an ethical life. If Agamben's thought cannot speak to these issues and these people, then I would question whether his political solutions are actually worth pursuing in the world in which we all live. But all this must wait for another study and another project. This will be my task in the coming years. If there is content here which can help others pursue a similar path to the one I will take myself, then this book has done its job.

Notes

1 Agamben (2016a) xiii.
2 Levinas (1969) 52.
3 Agamben and Ferrando (2014) 47.

Bibliography

Abbott, M (2012) 'No Life is Bare, The Ordinary is Exceptional: Giorgio Agamben and the Question of Political Ontology', *Parrhesia*, 14, 23–36.

Abbott, M (2014) *The Figure of This World: Agamben and the Question of Political Ontology*, Edinburgh: Edinburgh University Press.

Adorno, T (1974) *Minima Moralia: Reflections from Damaged Life*, London: Verso.

Agamben, G (1993) *Stanzas: Word and Phantasm in Western Culture*, Martinez, R (tr.), Minneapolis: University of Minnesota Press.

Agamben, G (1995) *Idea of Prose*, Whitsitt, S and Sullivan, M (tr.), Albany: SUNY Press.

Agamben, G (1998) *Homo Sacer: Sovereign Power and Bare Life*, Heller-Roazen, D (tr.), Stanford: Stanford University Press.

Agamben, G (1999a) 'Absolute Immanence' in *Potentialities: Collected Essays in Philosophy*, Heller-Roazen, D (tr.), Stanford: Stanford University Press, 220–239.

Agamben, G (1999b) 'Bartleby, or On Contingency' in *Potentialities: Collected Essays in Philosophy*, Heller-Roazen, D (tr.), Stanford: Stanford University Press, 243–271.

Agamben, G (1999c) 'On Potentiality' in *Potentialities: Collected Essays in Philosophy*, Heller-Roazen, D (tr.), Stanford: Stanford University Press, 177–184.

Agamben, G (1999d) 'Pardes: The Writing of Potentiality' in *Potentialities: Collected Essays in Philosophy*, Heller-Roazen, D (tr.), Stanford: Stanford University Press, 205–219.

Agamben, G (1999e) 'The Messiah and the Sovereign: The Problem of Law in Walter Benjamin' in *Potentialities: Collected Essays in Philosophy*, Heller-Roazen, D (tr.), Stanford: Stanford University Press, 160–174.

Agamben, G (1999f) 'The Thing Itself' in *Potentialities: Collected Essays in Philosophy*, Heller-Roazen, D (tr.), Stanford: Stanford University Press, 27–38.

Agamben, G (1999g) *The End of the Poem: Studies in Poetics*, Heller-Roazen, D (tr.), Stanford: Stanford University Press.

Agamben, G (1999h) *The Man Without Content*, Albert, G (tr.), Stanford: Stanford University Press.

Agamben, G (2000) *Means Without End: Notes on Politics*, Binetti, V and Casarino, C (tr.), Minneapolis: University of Minnesota Press.

Agamben, G (2001) 'For a Philosophy of Infancy', *Public*, 21, 120–122.

Agamben, G (2002) *Remnants of Auschwitz: The Witness and the Archive*, Heller-Roazen, D (tr.), New York: Zone Books.

Agamben, G (2004a) 'Difference and Repetition: On Guy Debord's Film' in *Guy Debord and the Situationist International: Texts and Documents*, McDonough, T (ed.), Cambridge: MIT Press, 313–319.

Agamben, G (2004b) *The Open: Man and Animal*, Attell, K (tr.), Stanford: Stanford University Press.
Agamben, G (2005a) 'Introduzione' in Carl Schmitt, *Un giurista davanti a se stesso: Saggi e interviste*, Vicenza: Neri Pozza.
Agamben, G (2005b) 'La potenza del pensiero' in *La potenza del pensiero: Saggi e conferenze*, Venezia: Neri Pozza, 273–288.
Agamben, G (2005c) *State of Exception*, Attell, K (tr.), Chicago: University of Chicago Press.
Agamben, G (2005d) *The Time That Remains: A Commentary on the Letter to the Romans*, Dailey, R (tr.), Stanford: Stanford University Press.
Agamben, G (2006) *Language and Death: The Place of Negativity*, Pinkus, K and Hardt, M (tr.), Minneapolis: University of Minnesota Press.
Agamben, G (2007a) *Infancy and History: On the Destruction of Experience*, Heron, L (tr.), London: Verso Books.
Agamben, G (2007b) *The Coming Community*, Hardt, M (tr.), Minneapolis: University of Minnesota Press.
Agamben, G (2007c) *Profanations*, Fort, J (tr.), Princeton: Princeton University Press.
Agamben, G (2007d) 'The Work of Man' in *Giorgio Agamben: Sovereignty and Life*, Calarco, M and DeCaroli, S (eds.), Stanford: Stanford University Press, 1–10.
Agamben, G (2009a) 'On the Limits of Violence', *Diacritics*, 39, 103–111.
Agamben, G (2009b) 'Philosophical Archaeology', *Law and Critique*, 20, 211–231.
Agamben, G (2009c) *The Signature of All Things: On Method*, D'Isanto, L and Attell, K (tr.), New York: Zone Books.
Agamben, G (2009d) *What is an Apparatus? and Other Essays*, Kishik, D and Pedatella, S (tr.), Stanford: Stanford University Press.
Agamben, G (2010) *Nudities*, Kishik, D and Pedatella, S (tr.), Stanford: Stanford University Press.
Agamben, G (2011) *The Kingdom and the Glory: For a Theological Genealogy of Economy and Government*, Chiesa, L and Mandarini, M (tr.), Stanford: Stanford University Press.
Agamben, G (2012) *The Church and the Kingdom*, de la Durantaye (tr.), London: Seagull Books.
Agamben, G (2013a) *Opus Dei: An Archaeology of Duty*, Kotsko, A (tr.), Stanford: Stanford University Press.
Agamben, G (2013b) *The Highest Poverty: Monastic Rules and Form-of-Life*, Kotsko, A (tr.), Stanford: Stanford University Press.
Agamben, G (2014) 'What is a Destituent Power?', *Environment and Planning D: Society and Space*, 32, 65–74.
Agamben, G (2015a) *Pilate and Jesus*, Kotsko, A (tr.), Stanford: Stanford University Press.
Agamben, G (2015b) *Stasis: Civil War as a Political Paradigm*, Heron, N (tr.), Edinburgh: Edinburgh University Press.
Agamben, G (2016a) *The Use of Bodies*, Kotsko, A (tr.), Stanford: Stanford University Press.
Agamben, G (2016b) *What is Real?*, Chiesa, L (tr.), Stanford: Stanford University Press.
Agamben, G (2017a) *Taste*, Francis, C (tr.), London: Seagull Books.
Agamben, G (2017b) *The Fire and the Tale*, Chiesa, L (tr.), Stanford: Stanford University Press.
Agamben, G (2017c) *The Mystery of Evil: Benedict XVI and the End of Days*, Kotsko, A (tr.), Stanford: Stanford University Press.
Agamben, G (2017d) *The Omnibus Homo Sacer*, Stanford: Stanford University Press.

Agamben, G (2018a) *Karman: A Brief Treatise on Action, Guilt and Gesture*, Kotsko, A (tr.), Stanford: Stanford University Press.

Agamben, G (2018b) *Pulcinella: Or Entertainment for Kids in Four Scenes*, Attell, K (tr.), East Peoria, Seagull Books.

Agamben, G (2018c) *The Adventure*, Chiesa, L (tr.), Cambridge: MIT Press.

Agamben, G (2018d) *What Is Philosophy?*, Chiesa, L (tr.), Stanford: Stanford University Press.

Agamben, G (2019) *Creation and Anarchy: The Work of Art and the Religion of Capitalism*, Stanford: Stanford University Press.

Agamben, G (2020a) 'Biosicurezza e politica', *Quodlibet* (11 May 2020), https://www.quodlibet.it/giorgio-agamben-biosicurezza/.

Agamben, G (2020b) 'Chiarimenti', *Quodlibet* (17 March 2020), https://www.quodlibet.it/giorgio-agamben-chiarimenti/.

Agamben, G (2020c) 'L'invenzione di un'epidemia', *Quodlibet* (26 February 2020), https://www.quodlibet.it/giorgio-agamben-l-invenzione-di-un-epidemia/.

Agamben, G (2020d) 'La medicina come religione', *Quodlibet* (2 May 2020), https://www.quodlibet.it/giorgio-agamben-la-medicina-come-religione.

Agamben, G (2020e) 'Quando la casa brucia', *Quodlibet* (5 October 2020), https://www.quodlibet.it/giorgio-agamben-un-paese-senza-volto.

Agamben, G (2020f) 'Riflessioni sulla peste', *Quodlibet* (27 March 2020), https://www.quodlibet.it/giorgio-agamben-riflessioni-sulla-peste/.

Agamben, G (2020g) 'Un paese senza volto', *Quodlibet* (8 October 2020), https://www.quodlibet.it/giorgio-agamben-un-paese-senza-volto.

Agamben, G (2020h) *The Kingdom and the Garden*, Kotsko, A (tr.), East Peoria, Seagull Books.

Agamben, G and Ferrando, M (2014) *The Unspeakable Girl: The Myth and Mystery of Kore*, de la Durantaye, L and Wyman, A (tr.), East Peoria, Seagull Books.

Alford, F (2004) 'Levinas and Political Theory', *Political Theory*, 32, 146–171.

Anidjar, G (2011) 'The Meaning of Life', *Critical Inquiry*, 37, 697–723.

Anozie, M (2020) 'Abortion and Homosexuality Prohibitory Regimes Versus the Right to Privacy in Nigeria', *Commonwealth Law Bulletin*, 46, 483–510.

Aristotle (1984a) 'On the Parts of Animals' in *The Complete Works of Aristotle, Volume One*, Barnes, J (ed.), Princeton: Princeton University Press.

Aristotle (1984b) 'On the Soul' in *The Complete Works of Aristotle, Volume One*, Barnes, J (ed.), Princeton: Princeton University Press.

Aristotle (1984c) 'Politics' in *The Complete Works of Aristotle, Volume Two*, Barnes, J (ed.), Princeton: Princeton University Press.

Aristotle (1984d) 'Poetics' in *The Complete Works of Aristotle, Volume Two*, Barnes, J (ed.), Princeton: Princeton University Press.

Aristotle (1984e) 'Nicomachean Ethics' in *The Complete Works of Aristotle, Volume Two*, Barnes, J (ed.), Princeton: Princeton University Press.

Aristotle (1984f) 'Metaphysics' in *The Complete Works of Aristotle, Volume One*, Barnes, J (ed.), Princeton: Princeton University Press.

Armstrong, A (2008) 'Beyond Resistance: A Response to Žižek's Critique of Foucault's Subject of Freedom', *Parrhesia: A Journal of Critical Philosophy*, 5, 19–31.

Attell, K (2009) 'Potentiality, Actuality, Constituent Power', *Diacritics*, 39, 35–53.

Attell, K (2015) *Giorgio Agamben: Beyond the Threshold of Deconstruction*, New York: Fordham University Press.

Badiou, A (2001) *Saint Paul: The Foundation of Universalism*, Brassier, R (tr.), Stanford: Stanford University Press.

Badiou, A (2005) 'Universal Truths and the Question of Religion', *Journal of Philosophy and Scripture*, 3, 38–42.

Badiou, A (2009) *Logic of Worlds*, Toscano, A (tr.), London: Continuum.

Bartoloni, P (2004) 'The Stanza of the Self: on Agamben's Potentiality', *Contretemps*, 5, 8–15.

Ben-Dor, O (2007) *Thinking About Law: In Silence with Heidegger*, Oxford: Hart Publishing.

Benjamin, W (1996) 'Letter to Florens Christian Rang, December 9, 1923' in *Selected Writings, volume 1, 1913–1926*, Bullock, M and Jennings, M (eds.), Cambridge: Harvard University Press, 389.

Benjamin, W (1999) 'Theses on the Philosophy of History' in *Illuminations*, Zorn, H (tr.), London: Pimlico, 245–255.

Benjamin, W (2002) *The Arcades Project*, Elland, H and McLaughlin, K (tr.), Cambridge: Harvard University Press.

Benjamin, W (2003) 'On the Concept of History' in *Walter Benjamin, Selected Writings, Volume 4: 1938–1940*, Jennings M (ed.), Cambridge: Harvard University Press, 389–400.

Benjamin, W (2004) 'Critique of Violence' in *Selected Writings, volume 1, 1913–1926*, Bullock, M and Jennings, M (eds.), Cambridge: Harvard University Press, 236–252.

Benjamin, W (2011) 'Notes toward a Work on the Category of Justice' in Fenves, P, *The Messianic Reduction: Walter Benjamin and the Shape of Time*, Stanford: Stanford University Press, 257–258.

Bergo, B (2005) 'Ontology, Transcendence, and Immanence in Emmanuel Levinas', *Research in Phenomenology*, 25, 141–177.

Bergo, B (2009) 'Levinas's Weak Messianism in Time and Flesh, or The Insistence of Messiah Ben David', *Journal for Cultural Research*, 15, 225–248.

Bernasconi, R (1998) 'Different Styles of Eschatology: Derrida's Take on Levinas's Political Messianism', *Research in Phenomenology*, 28, 3–19.

Bernasconi, R (2005) 'No Exit: Levinas' Aporetic Account of Transcendence', *Research in Phenomenology*, 35, 101–117.

Biddick, K (2016) *Make and Let Die: Untimely Sovereignties*, Punctum Books.

Bierlein, M (2007) 'Seeing the Face of the Patient: Considerations in Applying Bioethics Mediation to Non-Competent End-of-Life Decision Making', *Ohio State Journal on Dispute Resolution*, 23, 61–88.

Bird, G (2016) *Containing Community: From Political Economy to Ontology in Agamben, Esposito, and Nancy*, New York: SUNY Press.

Bloch, E (1972) *Atheism in Christianity: the Religion of the Exodus and the New Kingdom*, Swann, J (tr.), New York: Herder and Herder.

Bobb-Semple, C (2007) 'English Common Law, Slavery, and Human Rights', *Texas Wesleyan Law Review*, 13, 659–684.

Boonan, D (2012) *A Defense of Abortion*, Cambridge: Cambridge University Press.

Bordeleau, E (2017) 'Initiating Life: Agamben and the Political Use of Intimacy', *The Journal of Speculative Philosophy*, 31, 481–492.

Brower, V (2017) 'Jacques Derrida' in *Agamben's Philosophical Lineage*, Kotsko, A and Salzani, C (eds.), Edinburgh: Edinburgh University Press, 230–241.

Brown, W (1995) *States of Injury: Power and Freedom in Late Modernity*Princeton: Princeton University Press.

Buckley Dyer, J (2013) *Slavery, Abortion, and the Politics of Constitutional Meaning*, Cambridge: Cambridge University Press.

Burchell, G (2006) 'Introduction' in *Michel Foucault, Psychiatric Power, Lectures at the Collège de France, 1973–1974*, Basingstoke: Palgrave Macmillan.

Burge, T (1992) 'Philosophy of Language and of Mind: 1950–1990', *The Philosophical Review*, 101, 3–51.

Burggraeve, R (1999) 'Violence and the vulnerable face of the other: The vision of Emmanuel Levinas on moral evil and our responsibility', *Journal of Social Philosophy*, 30, 29–45.

Bush, J (1997) '*The British Constitution and the Creation of American Slavery*' in *Slavery & the Law*, Finkelman. P (ed.), Madison: Madison House, 379–418.

Bussolini, J (2010) 'What is a Dispostive?', *Foucault Studies*, 10, 85–107.

Calarco, M (2008) *Zoographies: The Question of the Animal from Heidegger to Derrida*, New York: Columbia University Press.

Calarco, M and De Caroli, S (eds.) (2007) *Giorgio Agamben: Sovereignty & Life*, Stanford: Stanford University Press.

Campbell, T (2011) *Improper Life: Technology and Biopolitics from Heidegger to Agamben*, Minneapolis: University of Minnesota Press.

Campbell, T (2012) '"Enough of a Self": Esposito's Impersonal Biopolitics', *Law, Culture and the Humanities*, 8, 31–46.

Carlisle, C (2005) 'Kierkegaard's Repetition: The Possibility of Motion', *British Journal for the History of Philosophy*, 13, 521–541.

Cavarero, A (1992) 'Equality and Sexual Difference: Amnesia in Political Thought' in *Beyond Equality and Difference: Citizenship, Feminist Politics and Female Subjectivity*, Bock, G and James, S (eds.), New York: Routledge, 32–47.

Chiesa, L (2009) 'Giorgio Agamben's Franciscan Ontology', *Cosmos and History: The Journal of Natural and Social Philosophy*, 5, 105–116.

Chiesa, L and Ruda, F (2011) 'The Event of Language as Force of Life: Agamben's Linguistic Vitalism', *Angelaki: Journal of the Theoretical Humanities*, 16, 163–180.

Cimino, A (2016) 'Agamben's Political Messianism in 'The Time That Remains'', *International Journal of Philosophy and Theology*, 77, 102–118.

Colebrook C and Maxwell, J (2016) *Agamben*, Cambridge: Polity Press.

Colony, T (2007) 'Before the abyss: Agamben on Heidegger and the Living', *Continental Philosophy Review*, 40, 1–16.

Connolly, W (2007) 'The Complexities of Sovereignty', in *Giorgio Agamben: Sovereignty and Life*, Calarco, M and DeCaroli, S (eds.), Stanford: Stanford University Press, 23–42.

Cooper, M (2009) 'The Silent Scream – Agamben, Deleuze and the Politics of the Unborn' in *Deleuze and Law*, Braidotti, R, Colebrook, C and Hanafin, P (eds.), London: Palgrave Macmillan.

Cornell, D (1988) 'Post-Structuralism, the Ethical Relation, and the Law', *Cardozo Law Review*, 9, 1591–1628.

Cornell, D (1990a) 'From the Lighthouse: The Promise of Redemption and the Possibility of Legal Interpretation', *Cardozo Law Review*, 11, 1687–1714.

Cornell, D (1990b) 'The Violence as the Masquerade: Law Dressed Up As Justice', *Cardozo Law Review*, 11, 1047–1064.

Cornell, D (1992) *The Philosophy of the Limit*, London: Routledge.

Critchley, S (1992) *The ethics of deconstruction: Derrida and Levinas*, Edinburgh: Edinburgh University Press.

Critchley, S (1999) *Ethics, Politics, Subjectivity: Essays on Derrida, Levinas and Contemporary French Thought*, London: Verso.

Critchley, S (2004) *Very Little … Almost Nothing*, London: Routledge.
Critchley, S (2010) *The Problem with Levinas*, Oxford: Oxford University Press.
Critchley, S and Bernasconi, R (2002) 'Introduction' in *The Cambridge Companion to Levinas*, Critchley, S and Bernasconi, R (eds.), Cambridge: Cambridge University Press, 1–32.
Crowe, J (2006) 'Levinasian Ethics and Legal Obligation', *Ratio Juris*, 19, 421–435.
Dahnke, M (2012) 'Emmanuel Levinas and the Face of Terri Schiavo: Bioethical and Phenomenological Reflections on a Private Tragedy and Public Spectacle', *Theoretical Medicine and Bioethics*, 33, 405–420.
de Boever, A (2010) 'Bio-Paulitics', *Journal for Cultural and Religious Theory*, 11, 35–51.
de Boever, A (2015) *Plastic Sovereignties: Agamben and the Politics of Aesthetics*, Edinburgh: Edinburgh University Press.
de la Durantaye, L (2009) *Giorgio Agamben: A Critical Introduction*, Stanford: Stanford University Press.
Dean, M (2004) 'Four Theses on the Powers of Life and Death', *Contretemps*, 5, 16–29.
Dean, M (2013) *The Signature of Power: Sovereignty, Governmentality and Biopolitics*, London: SAGE Publications.
DeCaroli, S (2012) 'The Idea of Awakening: Giorgio Agamben and the Nāgārjuna References', *Res Publica: Revista de Filosofía Política*, 28, 101–138.
DeCaroli, S (2020) 'That Which Is Born Generates Its Own Use. Giorgio Agamben and Karma', *Etica & Politica / Ethics & Politics*, 22, 247–273.
Deleuze, G (1994) *Difference and Repetition*, Patton, P (tr.), New York: Columbia University Press.
Deleuze, G (2001) *Pure Immanence: Essays on A Life*, Boyman, A (tr.), New York: Zone Books.
Deleuze, G (2006) *Foucault*, Hand, S (tr.), Minneapolis: University of Minnesota Press.
Deleuze G and Guattari F (1994) *What is Philosophy?*, Tomlinson H and Burchell G (tr.), New York: Columbia University Press.
Derrida, J (1978) *Writing and Difference*, Bass, A (tr.), New York: Routledge.
Derrida, J (1980) *The Post Card*, Bass, A (tr.), Chicago: University of Chicago Press.
Derrida, J (1982) *Margins of Philosophy*, Bass, A (tr.), Chicago: University of Chicago Press.
Derrida, J (1986) *Glas*, Leavey, J and Rand, R (trs.), Lincoln: University of Nebraska Press.
Derrida, J (1988) 'Afterword: Toward an Ethic of Discussion' in *Limited Inc.*, Graff, G (ed.), Evanston: Northwestern University Press, 111–150.
Derrida, J (1990) 'Force of Law: The "Mystical Foundation of Authority"', *Cardozo Law Review*, 11, 919–1045.
Derrida, J (1991) 'At This Very Moment in This Text Here I Am' in *Re-reading Levinas*, Bernasconi, R and Critchley, S (eds.), Bloomington: Indiana University Press.
Derrida, J (1994) *Specters of Marx: The State of the Debt, the Work of Mourning, & the New International*, Kamuf, P (tr.), London: Routledge.
Derrida, J (1997) *Of Grammatology*, Spivak, G (tr.), Baltimore: Johns Hopkins University Press.
Derrida, J (2008) *The Animal That Therefore I Am*, Willis, D (tr.), New York: Fordham University Press.
Derrida, J (2009) *The Beast and the Sovereign, vol 1*, Bennington, G (tr.), Chicago: The University of Chicago Press.
Deutscher, P (2008) '*The Inversion of Exceptionality: Foucault, Agamben and "Reproductive Rights"*' *South Atlantic Quarterly*, 108, 55–70.

Deutscher, P (2017) *Foucault's Futures: A Critique of Reproductive Reason*, New York: Columbia University Press.

Diamantides, M (1995) 'Ethics in Law: Death Marks on a "Still Life" a Vision of Judgement as Vegetating', *Law and Critique*, 6, 209–228.

Diamantides, M (2000) *The Ethics of Suffering: Modern Law, Philosophy and Medicine*, Farnham: Ashgate.

Diamantides, M (2017) 'Law and Compassion: Between Ethics and Economy, Philosophical Speculation and Arche-ology', *International Journal of Law in Context*, 13, 197–211.

Dickinson, C (2011) *Agamben and Theology*, London: T & T Clark.

Dickinson, C (2014) *Between the Canon and the Messiah: The Structure of Faith in Contemporary Continental Thought*, London: Bloomsbury.

Dickinson, C (2015a) 'Citing 'Whatever Authority" in *Agamben's Coming Philosophy: Finding a New Use for Theology*, Dickinson C and Kotsko A (eds.), London: Rowman & Littlefield International, 67–84.

Dickinson, C (2015b) 'On the 'Coming Philosophy" in *Agamben's Coming Philosophy: Finding a New Use for Theology*, Dickinson C and Kotsko A (eds.), London: Rowman & Littlefield International, 21–39.

Dickinson, C (2015c) 'The 'Absence' of Gender' in Agamben's Coming Philosophy: Finding a New Use for Theology, Dickinson, C and Kotsko, A, London: Rowman & Littlefield International, 167–182.

Dillon, M (2005) 'Cared to Death: The Biopoliticised Time of Your Life', *Foucault Studies*, 2, 37–46.

Douglass, F (1986) *Narrative of the Life of Frederick Douglass, an American Slave*, New York: Penguin Books.

Douzinas, C (2000) *The End of Human Rights: Critical Legal Thought at the Turn of the Century*, Oxford: Hart Publishing.

Douzinas, C and Warrington, R (1994) *Justice Miscarried: Ethics and Aesthetics in Law*, London: Harvester Wheatsheaf.

Drescher, S (1989) 'Manumission in a Society without Slave Law: Eighteenth century England', *Slavery & Abolition*, 10, 85–101.

Drescher, S (2009) *Abolition: A History of Slavery and Antislavery*, New York: Cambridge University Press.

Dworkin, R (1993) *Life's Dominion: An Argument About Abortion, Euthanasia, and Individual Freedom*, New York: Alfred A Knopf.

Edelglass, W (2006) 'Levinas on Suffering and Compassion', *Sophia*, 45, 39–56.

Eriksson, K (2005) 'Foucault, Deleuze and the Ontology of Networks', *The European Legacy*, 10, 595–610.

Esposito, R (2008) *Bíos: Biopolitics and Philosophy*, Campbell, T (tr.), Minneapolis: Minnesota University Press.

Esposito, R (2009) *Communitas: The Origin and Destiny of Community*. Campbell, T (tr.), Stanford: Stanford University Press.

Esposito, R (2011) *Immunitas: The Protection and Negation of Life*. London: Polity Press.

Esposito, R (2012) 'The *Dispositif* of the Person', *Law, Culture and the Humanities*, 8, 17–30.

Evans, M (2017) 'Levinas, Derrida and the Ethics and Politics of Reproduction', *Journal of the British Society of Phenomenology*, 48, 44–62.

Febbri, L (2011) 'From Inoperativeness to Action: On Giorgio Agamben's Anarchism', *Radical Philosophy*, 14, 85–100.

Finkelman, P (1994) 'Let Justice Be Done, Though the Heavens May Fall: The Law of Freedom', *Chicago-Kent Law Review*, 70, 325–368.
Finkelman, P and Drescher, S (2017) 'The Eternal Problem of Slavery in International Law: Killing the Vampire of Human Culture', *Michigan State Law Review*, 755–803.
Finlayson, J (2010) '"Bare life" and politics in Agamben's reading of Aristotle', *The Review of Politics*, 72, 97–126.
Foucault, M (1978) *The History of Sexuality, Volume One: An Introduction*, Hurley, D (tr.), London: Penguin Books.
Foucault, M (1980a) 'Body/Power' in *Power/Knowledge: Selected Interviews and Other Writings, 1972–1977*, Gordon, C (ed.), New York: Pantheon, 55–62.
Foucault, M (1980b) 'The Confession of the Flesh' in *Power/Knowledge: Selected Interviews and Other Writings, 1972–1977*, Gordon, C (tr.), Brighton: Harvester Press, 194–228.
Foucault, M (1982a) 'The Subject and Power' in *Michel Foucault: Beyond Structuralism and Hermeneutics*, Dreyfus, H and Rabinow, P (eds.), Brighton: Harvester Press, 208–226.
Foucault, M (1982b) 'The Subject and Power', *Critical Inquiry*, 8, 777–795.
Foucault, M (1991a) *Discipline and Punish: The Birth of the Prison*, Sheridan, A (tr.), London: Penguin Books.
Foucault, M (1991b) 'On the Genealogy of Ethics: An Overview of the Work in Progress' in *The Foucault Reader: An Introduction to Foucault's Thought*, Rabinow, P (ed.), London: Penguin Books, 340–372.
Foucault, M (1991c) 'Polemics, Politics, and Problematizations: An Interview with Michel Foucault' in *The Foucault Reader: An Introduction to Foucault's Thought*, Rabinow, P (ed.), London: Penguin Books, 381–390.
Foucault, M (1994) 'Prisons et asiles dans le mécanisme du pouvoir' in *Dits et Ecrits: 1954–1988, vol. II*, Paris: Gallimard, 523–524.
Foucault, M (1998a) 'A Preface to Transgression' in *Essential Works of Foucault 1954–1984, Vol 2: Aesthetics, Ethics and Epistemology*, Hurley, R (tr.), Rabinow, P (ed.), Harmondsworth: Penguin Books, 69–87.
Foucault, M (1998b) 'Life, Experience and Science' in *Essential Works of Foucault 1954–1984, Vol 2: Aesthetics, Ethics and Epistemology*, Hurley, R (tr.), Rabinow, P (ed.), Harmondsworth: Penguin Books, 465–478.
Foucault, M (1998c) *The Order of Things: Archaeology of the Human Science*, Abingdon: Routledge.
Foucault, M (2000a) 'Sex, Power and the Politics of Identity' in *Essential Works of Foucault 1954–1984, Vol. 1: Ethics, Subjectivity and Truth*, Hurley, R (tr.), Rabinow, P (ed.), Harmondsworth: Penguin Books, 157–173.
Foucault, M (2000b) 'Technologies of the Self' in *Essential Works of Foucault 1954–1984, Vol. 1: Ethics, Subjectivity and Truth*, Hurley, R (tr.), Rabinow, P (ed.), Harmondsworth: Penguin Books, 223–251.
Foucault, M (2000c) 'The Ethics of the Concern for Self as a Practice of Freedom' in *Essential Works of Foucault 1954–1984, Vol. 1: Ethics, Subjectivity and Truth*, Hurley, R (tr.), Rabinow, P (ed.), Harmondsworth: Penguin Books, 281–301.
Foucault, M (2000d) 'What is Enlightenment?' in *Essential Works of Foucault 1954–1984, Vol. 1: Ethics, Subjectivity and Truth*, Hurley, R (tr.), Rabinow, P (ed.), Harmondsworth: Penguin Books, 303–319.
Foucault, M (2002a) 'Interview with Michel Foucault' in *Essential Works of Foucault 1954–1984, Vol. 3: Power*, Hurley, R (tr.), Rabinow, P (ed.), Harmondsworth: Penguin Books, 239–297.

Foucault, M (2002b) 'Useless to Revolt?' in *Essential Works of Foucault 1954–1984, Vol. 3: Power*, Hurley, R (tr.), Rabinow, P (ed.), Harmondsworth: Penguin Books, 449–453.
Foucault, M (2003a) *Society Must Be Defended, Lectures at the Collège de France, 1975–76*, Macey, D (tr.), London: Penguin Books.
Foucault, M (2003b) *The Birth of the Clinic*, Abingdon: Routledge.
Foucault, M (2007) *Security, Territory, Population: Lectures at the Collège de France, 1978–1979*, London: Palgrave Macmillan.
Fox, C (2011) 'The Novelty of Religion and the Religiosity of Substitution in Levinas and Agamben', *Levinas Studies*, 6, 131–158.
Frost, T (2010) 'Agamben's Sovereign Legalization of Foucault', *Oxford Journal of Legal Studies*, 30, 545–577.
Frost, T (2013) 'The Hyper-Hermeneutic Gesture of a Subtle Revolution', *Critical Horizons: A Journal of Philosophy and Social Theory*, 14, 70–92.
Frost, T (2014) 'Thinking relationality in Agamben and Levinas', *Griffith Law Review*, 23, 210–231.
Frost, T (2019) 'The *Dispositif* between Foucault and Agamben', *Law, Culture and the Humanities*, 15, 151–171.
Frost, T (2020) 'Destituent Power and the Problem of the Lives to Come', *Etica & Politica / Ethics & Politics*, 22, 211–234.
Frost, T (2021) 'Kierkegaard and the Figure of Form-of-Life' in *Agamben and the Existentialists*, Norris, M and Dickinson, C (eds.), Edinburgh: Edinburgh University Press (in press).
Fuggle, S (2009) 'Excavating Government: Giorgio Agamben's Archaeological Dig', *Foucault Studies*, 7, 81–98.
Fukuyama, F (2006) *The End of History and the Last Man*, New York: Free Press.
Genel, K (2006) 'The Question of Biopower: Foucault and Agamben', *Rethinking Marxism*, 18, 43–62.
George, R (1999) 'Law, Democracy, and Moral Disagreement' in *Deliberative Politics: Essays on Democracy and Disagreement*, Macedo, S (ed.), Oxford: Oxford University Press.
Giacino, J and Kalmar, K (1997) 'The Vegetative and Minimally Conscious States: A comparison of clinical features and outcome', *Journal of Head Trauma Rehabilitation*, 12, 36–51.
Giacino, J and Kalmar, K (2005) 'Diagnostic and Prognostic Guidelines for the Vegetative and Minimally Conscious States', *Neuropsychological Rehabilitation*, 15, 166–177.
Gibbs, R (2006) 'Law and Ethics', *Revista Portuguesa de Filosofia*, 62, 395–402.
Giubilini, A and Minerva, F (2013) 'After-birth Abortion: Why Should the Baby Live?', *Journal of Medical Ethics*, 39, 261–263.
Golden, M (1985) 'Pais, «Child» and «Slave»', *L'Antiquité Classique*, 54, 91–104.
Goldenberg, D (1973) 'The Right to Abortion: Expansion of the Right to Privacy Through the Fourteenth Amendment', *The Catholic Lawyer*, 19, 336–357.
Golder, B and Fitzpatrick, P (2009) *Foucault's Law*, Abingdon: Routledge.
Gould, R (2013) 'Laws, Exceptions, Norms: Kierkegaard, Schmitt, and Benjamin on the Exception', *Telos*, 162, 77–96.
Greasley, K (2017) *Arguments about Abortion: Personhood, Morality, and Law*, Oxford: Oxford University Press.
Guenther, L (2006a) '"Like a Maternal Body": Emmanuel Levinas and the Motherhood of Moses', *Hypatia*, 21, 119–136.
Guenther, L (2006b) *The Gift of the Other: Levinas and the Politics of Reproduction*, Albany: State University of New York Press.

Guenther, L (2009) '"Nameless Singularity": Levinas on Individuation and Ethical Singularity', *Epoché*, 14, 167–187.

Guenther, L (2011) 'Shame and the Temporality of Social Life', *Continental Philosophy Review*, 44, 23–39.

Guenther, L (2012) 'Resisting Agamben: The Biopolitics of Shame and Humiliation', *Philosophy and Social Criticism*, 38, 59–79.

Gutting, G (2003) 'Foucault and the History of Madness' in *The Cambridge Companion to Foucault*, Gutting, G (ed.), 2nd edn, Cambridge: Cambridge University Press, 49–73.

Hägglund, M (2008) *Radical Atheism: Derrida and the Time of Life*, Stanford: Stanford University Press.

Heidegger, M (1962) *Being and Time*, Macquarrie, J and Robinson, E (tr.), New York: Harper Row.

Heidegger, M (1968) *What is Called Thinking?*, Gray, J (tr.), New York: Harper Row.

Heidegger, M (1971) *On the Way to Language*, Hertz, P (tr.), New York: Harper Row.

Heidegger, M (1982) *The Basic Problems of Phenomenology*, Hofstadter, A (tr.), Indianapolis: Indiana University Press.

Heidegger, M (1992) *Parmenides*, Schuwer, A and Rojcewicz, R (tr.), Bloomington: Indiana University Press.

Heidegger, M (1993) 'Letter on Humanism' in *Basic Writings: Martin Heidegger*, Krell, D (ed.), Abingdon: Routledge, 213–265.

Heidegger, M (1994) *Hegel's Phenomenology of Spirit*, Indianapolis: Indiana University Press.

Heidegger, M (1995) *The Fundamental Concepts of Metaphysics: World, Finitude, Solitude*, McNeill, W and Walker, N (tr.), Indianapolis: Bloomington University Press.

Heidegger, M (2012) *Contributions to Philosophy: Of the Event*, Rojcewicz, R and Vallega-Neu (tr.), Bloomington: Indiana University Press.

Heller-Roazen, D (1999) 'Editor's Introduction: "To Read What Was Never Written"' in *Potentialities: Collected Essays in Philosophy*, Heller-Roazen, D (tr.), Stanford: Stanford University Press, 1–23.

Hewson, B (2001) 'Reproductive Autonomy and the Ethics of Abortion', *Journal of Medical Ethics*, 27, 10–14.

Hill, L (2007) *The Cambridge Introduction to Jacques Derrida*, Cambridge: Cambridge University Press.

Hudson, B (2003) *Justice in the Risk Society*, London: Sage Publications.

Hulsebosch, D (2006) 'Nothing But Liberty: *Somerset's Case* and the British Empire', *Law and History Review*, 24, 647–657.

Kang, Y A (1997) 'Levinas on Suffering and Solidarity', *Tijdshrift voor Filosofie*, 59, 482–504.

Kaufman, E (2008), 'The Saturday of Messianic Time (Agamben and Badiou on the Apostle Paul)', *South Atlantic Quarterly*, 107, 37–54.

Kavanaugh, J (2001) *Who Counts as Persons? Human Identity and the Ethics of Killing*, Washington: Georgetown University Press.

Keenan, D (1999) *Death and Responsibility: The 'Work' of Levinas*, Albany: State University of New York Press.

Kelly, J N D (1977) *Early Christian Doctrine*, 5th edn, London: Adam & Charles Black.

Kierkegaard, S (1980) *The Sickness unto Death*, Hong, H and Hong, E (tr.), Princeton: Princeton University Press.

Kierkegaard, S (1983) 'Repetition: A Venture in Experimenting Psychology' in *Fear and Trembling/Repetition*, Hong, H and Hong, E (tr.), Princeton: Princeton University Press.

Kierkegaard, S (1991) *Practice in Christianity*, Hong, H and Hong, E (tr.), Princeton: Princeton University Press.

Kierkegaard, S (1995) *Works of Love*, Hong, H and Hong, E (tr.), Princeton: Princeton University Press.

Kierkegaard, S (2015) *Christian Discourses*, Lowrie, W (tr.), Princeton: Princeton University Press.

Kishik, D (2012) *The Power of Life: Agamben and the Coming Politics*, Stanford: Stanford University Press.

Kishik, D (2020) 'Homo Schizoid. Destituent Power and Nonrelational Life', *Etica & Politica / Ethics & Politics*, 22, 287–296.

Kojève, A (1969) *Introduction to the Reading of Hegel*, Nichols Jr, J (tr.), Ithaca: Cornell University Press.

Kotsko, A (2020) *Agamben's Philosophical Tradition*, Edinburgh: Edinburgh University Press.

LaCapra, D (1990) 'Justice and the Force of Law', *Cardozo Law Review*, 11, 1065–1078.

LaCapra, D (2009) *History and Its Limits: Human, Animal, Violence*, Ithaca: Cornell University Press.

Laclau, E (2007) 'Bare Life or Social Indeterminacy' in *Giorgio Agamben: Sovereignty and Life*, Calarco, M and DeCaroli, S (eds.), Stanford, Stanford University Press, 11–22.

Laes, C (2008) 'Child Slaves at Work in Roman Antiquity', *Ancient Society*, 38, 235–283.

Lagaay, A and Rauch, M (2020) 'Scenes of Indifference, The Addressee of the Adventure', *Etica & Politica / Ethics & Politics*, 22, 87–108.

Lagaay, A and Schiffers, J (2009) 'Passivity at Work. A Conversation on an Element in the Philosophy of Giorgio Agamben', *Law and Critique*, 20, 325–337.

Laureys, S et al (2010) 'Unresponsive Wakefulness Syndrome: A New Name for the Vegetative State or Apallic Syndrome', *BMC Medicine*, 8, 68.

Lazzarato, M (2006) 'Immaterial Labor' in *Radical Thought in Italy: A Potential Politics*, Virno, P and Hardt, M (eds.), Minneapolis: University of Minnesota Press, 133–147.

Lazzarato, M (2012) *The Making of the Indebted Man*, Amsterdam: Semiotext(e).

Levinas, E (1969) *Totality and Infinity*, Lingis, A (tr.), Pittsburgh: Duquesne University Press.

Levinas, E (1978) *Existence and Existents*, Lingis A (tr.), The Hague: Martinus Nijhoff

Levinas, E (1985) *Ethics and Infinity: Conversations with Phillipe Nemo*, Cohen R (tr.), Pittsburgh: Duquesne University Press.

Levinas, E (1987) *Time and the Other*, Cohen, R (tr.), Pittsburgh: Duquesne University Press.

Levinas, E (1988a) 'The Paradox of Morality: An Interview with Emmanuel Levinas' in *The Provocation of Levinas: Rethinking the Other*, Bernasconi, R and Wood, D (eds.), London: Routledge, 168–180.

Levinas, E (1988b) 'Useless Suffering' in *The Provocation of Levinas: Rethinking the Other*, Bernasconi, R and Wood, D (eds.), London: Routledge, 156–167.

Levinas, E (1988c) *Is it Righteous to Be?: Interviews with Emmanuel Levinas*, Robbins, J (ed.), Stanford: Stanford University Press.

Levinas, E (1989a) 'Ethics as First Philosophy' in *The Levinas Reader*, Hand, S and Temple, M (tr.), Oxford: Blackwell, 75–87.

Levinas, E (1989b) *The Levinas Reader*, Hand, S and Temple, M (tr.), Oxford: Blackwell.

Levinas, E (1990) *Nine Talmudic Readings*, Aronowicz, A (tr.), Bloomington: Indiana University Press.

Levinas, E (1993) *Outside the Subject*, London: The Athlone Press.

Levinas, E (1994a) *Beyond the Verse: Talmudic Readings and Lectures*, Mole, G (tr.), Bloomington: Indiana University Press.

Levinas, E (1994b) *In the Time of the Nations*, Smith, M (tr.), Bloomington: Indiana University Press.

Levinas, E (1996a) 'Is Ontology Fundamental?' in *Emmanuel Levinas: Basic Philosophical Writings*, Peperzak, A, Critchley, S and Bernasconi, R (eds.), Bloomington: University of Indiana Press, 1–10.

Levinas, E (1996b) 'Meaning and Sense' in *Emmanuel Levinas: Basic Philosophical Writings*, Peperzak, A, Critchley, S and Bernasconi, R (eds.), Bloomington: University of Indiana Press, 33–64.

Levinas, E (1996c) 'Substitution' in *Emmanuel Levinas: Basic Philosophical Writings*, Peperzak, A, Critchley, S and Bernasconi, R (eds.), Bloomington: University of Indiana Press, 79–96.

Levinas, E (1996d) 'Transcendence and Height' in *Emmanuel Levinas: Basic Philosophical Writings*, Peperzak, A, Critchley, S and Bernasconi, R (eds.), Bloomington: University of Indiana Press, 11–31.

Levinas, E (1998a) *Entre Nous: Thinking-of-the-other*, Smith, M and Harshav, B (trs.), New York: Columbia University Press.

Levinas, E (1998b) *Of God Who Comes to Mind*, Bergo, B (tr.), Stanford: Stanford University Press.

Levinas, E (1999) *Alterity and Transcendence*, Smith, M (tr.), New York: Columbia University Press.

Levinas, E (2000) *God, Death and Time*, Bergo, B (tr.), Stanford: Stanford University Press.

Levinas, E (2001a) 'Judaism and the Feminine' in *Difficult Freedom: Essays in Judaism*, Hand, S (tr.), Baltimore: Johns Hopkins University Press, 30–38.

Levinas, E (2001b) *Difficult Freedom: Essays in Judaism*, Hand, S (tr.), Baltimore: Johns Hopkins University Press.

Levinas, E (2003a) *Humanism and the Other*, Urbana: University of Illinois Press/

Levinas, E (2003b) *On Escape*, Bergo, B (tr.), Stanford: Stanford University Press.

Levinas, E (2008) *Otherwise Than Being, Or Beyond Essence*, Lingis, A (tr.), Pittsburgh: Duquesne University Press.

Lingis, A (1994) *The Community of Those Who Have Nothing in Common*, Bloomington: Indiana University Press.

Lorimer, D (1984) 'Black Slaves and English Liberty: A Re-examination of Racial Slavery', *Immigrants & Minorities: Historical Studies in Ethnicity, Migration and Diaspora*, 3, 121–150.

Loumansky, A (2006) 'Levinas and the Possibility of Justice', *Liverpool Law Review*, 27, 147–171.

Luaute, J, Maucort-Boulch, Det al (2010) 'Long-term outcomes of chronic minimally conscious and vegetative states', *Neurology*, 75, 246–252.

Lukács, G (1999) *History and Class Consciousness: Studies in Marxist Dialectics*, Livingstone R (tr.), Cambridge: MIT Press.

Magill, S (2020) 'The Right to Privacy and Access to Abortion in a Post-*Puttaswamy* World', *University of Oxford Human Rights Hub Journal*, 3, 160–194.

Manderson, D (2006) *Proximity, Levinas and the Soul of Law*, London: McGill-Queen's University Press.

Manderson, D (2007) 'Here I Am: Illuminating and Delimiting Responsibility' in *Levinas, Law, Politics*, Diamantides, M (ed.), Abingdon: Routledge.

Martel, J (2015) 'The Anarchist Life we are Already Living: Benjamin and Agamben on Bare Life and the Resistance to Sovereignty' in *Toward a Critique of Violence: Walter Benjamin and Giorgio Agamben*, Moran, B and Salzani, C (eds.), London: Bloomsbury, 125–138.

Mbembé, A (2003) 'Necropolitics', *Public Culture*, 15, 11–40.

McHale, J and Jones, J (2012) 'Privacy, Confidentiality and Abortion Statistics: A Question of Public Interest?', *Journal of Medical Ethics*, 38, 31–34.

Mills, C (2008a) 'Playing with Law: Agamben and Derrida on Postjuridical Justice', *South Atlantic Quarterly*, 107, 15–36.

Mills, C (2008b) *The Philosophy of Agamben*, Stocksfield: Acumen Publishing.

Minkkinen, P (2009) *Sovereignty, Knowledge, Law*, Abingdon: Routledge.

Mokrosinka, D (2018) 'Privacy and Autonomy: On Some Misconceptions Concerning the Political Dimensions of Privacy', *Law and Philosophy*, 37, 117–143.

Morgan, M (2014) 'Levinas and Messianism' in *Rethinking the Messianic Idea in Judaism*, Morgan, M and Weitzman, S (eds.), Indianapolis: Indiana University Press, 195–225.

Murray, A (2010) *Giorgio Agamben*, London: Routledge.

Nancy, J-L and Fabbri, L (2007) 'Philosophy as Chance: An Interview with Jean-Luc Nancy', *Critical Inquiry*, 33, 427–440.

Negri, A (2003) 'The Ripe Fruit of Redemption: Review of Giorgio Agamben, The State of Exception', *Il Manifesto*.

Norris, A (2005) 'The Exemplary Exception: Philosophical and Political Decisions in Giorgio Agamben's Homo Sacer' in *Politics, Metaphysics, and Death: Essays on Giorgio Agamben's Homo Sacer*, Norris, A (ed.), Durham: Duke University Press, 262–283.

Nortvedt, P (2003) 'Levinas, Justice and Health Care', *Medicine, Health Care and Philosophy*, 6, 25–34.

Noys, B (2005) *The Culture of Death*, New York: Berg Press.

Ojakangas, M (2005) 'Impossible Dialogue on Biopower: Agamben and Foucault', *Foucault Studies*, 2, 5–28.

Oldham, J (2007) 'Insurance Litigation Involving the *Zong* and Other British Slave Ships, 1780–1807', *The Journal of Legal History*, 28, 299–318.

Oliver, K (2007) 'Stopping the Anthropological Machine: Agamben with Heidegger and Merleau-Ponty', *PhænEx: Journal of Existential and Phenomenological Theory and Culture*, 2, 1–23.

Palladino, P (2011) 'Miranda's Story: Molecules, Populations and the Mortal Organism', *History of the Human Sciences*, 24, 1–20.

Palladino, P (2013) 'Blessed Life…' in *Giorgio Agamben: Legal, Political and Philosophical Perspectives*, Frost, T (ed.), Abingdon: Routledge, 207–222.

Parry, J (2005) '"Society Must Be [Regulated]": Biopolitics and the Commerce Clause in *Gonzalez v Raich*', *Lewis and Clark Law Review*, 9, 853–877.

Parsley, C (2010) 'The Mask and Agamben: The Transitional Juridical Technics of Legal Relation', *Law, Text, Culture*, 14, 12–39.

Passavant, P (2007) 'The Contradictory State of Giorgio Agamben', *Political Theory*, 35, 147–174.

Peperzak, A (1993) *To the Other: An Introduction to the Philosophy of Emmanuel Levinas*, West Lafayette: Purdue University Press.

Perpich, D (2008) *The Ethics of Emmanuel Lévinas*, Stanford: Stanford University Press.

Perry, J (2006) 'Biblical BioPolitics: Judicial Process, Religious Rhetoric, Terri Schiavo and Beyond', *Health Matrix*, 16, 553–560.

Pitkin, A (2001) 'Scandalous Ethics: Infinite Presence with Suffering', *Journal of Consciousness Studies*, 8, 231–246.

Poleshchuk, I (2014) 'The Ethics of Futurity: Messianism and Intersubjectivity', *International Journal of Humanities and Social Science*, 4, 56–66.
Prozorov, S (2009a) 'Giorgio Agamben and the End of History', *European Journal of Social Theory*, 12, 523–542.
Prozorov, S (2009b) 'The Appropriation of Abandonment: Giorgio Agamben on the State of Nature and the Political', *Continental Philosophy Review*, 42, 327–353.
Prozorov, S (2010) 'Why Giorgio Agamben Is an Optimist', *Philosophy and Social Criticism*, 36, 1053–1073.
Prozorov, S (2014) *Agamben and Politics: A Critical Introduction*, Edinburgh: Edinburgh University Press.
Prozorov, S (2017) 'Agamben, Badiou and Affirmative Biopolitics' in *Agamben and Radical Politics*, McLoughlin, D (ed.), Cambridge: Cambridge University Press, 165–188.
Putnam, H (2002) 'Levinas and Judaism' in *The Cambridge Companion to Levinas*, Critchley, S and Bernasconi, R (eds.), Cambridge: Cambridge University Press, 33–62.
Rabinow, P (ed.) (1991) *The Foucault Reader: An Introduction to Foucault's Thought*, London: Penguin Books, 7–11.
Rabinow, P (1999) *French DNA: Trouble in Purgatory*, Chicago: University of Chicago Press.
Rabinow, P and Rose, N (2006) 'Biopower Today', *BioSocities*, 1, 195–217.
Rae, G (2018) 'Agency and Will in Agamben's Coming Politics', *Philosophy & Social Criticism*, 44, 978–996.
Raulff, U and Agamben, G (2004) 'An Interview with Giorgio Agamben', *German Law Journal*, 5, 609–614.
Rawls, J (2005) *Political Liberalism*, New York: Columbia University Press.
Raymont, V et al (2004) 'Prevalence of Mental Incapacity in Medical Inpatients and Associated Risk Factors: Cross-sectional Study', *The Lancet*, 364, 1421–1427.
Restuccia, F (2017) 'Jacques Lacan' in *Agamben's Philosophical Lineage*, Kotsko, A and Salzani, C (eds.), Edinburgh: University of Edinburgh Press, 252–261.
Reumann, J (1959) 'Oikonomia = "Covenant": Terms For Heilsgeschichte in Early Christian Usage', *Novum Testamentum*, 3, 282–292.
Rosenfeld, M (1990) 'Temptations of the New Legal Formalism', *Cardozo Law Review*, 11, 1211–1268.
Ross, A (2008) 'Introduction', *South Atlantic Quarterly*, 108, 1–13.
Royal College of Physicians (RCP) (2020) *Prolonged Disorders of Consciousness: National Clinical Guidelines*, London: Royal College of Physicians.
Salzani, C (2020a) 'Beyond Human and Animal: Giorgio Agamben and Life as Potential' in *Animality in Contemporary Italian Philosophy*, Cimatti, F and Salzani, C (tr.), Basingstoke: Palgrave Macmillan, 97–113.
Salzani, C (2020b) 'Outside of Being: Agamben's Potential Beyond Anthropocentrism', *Etica & Politica / Ethics & Politics*, 22, 71–86.
Savà, P (2012) '"God Didn't Die, He Was Transformed into Money" – An interview with Giorgio Agamben' (16 August 2012) http://libcom.org/library/god-didnt-die-he-was-transformed-money-interview-giorgio-agamben-peppe-sav%C3%A0?fb_action_ids=10101499911986209&fb_action_types=og.likes&fb_source=other_multiline&action_object_map=%5B459503257509635%5D&action_type_map=%5B%22og.likes%22%5D&action_ref_map=%5B%5D.
Schmitt, C (2003) *The Nomos of the Earth: In the International Law of the Jus Publicum Europaeum*, Ulmen, G.L. (tr.), Candor: Telos Press.

Schütz, A (2009) 'Imperatives without *Imperator*', *Law and Critique*, 20, 233–243.

Scott, D (1990) 'Platonic Recollection and Cambridge Platonism', *Hermathena*, 149, 73–97.

Sealey, K (2010) 'The Primacy of Disruption in Levinas' Account of Transcendence', *Research in Phenomenology*, 40, 363–377.

Seshadri, K (2014) 'Agamben, the Thought of *Sterēsis*: An Introduction to Two Essays', *Critical Inquiry*, 40, 470–479.

Simmons, W (1999) 'The Third: Levinas's Theoretical Move from An-archical Ethics to the Realm of Justice and Politics', *Philosophy & Social Criticism*, 25, 93–104.

Singer, P (1995) *Rethinking Life and Death: The Collapse of Our Traditional Ethics*, New York: St. Martin's.

Singer, P (2011) *Practical Ethics*, 3rd edn, New York: Cambridge University Press.

Spinoza (1996) *Ethics*, London: Penguin Books.

Stone, M (2010) 'Levinas and Political Subjectivity in an Age of Global Biopower', *Law, Culture and the Humanities*, 6, 105–123.

Stone, M (2016) *Levinas, Ethics and Law*, Edinburgh: Edinburgh University Press.

Thurschwell, A (2003) 'Specters of Nietzsche: Potential Futures for the Concept of the Political in Agamben and Derrida', *Cardozo Law Review*, 24, 1193–1260.

Thurschwell, A (2005) 'Cutting the Branches for Akiba: Agamben's Critique of Derrida', in Giorgio Agamben's Homo Sacer' in *Politics, Metaphysics, and Death: Essays on Giorgio Agamben's Homo Sacer*, Norris, A (ed.), Durham: Duke University Press, 173–197.

Tiermersma, D (1987) 'Ontology and Ethics in the Foundation of Medicine and the Relevance of Levinas' View', *Theoretical Medicine*, 8, 127–133.

Tooley, M (1972) 'Abortion and Infanticide', *Philosophy & Public Affairs*, 2, 37–65.

Unger, R (1983) 'The Critical Legal Studies Movement', *Harvard Law Review*, 96, 561–675.

Vacarme, (2004) '"I am sure that you are more pessimistic than I am…": An Interview with Giorgio Agamben' *Rethinking Marxism*, 16, 115–124.

van Cleve, G (2006) 'Somerset's Case and Its Antecedents in Imperial Perspective', *Law and History Review*, 24, 601–645.

Veitch, K (2006) 'Medical Law and the Power of Life and Death', *International Journal of Law in Context*, 2, 137–157.

Wall, T (1999) *Radical Passivity: Levinas, Blanchot and Agamben*, New York: SUNY Press.

Watkin, W (2014) *Agamben and Indifference: A Critical Overview*, London and New York: Rowman & Littlefield.

Weber, S (1990) 'In the Name of the Law', *Cardozo Law Review*, 11, 1515–1538.

Webster, J (2007) 'The *Zong* in the Context of the Eighteenth-Century Slave Trade', *The Journal of Legal History*, 8, 285–298.

White, R (2012) 'Levinas, The Philosophy of Suffering, and the Ethics of Compassion', *The Heythrop Journal*, 53, 111–123.

Whyte, J (2013) *Catastrophe and Redemption: The Political Thought of Giorgio Agamben*, Albany: SUNY Press.

Wiecek, W (1974) 'Somerset: Lord Mansfield and the Legitimacy of Slavery in the Anglo-American World', *The University of Chicago Law Review*, 42, 86–126.

Wijdicks, E (2006) 'Minimally Conscious State vs. Persistent Vegetative State: The Case of Terry (Wallis) vs. the Case of Terri (Schiavo)', *Mayo Clinic Proceedings*, 81, 1155–1158.

Wilkinson, I (2017) 'The Controversy of Compassion as an Awakening to our Conflicted Social Condition', *International Journal of Law in Context*, 13, 212–224.

Wolcher, L (2003) 'Ethics, Justice, and Suffering in the Thought of Levinas: The Problem of the Passage', *Law and Critique*, 14, 93–116.

Wright, N.T. (2013a) 'Paul and Empire (2010)' in *Pauline Perspectives: Essays on Paul, 1978–2013*, London: SPCK, 439–452.
Wright, N.T. (2013b) 'Paul in Current Anglophone Scholarship (2012)' in *Pauline Perspectives: Essays on Paul, 1978–2013*, London: SPCK, 474–488.
Wright, N.T. (2013c) 'The Law and Romans 2 (1996)' in *Pauline Perspectives: Essays on Paul, 1978–2013*, London: SPCK, 134–151.
Wright, N.T. (2013d) *Paul and the Faithfulness of God, Parts III and IV*, London: SPCK.
Wright, N.T. (2015) *Paul and His Recent Interpreters: Some Contemporary Debates*, London: SPCK.
Wright, T (1997) *What Saint Paul Really Said: Was Paul of Tarsus the Real Founder of Christianity?*, Oxford: Lion Publishing.
Yates, C (2011) 'The Double Fidelity: The Messianic Lens for Lévinas's Eschatological Vision', *Journal of the British Society for Phenomenology*, 42, 160–175.
Zartaloudis, T (2002) 'Without Negative Origins and Absolute Ends: A Jurisprudence of the Singular', *Law and Critique*, 13, 197–230.
Zartaloudis, T (2010) *Giorgio Agamben: Power, Law and the Uses of Criticism*, Abingdon: Routledge.
Ziarek, E (2008) 'Bare Life on Strike: Notes on the Biopolitics of Race and Gender', *South Atlantic Quarterly*, 108, 89–106.
Ziarek, K (2008) 'After Humanism: Agamben and Heidegger', *South Atlantic Quarterly*, 107, 187–209.

Index

For Product Safety Concerns and Information please contact our EU
representative GPSR@taylorandfrancis.com
Taylor & Francis Verlag GmbH, Kaufingerstraße 24, 80331 München, Germany

www.ingramcontent.com/pod-product-compliance
Ingram Content Group UK Ltd.
Pitfield, Milton Keynes, MK11 3LW, UK
UKHW020147200926
475702UK00016B/2594

* 9 7 8 1 0 3 2 0 5 7 1 5 6 *